Embodied Archive

Corporealities: Discourses of Disability

Series editors: David T. Mitchell and Sharon L. Snyder

A complete list of titles in the series can be found at www.press.umich.edu

Embodied Archive

❦

*Disability in Post-Revolutionary Mexican
Cultural Production*

Susan Antebi

University of Michigan Press
Ann Arbor

Published in the United States of America by the
University of Michigan Press
Manufactured in the United States of America
Printed on acid-free paper
First published April 2021

A CIP catalog record for this book is available from the British Library.

Library of Congress Cataloging-in-Publication Data

Names: Antebi, Susan, author.
Title: Embodied archive : disability in post-revolutionary Mexican cultural production / Susan Antebi.
Description: Ann Arbor : University of Michigan Press, 2021. | Series: Corporealities: discourses of disability | Includes bibliographical references (pages 245–260) and index.
Identifiers: LCCN 2020054687 (print) | LCCN 2020054688 (ebook) | ISBN 9780472038503 (paperback) | ISBN 9780472902422 (ebook other)
Subjects: LCSH: People with disabilities in mass media. | People with disabilities—Mexico—Social conditions. | Race in mass media. | Racism—Mexico—20th century. | Mexico—Social conditions—20th century.
Classification: LCC HV1559.M4 A58 2021 (print) | LCC HV1559.M4 (ebook) | DDC 305.9/0809720904'z—dc23
LC record available at https://lccn.loc.gov/2020054687
LC ebook record available at https://lccn.loc.gov/2020054688

ISBN 978-0-472-90242-2 (OA e-book)

DOI: https://doi.org/10.3998/mpub.11644714

This open access version made available by Victoria College at the University of Toronto

Cover: Drawing illustrating the Special Education Service within the National Institute of Psychopedagogy, 1936. *Instituto Nacional de Psicopedagogía*. Secretaría de Educación Pública, Departamento de Psicopedagogía y Médico Escolar.

Cover description: Black and white drawing of a woman wearing a long, sleeveless dress, standing upright, her arms slightly outstretched. She rests each of her hands on the shoulders of two small boys, one of whom leans on a crutch. A third, smaller boy stands close to her legs. Above the illustration, to the left, the words "Embodied Archive" are printed in green, with the words "Disability in Post-Revolutionary Mexican Cultural Production" printed in black, slightly to the right. Below the illustration, the name "Susan Antebi" is printed in white on a red background.

For Sergio and Camilo

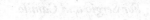

Acknowledgments

It occurs to me in writing these pages that the genre of "acknowledgments" tends to create a strange taxonomy of persons, placing each in a singular category, when in fact there are many who fit into more than one role, as friends, colleagues, interlocutors, supporters, scholars of one or several disciplines, and those who hail from one or several locations. In ways far beyond this acknowledgment taxonomy, I am grateful to everyone who has knowingly or unknowingly shaped this book. Contingency, the idea that one thing, such as an event, a feeling, or a sense of identity, depends on outside factors or circumstances, appears frequently in the pages to come. Yet the gratitude I wish to express here is not contingent on the publication of my book; rather, this project offers me a serendipitous excuse to offer my thanks.

I have been fortunate to work with generous colleagues at the University of Toronto, including my many fellow travelers in the Department of Spanish and Portuguese and in the Latin American Studies Program, who have contributed to a vibrant academic environment. I especially wish to thank Rosa Sarabia, Eva-Lynn Jagoe, Néstor Rodríguez, Victor Rivas, Sanda Munjic, Robert Davidson, Stephen Rupp, Yolanda Iglesias, Ricardo Sternberg, Josiah Blackmore, Mariana Mota Prado, Kevin Coleman, Anne-Emanuelle Birn, Luis van Isschot, Melanie Newton, Donald Kingsbury, Bernardo García Domínguez, and Juan Marsiaj. Portions of this research were presented in earlier forms to colleagues in disability studies, and I am particularly grateful to Tanya Titchkosky, Rod Michalko, and Anne McGuire for facilitating space and offering knowledgeable feedback on my work in progress. I also thank my colleagues in the Racial Technologies Working Group, Tamara Walker, Valentina Napolitano, Luisa Schwartzman, Antonio Torres-Ruiz, Nae Hanashiro Ávila, and Ted Sammons, who provided invaluable insight on an earlier draft of chapter 1, as well as a welcoming space in which to share work in progress. Thanks are due as well to participants in the Tepoztlán Institute for Transnational History of the Americas, of 2016, who productively engaged with an earlier version of a portion of the manuscript. I am immensely grateful to Salvador Alanis and Ximena Berecochea, codirectors of the Toronto-based Institute for Creative Exchange (ICE), for their innovative work in the creation and facilitation of artistic and cultural initiatives, and particularly for the opportunity to participate along with Mario Bellatin and Daniel Canty in the workshop Art and Orthopedics, which allowed me to work through some of the concepts presented in this book. I extend my appreciation to Héctor Domínguez Ruvalcaba, Ana Ugarte, Kristina Mitchell, Carolyn Fornoff, Ryan Prout, and their colleagues for additional opportunities to present and improve on versions of this work in various venues over a number of years.

Disability studies is sometimes defined as a field, yet it tends to operate as a multiplicity of shifting and partially entangled fields, with dynamic sites of encounter between varied disciplines and forms of knowledge. Approaching disability studies through literature, and more specifically through Mexican literary and cultural studies, has allowed me to learn from many generous colleagues, each of whom engages the work of disability studies from a uniquely informed angle. I am indebted to Beth Jörgensen, Susanne Hartwig, Sander Gilman, Susan Schweik, Rachel Adams, Petra Kuppers, Nirmala Erevelles, Robert McRuer, Encarnación Juárez Almendros, Jay Dolmage, Julie Avril Minich, Eunjung Kim, and Benjamin Fraser for their perceptive readings and commitment to a dynamic academic community that has sustained me in many ways over the years. I wish to express my appreciation to David Mitchell and Sharon Snyder, Corporealities series editors, for their generous enthusiasm for this book. It has been a privilege to work with them recently, and to learn from them through their many projects. As a starstruck reader of *Narrative Prosthesis*, I continue to recognize the ways that their evolving research has influenced my approach to disability studies. I also deeply appreciate the immensely generous efforts of the two anonymous readers of the book manuscript, who offered both encouragement and productive criticism that enabled me to improve the work.

The research and writing of this book, along with some other complementary projects, have been enriched by conferences and other exchanges with my "Mexicanista" colleagues. I am thankful for the ongoing support and intellectual energy of Ignacio Sánchez Prado, Debra Castillo, Ryan Long, John Ochoa, Emily Hind, Rebecca Janzen, Adela Pineda, Horacio

Legrás, Oswaldo Zavala, Sara Potter, Jorge Quintana Navarrete, Amanda Petersen, Cheyla Samuelson, Alberto Ribas, Antonio Córdoba, Ilana Dann Luna, Oswaldo Estrada, Tamara Williams, Pedro Ángel Palou, Maarten van Delden, Dan Russek, Niamh Thornton, Viviane Mahieux, Sara Poot-Herrera, Jacobo Sefamí, José Ramón Ruisánchez, Rafael Acosta, David Dalton, Laura Torres-Rodríguez, Ana Sabau, Christina Soto van der Plas, Brian Price, Analisa Taylor, and Shelley Garrigan. I extend a special thanks to Berenice Villagómez, whose expertise and generous spirit, both as a Mexicanista and an administrator, have helped keep so many academic endeavors afloat.

Much of the research for this book was conducted in Mexico, and I particularly wish to express my gratitude to colleagues there for their insightful thoughts on this project in its various stages, and for opportunities both to present my work and to learn from their expertise. I thank Benjamín Mayer-Foulkes, director of the 17 Instituto de Estudios Críticos, and Beatriz Miranda Galarza, head of research and the "disability" area at 17, for their unwavering and energetic commitment to disability studies and to forging connections beyond traditional academic spaces. I also want to thank Patricia Brogna, Carlos López Beltrán, Ana María Carrillo, Federico Navarrete, Andrés Ríos Molina, Eloisa Alcócer, and Carlos Bojórquez Urzaiz, each of whom directly or indirectly supported and inspired this work.

Further thanks are due to those who assisted me in various ways with archival research and securing digitized images and permissions. These include Rogelio Vargas Olvera, of the Archivo Histórico de la Secretaría de Salud Pública; Juan Gerardo López Hernández, of the Archivo Histórico de la Ciudad de México; Jorge Daniel Ciprés Ortega, of the Hemeroteca Nacional de México; Luis Alberto Cruz Hernández, of the Biblioteca Nacional de México; Francisco Mondragón, of the Archivo Fotográfico México Indígena; Dr. Jesús Francisco García Pérez, of the Instituto de Investigaciones Sociales, UNAM; and Roberto Erick Arceo López, of the *Revista Mexicana de Sociología*. Among those who assisted me at the Archivo General de la Nación (AGN), I especially thank Marlene Pérez García, Bertha Lilliam Pimentel Bernal, Alan Antonio Morales Martínez, Abraham Maldonado Ruiz, and José Samuel Guzmán Palomera. In Toronto, I have been fortunate to count on the expert assistance of librarians Miguel Torrens and David Fernández, and the outstanding administrative support of Blanca Talesnik, Paula Triana, and Sara Solis. I would also like to express my gratitude to my current student, Veronika Brejkaln, and my former student, Rebecca Janzen, each of whom assisted me at different points in archival research for this project. I owe thanks as well to Andrew Ascherl for his expertise in creating an index for this book and previous ones, to Sara Cohen, my editor at the University of Michigan Press, her assistant, Flannery Wise, my production editor Melissa Scholke, and copy-editor Daniel Otis for their tireless work on this project.

During my research trips to Mexico City I enjoyed the support of my extended family members, Raúl Rivera Ayala, María Guadalupe Rivera Ayala, Antonia Rivera Ayala, and Estela Rivera Ayala, who fed me (or at least called to tell me what they were cooking in my absence), drove me to one place or another, and kept me laughing even after long hours chasing documents. I am thankful as well to the friends who remind me it's worthwhile to unglue my eyes from screens and pages: Kate Holland, Iván Fernández Peláez, Christine Stiffler Nayal, Ivy Baron, Melanie Temin, Adnai Mendez, Lital Levy, Shelley Lumba, Georgia Marman, Marilyn Miller, Wanda Rivera-Rivera, Abdón Ubidia, Scott Miller, Laura Cueva-Miller, and Freya Schiwy. My beautiful cat, Pascal, accompanied me through much of the writing of these chapters, but sadly did not make it to the final stretch. If he were here today, he would not be impressed by this book in the least, but would jump onto my keyboard, indifferent to deadlines, theories, and syntax. I miss his commitment to unfettered enjoyment.

The last months of preparation of this manuscript, including a trip to Mexico City that was cut short by the global pandemic and followed by two weeks of self-isolation, have reminded me of the tremendous support I have received from my family over the many years during which this book developed. I am immensely grateful to Joseph and Joanna Antebi, and to William Antebi, for their unfailing encouragement and humor. Finally, I wish to offer a profound thanks to Sergio Rivera Ayala and Camilo Rivera-Antebi, who have so closely witnessed and patiently sustained the labor that intermittently or frenetically produced this book.

Funding for the research and writing of this book was generously provided by the Social Sciences and Humanities Research Council of Canada, the Jackman Humanities Institute at the University of Toronto, and a Victoria College Grant.

Chapter 3 is derived from an article published in *Journal of Latin American Cultural Studies*, December 2012, ©Taylor and Francis, available online at https://www.tandfonline.com/doi/full/10.1080/13569325.2012.711749. A portion of chapter 2 appeared in the *Arizona Journal of Hispanic Cultural Studies* (vol. 17, 2013, pp. 163–80) and is republished here with the journal's permission.

Contents

Digital materials related to this title can be found on
the Fulcrum platform via the following citable URL:
https://doi.org/10.3998/mpub.11644714

Introduction

Contingent Disabilities

⁂

Diagnoses

This is the part of a book in which many readers would expect to find some kind of confession, or at the very least a more personal touch. Although this book focuses on disability in Mexican literary and archival sources, and not on its author, contemporary readers often wish to know something more. Why, they discreetly ask, did you become interested in disability studies? I have long wondered whether or not to comply with this implied request for more personal information. I wonder, too, as I write this, to whom I am answering, and whether there is anything at stake in the transaction. I am not offended by the question, nor do I always know quite what to say. I find myself in a strange space of hesitation, that might only give way to silence, or imaginative wandering, though I have always hoped it would lead to a little bit more of the truth. What is it that you would like to know? If there were a link here, I would click on it, and suggest you do the same, even though we don't know where it would take us. If I sound cryptic, it is probably out of fear. One answer might go something like this:

> On a humid spring afternoon, I exited the campus where I was a grad-
> uate student and pedaled towards Belmont. The psychiatrist at the
> hospital would see me for twenty minutes. I was late and out of breath.
> He asked me to begin at one hundred and count backwards, subtract-
> ing seven each time. I told him I resented being asked to do arithmetic
> after coming all this way. I wondered, in silence, if his instant diag-
> nosis was based on my uncooperative remark, and whether it was a

coincidence that it matched the specialty of that institution. The brick buildings were artfully spread over the landscape, similar to the place where I had attended a seminar just an hour before, but somehow not the same at all.

Other physicians advised me to try a low dose of lithium or an antipsychotic. I would mention to them—again, uncooperatively—that Freud used to prescribe cocaine to his patients. It is true there had been classes where I stared out the window and willed myself to see or not to see miniature men darting across the rooftops, and also that one morning when I looked in the mirror, my eyes were square instead of round. These could be the manifestations of a problem, its treatment, or possibly both. I notice that such details only become symptoms when they are spoken or written down. There is always another version of the same story, perhaps more or less mundane or awkwardly revelatory, a series of experiences that could become a process of self-identification, or might not. There are words such as "basket case" or "borderline" that I take up or throw away, and that sometimes refuse to dissolve. Perhaps I should change the symptoms and their explanation in my story, or perhaps I have already done so. The reader, like the physician, might be looking for the specificity and the extremity of the anecdote, as well as clear yes-or-no answers to her questions, but I hope she will recognize that one doesn't always find what one is looking for. I have sometimes hoped to find the one confession that would finally answer every question, situating itself neatly in the past. But stories have a way of continuing, spreading themselves out into their many pasts and futures. This book is not about me, but through the long process of researching, thinking, and writing it has become part of a story I hope I can tell.

Embodied Archive explores literary and archival sources centered on the diagnosis, measurement, perception, and control of human differences, figured as pathologies, particularly in the first decades of the post-revolutionary period in Mexico, or from the 1920s to the 1940s—a time when the eugenics movement and its variants played an important role in national culture. It is about bodies that potentially fail to conform to a normative standard that was itself in the process of being defined, and about an impetus to observe and document the features of Mexican citizenry, in particular those of schoolchildren, so as to shape them toward a more productive and hygienic national future. It is about the question of racialized bodies and their potential absorption into the state, about the fragility of the injured or potentially injured, and the place of fragility in a national process of becoming. The book is shaped at its core by the dilemma of contingent differences, forms of disability that do not appear in an explicit or unmediated fashion, but are instead projected into the future or the past by uncertain causal processes, are framed by external perspectives, or are displaced by the data and methodology meant to express them. Contingent disability hovers on an uncertain temporal horizon, between cause and effect, outside perceptions and lived realities, central to the production of the desires, fears, and imaginations that shape national histories and futures. In my readings, I also attend to instances in which expressions of human difference impact state-sponsored discourses of national identity and future, as well as the experience of temporal progression, often in resistant or incongruent ways. This book is about disability, and reads history and literature from a disability studies perspective. It assumes the calculated risk of projecting contemporary terminology and concepts onto a past in which such concepts did not yet exist, gesturing toward a transnational and transhistorical disability genealogy with implications for the disability of our present and future.

The diagnosis and measurement of pathology were key features of the eugenics movement in its globally diverse manifestations, in many cases with horrific or fatal outcomes for the human subjects under its scrutiny. Contemporary patterns of institutionalization, incarceration, and involuntary sterilization worldwide continue to mark and shape disabled lives, reminding us of the prevailing high stakes of notions of the differential value of individuals and groups.[1] My briefly rendered account of an outpatient visit to a psychiatric facility is vastly removed from the spaces in which violent injustices shape or foreclose the futures of those deemed different, less valid, or of lesser worth. Yet each moment of diagnosis, however minor or mundane, and its evocation through the repetition of symptoms that collapse experience into description, marks the body as an expression of medical data, and data as the shape and echo of many bodies. These intercorporeal processes may remind us that diagnosis—and disability—do not occur in isolation, but situate individuals and populations within complex, interdependent, and shifting continuums, which shape our many possible stories and determine unequal patterns of perceived social worth and life prognoses.

The writing of *Embodied Archive* is posited as a critical intervention into eugenic spaces of observation, measurement, and diagnosis through attention to a series of archival and literary texts. It aims not only to document some instances in which bodies and eugenic discourse unequally shape one another, but also to reflexively examine how archival witnessing, and the reading of disability in cultural history, may participate in the resignification of bodies, texts, and the cultural fields they help to create. "Intercorporeality," a term I use here to refer to the mutual dependency and referentiality linking bodies to one another, suggests as well the role of critical reading as an embodied practice, an ongoing, transhistorical, living and textual encounter through which disability may still come to mean otherwise.[2]

Eugenics and Hygiene

The eugenics movement was a global phenomenon that occupied the attention of healthcare workers, educators, writers, artists, and political leaders who sought in various ways to understand and mold a collective biological future, often conceived through the framework of the nation-state. In the Mexican context, as was also the case in many other Latin American countries, the concept of eugenics was closely intertwined with that of hygiene, leading to a version of "soft eugenics" that has been amply studied by historians of science. The twin concepts of hygiene and eugenics and their mutually reinforcing duality are crucial to the project at hand, not only as the basis of an understanding of Mexican public-health history, but because of how the concepts work together in the expression of disability as a contingent feature of temporal and historical chronology.[3] My archival encounter with hygiene and eugenics in Mexico is exemplified by documents describing conditions such as "feeblemindedness" or epilepsy in children as the possible outcome of their parents' alcoholism, promiscuity, or illnesses, as well as by campaigns against behaviors that might contribute to "abnormalities" in children of the future. The double-edged quality of this causal trajectory points forward and backward in time, postulating but never fully locating the problems it describes.

"Eugenics," a term coined by the English scientist Sir Francis Galton in 1883, and meaning literally "well born," generally refers to programs designed to "improve" the population through reproductive control, including forced sterilization, institutionalization, immigration restrictions, and in some cases, genocide. Variants of eugenics also encompassed educational programs to discourage reproduction among poorer or racialized population sectors, while encouraging reproduction in more economically privileged sectors. Though often associated with Nazi Germany and the "final solution," eugenics received widespread attention and development in the United States, Canada, Europe, and Latin America through research and policy implementation, well before the rise of the Third Reich.[4] Eugenic discourse in these contexts included emphasis on associations between racial or ethnic differences and disability; hence the screening of immigrants in the US and Canada highlighted racialized physical features as indicative of mental weakness and other ills.[5] In most contexts, eugenic propaganda favored a whitening of the population, excluding non-Europeans as well as Jews and southern Europeans from its vision of a more perfect biological future.

As Nancy Leys Stepan has written, Latin American eugenics, specifically in Mexico, Brazil, and Argentina, tended to operate as a "softer" program, one geared more closely to the notion of hygiene. "Hygiene" emphasizes practical improvements in the health of the present population, including issues of reproductive health. However, hygiene and eugenics, or as some prefer, "soft" and "hard" eugenics, work in tandem, in particular when hygiene is posited as a means to improve the future population as well as the present one. In studies of the Mexican context, historians of science including Stepan have emphasized the impact of neo-Lamarckism, and in particular the notion of the inheritance of acquired characteristics, as central to the logic underpinning the prevalence of hygiene, or "soft" eugenics, in public-health discourse of the post-revolutionary period. The idea that individual behavior and environmental factors could influence future generations through changes to the "germ plasm" would mean that campaigns to combat alcoholism, syphilis, tuberculosis, or unsanitary living conditions could be understood as part of a broader eugenic initiative.[6] As Carlos López Beltrán notes, however, Mexican eugenics and hygiene of this period are complicated by a broad array of scientific influences, through which flexible notions of inheritance from a range of sources beyond Lamarck combine with more rigid theories of genetic continuity. In this sense, the separation between "hard" and "soft" eugenics becomes more variable and difficult to define.[7]

Archival documents in public health and education reveal a combined focus on the continuity of negatively perceived traits over generations, and the transformation of future generations through environmental influences. This difference does not always represent a conflict between two theories, such as Mendelian and Lamarckian genetics, but instead offers a discursive space in which various external factors might be considered influential in long- or short-term reproductive future, while some biological tendencies may be seen as deterministic and unchanging over time.[8] As Marta Saade Granados notes, eugenics in Mexico may be better understood in the Foucauldian sense as a "discursive formation" (28), rather than as a clearly defined scientific field or ideology; this is in part because of the range of practices and fields in which it operates, with links to social medicine, biological science, education, literature, and politics. More specifically, in Saade Granados's view, Mexican eugenics encompassed a dual, self-contradictory emphasis on biological determinism and social environment (27). In this sense, the discourse of eugenics suggests a dual temporality, caught between an irrevocable fatality that would, in theory, demand violent, extreme solutions, and an open horizon on which human action may work toward desired (or feared) outcomes.[9]

This complication is important because as hygiene and eugenics come to inhabit complementary and at times intertwined spaces in the shifting fields of public health, pedagogical discourse, and cultural production, they help shape national identity, and particularly the problems of temporal continuity and future as features of that identity. If hard eugenics aims to control reproduction and shape the future "race," soft eugenics, or hygiene, directs its attention to health issues of the present, while at once projecting this present into an always possible future, linked as well to a hypothetical past. The combined and at times contradictory influence of these spheres means that human difference and disability become uncertainly suspended, in some instances identified clearly and marked for erasure but at other times situated more tentatively, as the possible past cause of a current problem, or the potential, future outcome of behavior or environment. In this way, disability and other differences become temporally contingent, situated by a series of causal circumstances, and structured by the linking of past, present, and future. Contingency—a key concept throughout this book—also suggests the ambivalence of human efforts to shape the biological future, between the "soft" eugenic notion that initiatives to change behavior and environments will impact this future, and the "hard" eugenic idea that reproductive futures are definitively located in the "germ plasm," and thus cannot be changed, except by preventing the reproduction of those deemed unfit. If both tendencies are present in the documentation studied here, it is also true that the "softer" approach predominates in post-revolutionary Mexico, in contrast to the model of eugenics prevalent in the US, Canada, and many European countries during the same period.

To further clarify this distinction and its importance in the present book, it may be helpful to turn briefly to Ellen Samuels's influential work on the identifiability of disabled, gendered, and racialized bodies in the US context from the nineteenth century to the present. "Fantasies of identification," as Samuels aptly demonstrates, ground themselves in scientific authority, and work to mark identity as measurable and fixed within the body (18, 22). Disability, in this argument, paradoxically both resists classification and offers (or appears to promise) a solid, unchanging physicality (14). The public-health documents and literary texts of the Mexican post-revolution informing my readings in this book do at times operate through a desire for what Samuels calls "biocertificative legibility" (17), which would categorize bodies once and for all according to their "healthy" or "pathological," disabled or racialized status, in some cases removing or isolating those deemed undesirable. However, because as we have seen, discourses of hygiene in the Mexican context tend to situate disability on an uncertain temporal horizon, the fantasy ultimately relies less on absolute classifications and more on the production of a solidifying, collective national self, gradually purged of its racializations and pathologies.[10]

In addition to this temporal structure of contingency, notions of human difference are shaped by broader discourses of national history as the collective imagining of pivotal events and transformative processes. José Vasconcelos's *The Cosmic Race* serves as a relevant illustration here. For Vasconcelos, the history and future of Latin America are marked by a combination of messianic destiny and circumstances that might have been otherwise, or are still to be created in the future. Thus, Napoleon's ceding of Louisiana to the English, as a kind of accident of history, created the conditions for Latin America's relationship to the United States, conceived as a racial conflict between Anglo-Saxonism and Latinism. This conflict in turn gave rise to the mission of the "cosmic race," which was to forge a national and pan–Latin American reproductive future in which the idealized attributes of each "race" would prevail while negatively perceived racial attributes would disappear, eventually giving rise to a perfected mestizo society. Racialized bodies, along with attributes such as "ugliness" and "monstrosity," mark the trajectory of national history and destiny through their projected disappearance, but also through the impetus to collective effort to actively shape the future through and against these undesirable qualities. In this discourse, Mexican national identity is shaped by a vision of history suspended between destiny and contingency, in which disability and racialized difference are central to the desires and tensions surrounding this historical unfolding. In other words, one might say that the contingency of disability appears here within a historical structure as well as a more immediate temporal one.

The ambivalent location of disability in Mexican public-health and cultural discourses creates a dynamic in which differences are subsumed or bracketed by their presumed causes and possible locations, or in which disability itself reorients the expected role of causality. This contingency of disability in Mexican cultural contexts links the dilemmas of public health and cultural aesthetics to a broader philosophical debate on national identity, connected in turn to the question of *mestizaje*, or racial mixing. The concept of contingency is also a key feature of the Mexican existential tradition of the Hyperion Group, in which philosophy struggles between the specificity of Mexican contexts and universal thought (Sánchez 66). In accordance with this reading, *Mexicanidad*, or "Mexican-ness," oscillates between historically determined and materially conditioned national identity, and the broader, more open-ended coordinates of the universal human condition. This dilemma extends beyond the Hyperion philosophers and their key period of activity from 1948 to 1952, to encompass wide-ranging and fraught debates on Mexican history and national identity. In the case of Samuel Ramos's *Profile of Man and Culture in Mexico* (1934), at stake is the question of whether the diagnosis of a Mexican—and mestizo—inferiority complex and its consequences are in some sense integral to the Mexican self, or better understood as the products of historical and social causality. Perhaps the internationally best-known Mexican essay is Octavio Paz's *The Labyrinth of Solitude* (1950), in which the author, following Ramos's lead, further tackles the issue of cyclical historical causality and its impact on the Mexican psyche, as well as the tension between the Mexican and the universal human conditions. Turning to Roger Bartra's *The Cage of Melancholy* (1987), the reader must navigate the dilemma of national stereotypes and their theatrical, institutionalized, self-referentiality as elements that seem to shift between sites of identification and empty symbols, and that may continue to shape Mexican identity even as they are unmasked as artifice.

These canonical twentieth-century works on the tensions surrounding expressions of Mexican history and national identity each negotiate structures of contingency, whether through philosophical, psychoanalytic, literary, or historical approaches, cycling through the ambivalent roles of causality, historical and political circumstance, cultural specificity, and human agency in shaping a Mexican nation and self—or its phantoms. As this brief overview may suggest, the problem of contingency is not exclusive to the Mexican context, nor can it be resolved through a simple opposition between secondary conditioning factors and essential reality or identity. While these works do not focus on the question of disability in an explicit sense, they contribute to our understanding of contingency and of the pitfalls of national identity. In ways not unlike the discourses of eugenics and hygiene, these works delay, project, bracket, and repeat the wounds and fragilities they seek to overcome. They also engage closely with the issue of race as a feature of national identity, a dynamic I discuss in the next section.

Becoming Mestizo

The history of eugenics and hygiene in Mexico and worldwide is necessarily a history of racism, and of the racialization of human differences, as will become evident in the chapters to come. Michel Foucault clarifies the link between racism and eugenics in his discussion of biopower, which from the nineteenth century justified death, exclusion, and exposure to the risk of death through arguments of evolutionism and the purification of the race (*Society Must Be Defended*, 256–57). In Foucault's discussion, racism as inseparable from the workings of biopower and state sovereignty is exemplified by Nazism but not exclusive to it. It is interesting that Foucault makes a brief distinction between what he calls "ethnic racism" and "racism of the evolutionist kind, biological racism" (261). In this way, the racism of modern, eugenic societies comes to encompass a desire for biological purification through the elimination of a variety of perceived traits, including criminality, madness, and sexual deviance, as well as ethnically coded differences. It is worth attending to the connections Foucault offers here between modes of racism as "ethnic" or "biological," though without fully collapsing the two, as it allows us to read "race" in Mexican eugenic discourse in terms of ethnic origins but also as closely bound to notions of desirable or undesirable biological markers, including disability. This is not simply to suggest that racial difference may often be coded through tropes of disability, but moreover that the desire to eliminate disability from a national future works in itself as a complementary and parallel form of racism.

Scholarship in fields such as literary criticism, the history of science, sociology, and anthropology has analyzed the diverse roles of racism (in Foucault's "ethnic" sense) and the politics of *mestizaje*, or racial mixing, in Mexican national spaces; perhaps unsurprisingly, significantly less explicit attention has been devoted to the roles of disability in this context. One aim of this book is therefore to propose a critical emphasis on disability as inseparable from racial discourse and eugenics in history. This reading understands markers of pathologized difference as tropes in the service of racism in some cases, but also as part of a disability history, expressed through the dilemma of contingency that suspends bodies, conditions, and causes between uncertain pasts and possible futures, health and fragility, normalcy and aberration, diagnosis and embodied perception. The mestizo continues to be a key figure in this history, often illustrative of the ambivalence structuring the origin and location of particular human characteristics, as well as their perceived strengths and fragilities.

A lengthy trajectory of critical bibliography on *The Cosmic Race*, and more generally on the figure of the mestizo as central to national culture and identity, makes evident the primacy of racial discourse in this history, as well as the ongoing vicissitudes of a discursive space in which racism is alternately posited as unthinkable in Mexico because of a national mestizo, or mixed-race, identity, or as still prevalent in subtle or overt manifestations (Dalton xi). The "cult of *mestizaje*," to borrow Marilyn Miller's term, predates the revolution; as Miller notes, the nineteenth-century statesmen Vicente Riva Palacio and Justo Sierra both offered favorable views of racial mixture, while Andrés Molina Enríquez elaborated an analysis of Mexico as fundamentally mestizo in his 1909 text, *Los grandes problemas nacionales* (Miller 28).[11] *Mestizaje* as developed by Vasconcelos appears to offer a eugenic vision of a present and future nation in which racial differences are subsumed into a harmonious whole. Rather than a whitening of the population through the elimination of indigenous and African elements, *mestizaje* celebrates mixture and its outcomes. In this vision, afro-descendant populations play an ambivalent role, for while they are part of the general amalgamation envisioned by Vasconcelos, their presence and social value are minimized and denigrated in the text of *The Cosmic Race*. Scholarship on racism in Mexico also points to market and class-driven desire for whitening, frequent erasure and denigration of afro-descendant populations, and the commonplace denial of the existence of racism in national culture.[12]

Mestizaje is often taken up as a social and political construct in the service of state sovereignty (Lund xv). For Pedro Ángel Palou as well, the mestizo is a (failed) political project of the state and the revolution, through which the peasant had to be deterritorialized, urbanized, and acculturated so as to leave behind his indigeneity and become mestizo (13–14), while for David Dalton the process is extended to emphasize technological transformation that produces the modern, mestizo subject (2). In addition to the overwhelmingly weighted political task to which an abstract notion of *mestizaje* is put to work, the figure of the mestizo in Mexican eugenics and national culture retains a sense of biological grounding, linking the mythical union of the indigenous mother, *La Malinche*, with the Spanish father, Hernán Cortés (Navarrete 97).[13] The mestizo thus continues to bind history and identity to the notions of personal and collective DNA. As Carlos López Beltrán and Vivette García Deister have shown, the twenty-first-century rise of new technologies for DNA sequencing, exemplified in the Human Genome Project and the subsequent Mexican Genome Project, has led to renewed interest in the mestizo as a molecular and bioinformatic category (9–14).

The ambivalence shaping the figure of the mestizo stems in part from a temporal conundrum, in which as we have seen, fears of and desires for racial mixture project themselves uncertainly toward pasts and futures, causes and outcomes, that can never be fully ascertained. In addition, the restless quality of the mestizo is the result of its splintered signification, as at times a mappable biological marker or source of identity, and also the process and outcome of cultural transformation, and at once a state-centered and ultimately neoliberal capitalist mandate of (bio)political control. In this way, *mestizaje* unfolds in accordance with the uncertain divide between "hard" and "soft" eugenics, as a mandate to conformity in which differences hover between potential emergence and disappearance, the material and the ephemeral, absorption and eradication.

The mestizo, optimistically rendered, is a figure of utopic desire shaping the hegemonic collective (Janzen 6). Beatriz Urías Horcasitas associates the *mestizaje* of the 1920s and beyond with the notion of the New Man (*hombre nuevo*), as the incarnation of positive attributes associated with the postrevolutionary working class. Yet she notes as well that by the 1930s, contrasting notions of a more negative "Mexican character" would develop in a series of philosophical texts, including Samuel Ramos's 1934 work, *Profile of Man and Culture in Mexico* (28, 211n39). This contrast allows us to situate the question of disability more specifically in relation to that of the mestizo, not simply as a series of problematic anomalies to be gradually purged or excluded from an idealized national future, but rather as a significant and lasting component of national identity. As a contemporary example, we might consider the role of pathology and predisposition to disease in research on the Map of the Mexican Genome. Popular dissemination of the project tends to emphasize the concept of a mestizo genome, linking biological markers to national identity. In the same process, researchers associate the genome with an increased incidence of health conditions such as diabetes and hypertension, so that *mestizaje* becomes a site for the diagnosis of problems and the targeted, lucrative development of their cure (López Beltrán and García Deister 14). In other words, *mestizaje* here defines the ability to get sick. Earlier articulations of the mestizo, as found in documentation from the archives of public education and health to be discussed in subsequent chapters, while lacking the biomedical specificity of the new genomic technologies, similarly reveal associations between urban school populations, coded as mestizo, and the diagnosis of a range of negatively charged physical and cognitive conditions. These are commonly portrayed as outcomes of environmental factors, such as crowded urban living conditions or parental alcoholism, factors that may in turn be associated with the processes of becoming mestizo. Disability thus emerges in archival and literary texts as intimately linked in many instances to the question of *mestizaje*, sometimes as its opposite but elsewhere as its partial equivalent, shaping the unresolved contours of national becoming in its projected or delayed causality.

Embodied Archive

The notion of disability appears through the examination of Mexican literary and public-health texts of the post-revolutionary period, not as explicitly defined in the texts, but rather as the intentional and indeed unavoidable effect of a transhistorical approach. The reading of disability as a "crip displacement"—to borrow Robert McRuer's use of this term—allows for a contemporary rendering of these texts and histories that makes possible their dialogue both with ongoing debates on the historical underpinnings of Mexican national and cultural identities, and with twenty-first-century global discourses of disability and corporeal diversity. For McRuer, the notion of crip displacement, while referring to literal human displacement (as in cases of eviction) and its links to impairment, also allows us to think about disability in spaces where it has not been typically perceived (133). In my readings as well, literal displacements are at times present, as when cognitive testing of schoolchildren justifies their removal to different classrooms or different schools, and more generally as the post-revolutionary period and its process of *mestizaje* come to signify the transformation of rural populations to urban ones. In addition, displacement here suggests attending to the production and transitions of meaning that may occur in the reading of historical texts as they come to participate in a disability genealogy.

In our contemporary context, the definition of disability rarely enjoys an agreed-upon status. Widespread public perception tends to view disability as self-explanatory, suggesting a "problem," "difficulty," "limitation," or "restriction," and calling for sympathy, prayer, charity, or medical intervention.[14] Activists and academics in a variety of international and local settings have long sought to challenge or complicate these views through protest as well as legislative action, education, and scholarship. Among disability activists and disability studies scholars, the familiar distinction between medical and social models, or those that pathologize individual differences and those that emphasize complex environmental factors, including social perception, remains central in some spaces. The success of the social model and key gains it has promoted in areas of legislation for disability rights and shifts in public attitudes toward disability are significant.[15] Yet the predominance of this model has given way to various modes of return to the specificity of materiality and embodied experience, and to a blurring of divisions between materiality and discursivity, or what David Mitchell and Sharon Snyder term "the turn-to-the-body school of disability criticism and new materialisms" (*Biopolitics*, 31). Renewed emphasis on materiality has also incorporated a revalorization of disability and of the experiences of disabled people, as well as attention to the permeability between bodies and their environments, between human and nonhuman bodies, and between the material and the social.[16] Within these frameworks, disability offers multiple and fluid meanings and transformative possibilities, while nonetheless bearing the weight of historical and ongoing injustices that unequally shape and valorize human differences. From my disability studies–informed point of view, disability demands an ongoing, critical rethinking of (inter)corporeality and the value of human and nonhuman life. Disability actively reshapes the world in accordance with diverse embodiment and perception in continuous transformation. Then too, disability demands justice as inseparable from history and from an evolving present in which exploitation and inequality continue to impact many disabled lives.

My encounter with public-health and education archival materials and related sources is mediated by the shifting roles of disability in contemporary theory and in society more generally. These include increased global interest in the topic in the context of the UN Convention on the Rights of Persons with Disabilities, initially proposed and negotiated by Mexico, and adopted in 2006. My readings are also shaped by notable disparities between promising legislation, both at international and local levels, and the lived realities of infrastructure, accessibility, and common attitudes toward disability across many social sectors, which often translate to exclusion or exploitation.[17] In addition, in approaching this study, I have been guided by scholarship from the field of the history of science, including research on the topics of eugenics, hygiene, "madness" (*locura*), the education of the blind and the deaf, and on the pathologization of criminality and race. While such studies do not tend to take up "disability" as a focal point, they do offer a historicization of notions of abnormality, health, and illness in Mexico, all of which ultimately participate in shaping a disability genealogy. As Adriana Soto Martínez notes in her study of disability in Mexico, in reference to physicians of the early post-revolutionary decades, "for specialists in eugenics and hygiene, the condition of disability offered fertile ground for theorization and intervention" (223).

At many points, discourses of hygiene and eugenics in the archival and literary texts of this study evoke elements of debates pertaining to disability in our contemporary world, although with distinct terminology. For example, contemporary opposition to telethons and similar media that tend to promote pity and charity as a response to disability is echoed in accounts of Public Welfare (*Beneficencia Pública*) in Mexico, and its transition from a nineteenth-century charity-based model to a post-revolutionary "scientific" approach to social improvement and to the economic integration of "abnormals." In addition, the later twentieth-century social model's insistence on disability as determined by environmental and social barriers, rather than by problems with a person's body, suggests in some ways the post-revolutionary hygienic emphasis on contingency and causality, that is, on factors that have given rise to problems such as "feeblemindedness," rather than the problem as intrinsic to the person. And while some contemporary disability studies scholarship emphasizes colonialism and global capitalism as central to the production of both socioeconomic inequality and disability worldwide, early-twentieth-century Mexican sources on public health and hygiene also turn to poverty and economic injustice as key causal elements to explain differential rates of illness and developmental delays among schoolchildren. In addition, new materialist approaches to disability studies that emphasize fluidity or continuity between bodies and environments are curiously echoed in early-twentieth-century discussions of school infrastructure and students' bodies. As I discuss in chapter 3, descriptions of illness or anomaly in school inspection reports shift between buildings and bodies, suggesting a holistic notion of hygiene encompassing humans and their physical environments. Some contemporary scholarship in disability studies and queer theory takes up the question of futurity, at times optimistically rendered as the projection of a hopeful horizon for the disabled and queer life still to come. In a related sense, as I discuss in chapter 2, earlier discourses of eugenics and hygiene center on the future for their articulation of a more promising world, unfolding thanks to the tireless efforts of physicians and educators. This is certainly not to suggest that these approaches are the same across time and space, for there are radical differences in each case, but rather to gesture toward elements of a potential disability genealogy, a pathway that does not insist on its own precise historical causality or continuity, but witnesses and traces points of recognition, repetition, and opposition, shaping a necessarily unfinished story.

There is undoubtedly something lost in the transaction through which archived documents become academic research, an incompleteness that tends to propel another return. Much of the research for this book was initiated at two distinct physical sites, buildings in Mexico City that today house archival collections on public health and public education. I was not the first to locate many of these sources; prior scholarship on the history of eugenics in Mexico, such as the work of Alexandra Stern, Nancy Leys Stepan, Laura Suárez y López Guazo, Marta Saade Granados, Beatriz Urías Horcasitas, and others, establishes the central actors and institutions relevant to the eugenics movement and related efforts in hygiene and education, as well as key publications on these topics, establishing pathways though which these histories can be traced. While following these historical leads, I approach the archival documents with the intention of incorporating a literary and disability-studies perspective to my readings, remaining attuned as well to the experience of research as an intercorporeal encounter. This encounter—as *embodied archive*—emphasizes the contemporary moment of reading itself as productive of meaning, and considers documents not as fixed repositories of information, but as fluid, virtual spaces through which words, bodies, and data continue to project and re-enact their stories, making them new.[18] In accordance with this approach, history should not be freely imagined or invented; however, neither should academic research pretend to be entirely removed from the particular experiences, knowledge, sensations, desires, and fears of those who conduct it. Disability, in my archival and literary readings, is not reducible to particular diagnoses, but appears through the repeated engagement between perceived or experienced human differences, their potential causes and effects, and efforts to describe, limit, or erase them, as well as through an intentional witnessing of these processes and the actual or hypothetical injustices they encompass.

The Archive of the Ministry of Public Health

Number 39, Donceles, Mexico City, not far from the house where Carlos Fuentes sets his classic short novel *Aura*, is today the address of the Archivo Histórico de la Secretaría de Salud Pública, the historical archive of the Mexican Ministry of Public Health. Documents housed here include letters and records from social assistance programs, schools for the poor, blind, deaf, orphaned, or indigent, and from the psychiatric facility known as La Castañeda. A small painted tile to the right of the front door informs us that this was the site of the Hospital del Divino Salvador, previously known as the Hospital de mujeres dementes, and established at this site in 1700. The hospital would later come under the jurisdiction of Beneficencia Pública, or Public Welfare, as one of a series of hospitals and institutions administering to the poorest sectors of society.

As Juan de Dios Peza writes in his classic 1881 text, *La Beneficencia en México*, in a brief chapter dedicated to the history of this hospital, most physicians avoid the field of "enfermedades del cerebro" [illnesses of the brain]: ". . . por la natural repugnancia, por el desagrado que ocasiona mirar constantemente todos los padecimientos de esos séres más desdichados que los

Fig. 1. A plaque at the entrance to the Archive of the Ministry of Public Health, at #39 Donceles, in Mexico City. The text reads:

"Aquí se estableció en 1700 el Hospital del Divino Salvador para mujeres dementes, fundado en el siglo XVII por el carpintero José Sayago.
—Dirección de monumentos coloniales de la república"

[In 1700, the Hospital of the Divine Savior for insane women, founded in the seventeenth century by the carpenter José Sayago, was established here.
—Administration of colonial monuments of the republic]. Photo by the author.

ciegos, que no sienten penetrar en su espíritu los rayos de la inteligencia" (27); [because of natural repugnance, because of the disgust caused by constantly seeing all the suffering of those beings, more unfortunate than the blind, who feel no rays of intelligence penetrate their spirit].

There are risks of historical inaccuracy in collapsing the stories encountered and contained here, from the ostensibly benevolent work of Jesuit priests who backed the charitable initiative of taking in and caring for eighteenth-century "*mujeres locas*," to the decidedly secular labor of a nineteenth-century public-welfare physician, praised by Peza for his scientific rigor, to the numerous public-health documents of the twentieth century, now housed in the archive. Yet approaching and entering the building, to which a bright blue wheelchair ramp had been at one point been added to the stone and tile step, and later removed, necessarily means navigating the stages that take us from one century to another, though rarely in a clear-cut manner. The painted tile at the entrance serves as a reminder that disgust and bodies associated with that feeling were mutually produced here and inhabited this space, through the "mad" women and the blind people to whom they were compared. The twentieth-century documents within the building sometimes retrieve the thread of this story, often with practical and state-sanctioned education or rehabilitation programs that purport to replace misfortune with more productive outcomes.

Public health, or *salubridad*, and public welfare, or *beneficencia*, share a complexly interwoven bureaucratic history in nineteenth- and twentieth-century Mexico.[19] At times separate, competing, or codependent entities, both administered to areas of health and education, attended to marginalized social sectors, and in the first decades of the twentieth century incorporated the combined precepts of hygiene and eugenics into many of their endeavors. In the context of the contemporary Public Health Archive, *Beneficencia Pública* functions as an organizational category, a label assigned to a collection of historical documents that would ultimately fall under the mandate of Public Health. *Beneficencia*, or Welfare, is also an archaic concept, later replaced by the category of *Asistencia* [Assistance] with emphasis shifting toward the obligations of the state to its population, and away from its previous benevolent role.

The concept of the "socialmente débiles" or "socially weak" appears frequently in documents pertaining to Welfare or Assistance, referring, for example, to "huérfanos, viudas, mujeres abandonadas, u hombres incapacitados por cualquier causa física para el trabajo, circunstancias debidas al desequilibrio de las fuerzas productoras de la sociedad" [orphans, widows, abandoned women, men unable to work due to any physical cause, circumstances resulting from the destabilization of the productive forces of society], or to "las capas débiles de la población" [weak population sectors] (Aguilar Ferreira 17–18). The goal of these institutions was to reintegrate these sectors into society through economic productivity, or to care for them permanently in cases where integration was not possible ("Bases generales" 3).

The notion of abnormality is frequently evoked in reference to those receiving the services of Welfare or Assistance.[20] Writing in 1932, the head of Educative and Social Action, a department within Public Welfare, underscores abnormality as the defining characteristic of all institutional inmates: "Todos los asilados, de cualquier clase que sean, niños, adolescentes, o adultos, hombres o mujeres, deben ser considerados como anormales desde el punto de vista social." [All the inmates, whether children, adolescents, or adults, men or women, should be considered abnormal from a social perspective] (Esquivel 5). The author describes how this social abnormality tends to evolve toward further negative consequences, and insists on the goal of converting the abnormal into elements of social integration. This discussion, grounded in sequential logic, stresses intervention at the level of causal origins: "La labor más importante es descubrir las causas que originan el alcoholismo, la mendicidad profesional, la vagancia, las enfermedades venéreas, la toxicomanía, la desadaptación del hogar, la falta de ahorro y previsión, la fecundidad del proletariado, la falta de trabajo, la miseria, las aglomeraciones urbanas, la educación inadecuada, las enfermedades, la falta del seguro social, y otros males" (1). [The most important task is to discover the causes of alcoholism, professional begging, vagrancy, venereal diseases, drug addiction, maladjustment in the home, lack of savings and foresight, high birth rates of the proletariat, unemployment, misery, urban congestion, inadequate education, illnesses, lack of social security, and other problems]. The goal in short is to "detener la degeneración de la raza" (1) [detain the degeneration of the race].

As in this case, discourses of eugenics and hygiene emerge at many points in the archival documents, reminding the reader that the work of these institutions, engaged in the day-to-day operation of schools, hospitals, and asylums, was also shaped by larger projects directed toward the management of national reproductive futures. Rather than provoking disgust or sentiments of pious charity, as was the case in prior centuries, the "socially weak" individuals under the purview of assistance programs would be subject to a "conscious and scientific attitude of social service (Morones 10). The "science" of this approach is based in part on an emphasis, again, on causality. As the same author notes, "La población propia de esta Institución se considera anormal desde el punto de vista del desarrollo físico inferior, debido a causas económicas y desde el punto de vista social debido a la desorganización familiar y a la carencia de normas morales" (9). [The population of this Institution is itself considered abnormal from the perspective of inferior physical development, due to economic causes, and from the social perspective due to disorganization of the family unit and the lack of moral norms]. Abnormality is bracketed here by causes external to the individuals as physical bodies, yet still closely associated with them through social and family structures. In this way, abnormality is contingent on a series of circumstances, rather than intrinsic to a given body. Hygiene, or soft eugenics, intervenes to combat these causes and to establish a logic in which abnormal bodies are partially separated from their possible causes and effects.

Documents from the archive housed at #39 Donceles reveal the intertwined endeavors of health, welfare, and education in this period, as is most clearly apparent in discussion of schools for the "socially weak," or those for the blind and the deaf. These institutions emphasize children as the emblematically weak social sector, hence the group overall acquires an implicitly childlike status, to be healed and educated for the benefit of the future population. In accordance with Adriana Soto Martínez's discussion of eugenics and hygiene in this period, disability is subject to a dual framework of medical and pedagogical knowledge, associated with both illness and immorality (222). The evolving institutions of Welfare, Assistance, and Public Health thus participate in shaping a disability genealogy, centered on specifically marginalized sectors but extending toward the population as a whole through a child-centered discourse of pedagogy and hygiene. The colonial building of the archive houses these intertwined histories, shaping in turn a space in which disability begins to merge with an evolving and expanding process of classification.

The National Archive

Beyond these specifically marked social sectors, education policies for the population as a whole fell to the Ministry of Public Education, whose historical archives are now held in the Archivo General de la Nación (National Archive), housed in the massive former prison, Lecumberri. Research at this facility is an awe-inspiring experience, not least because of the sheer size and panopticon-like structure of the space itself, in stark contrast to the exquisitely restored colonial building at #39 Donceles. The galleries, distributed like the spokes of a wheel around a central rotunda, house boxes of papers rather than prisoners, yet authorities remain vigilant over these national treasures lest any suffer damage or be allowed to escape. During the months I conducted a major portion of the research for this book, the outdoor passageway to Gallery Eight was inhabited by a large number of cats. Archival staff explained that the feline community combat pests that might otherwise damage documents. On a more recent visit, however, I was disappointed to find that the cats had disappeared. Other changes to the archive included increased bureaucratization and more restricted access to some documents. The disappearance of the cats, and the restrictions, were apparently related to construction work and remodeling of the archive. This work also coincided with new legislation on archival management, initiated to better preserve archival materials, but criticized by some scholars for its restrictions on research access and its delimitation of what should count as historical documents.[21] These changes to the archival landscape, in which cats used to sun themselves on the cobblestones of an extended patio, are undoubtedly part of a more complex series of circumstances. Yet they become inseparable from the experience of research, which is always shaped in its daily unfolding by conditions of access, by what the reader encounters along the way, and by what she sees both in the documents and when she lifts her eyes from the page. As I wait for a box of documents, requested three business days in advance, it occurs to me that this archival landscape is marked by what remains unseen, by real or feared management practices that might reclassify some histories, or by the mice that may be chewing on the pages.

Research experience at Mexico's National Archive is also inevitably marked by reminders that the building of Lecumberri, "the Black Palace," served as a prison from its inauguration in 1900 until 1976. As Susana Draper writes in reference to Lecumberri as both prison and archive, "The space performs a struggle in which we move from the administration of maladjusted bodies to the administration of a calling forth of memory, truth regimes, and the nature of the public sphere" (353).[22] The privilege of conducting research at this impressive public facility is at once shaped by the contours of what counts as the public sphere, by an evolving dynamic of restriction and access. As Draper further suggests, borrowing from Derrida's *Archive Fever*, the archive is central to the problem of democracy; rather than revealing hidden truths, it operates through the paradoxical conditions in which "making public" becomes both possible and impossible (355–56). In this sense too, archival research for this book was shaped by a disability genealogy in which bodies and the documentation of those bodies are managed, sometimes partially revealed, and always potentially reshaped and rewritten.

The documents I consulted at the National Archive's Gallery Eight pertained to the Ministry of Public Education, and more specifically to its Department of Psychopedagogy and Hygiene, founded in 1925. These records often reveal discursive overlaps with the work of Welfare and Assistance, through intertwined notions of hygiene and education. Yet the Department of Psychopedagogy and Hygiene (later the National Institute of Psychopedagogy, founded in 1936) operated on a more massive scale, intended to benefit all Mexican public-school children. As further discussed in chapter 3, the work of Psychopedagogy and Hygiene included the large-scale physical and cognitive testing of schoolchildren, with the goals of creating homogeneous student groups and identifying the characteristics of "the Mexican child." Although the Education Ministry did not attend specifically to the "abnormal" and socially marginalized populations under the purview of Public Welfare, the work of Psychopedagogy and Hygiene was nonetheless closely tied to concerns with the issue of "abnormality," in particular with ways to identify, treat, and combat it. Activities included the training of teachers to identify mental abnormality, along with conferences on the topic, and the elaboration of "health cards" for each student that would include data on biometrics, health conditions of both the child and parents, a mental profile, and information about academic performance ["Informe de labores"]. As in the case of Public Welfare and Assistance, here too physicians emphasized the question of heredity and its various causal pathways, including the influences of alcohol, syphilis, and poor nutrition, among other factors.

A common concern regarding schoolchildren was the question of delay, or "*retraso escolar*," defined as a discrepancy of at least three years between the child's "chronological age" and his or her "mental age," ascertained through testing. Yet delay was immediately subdivided according to its causes, which could be social or physical, and were often traced to the family environment and to the economic context. Delay was thus described on a continuum, grouping students into those who could be taught to various degrees, and those who were unteachable and would receive medical care rather than education (Santamarina, "La cuestión de los anormales"). Another key area of interest was the physical environment of the schools, including furniture such as school desks, which were thought to cause spinal deformities if improperly proportioned, and textbooks, which were said to contribute to defects in vision if not properly printed (Arellano Belloc; Fernández Manero). The eugenically oriented work of Psychopedagogy and Hygiene generally implemented a quantitative and medicalized approach to the Mexican schoolchild, in which education was intrinsically bound to the promotion of health over an extended trajectory, applied both to children and to the greater present and future populations they would potentially become.

Public Health and Psychopedagogy and Hygiene both participated in the widespread implementation of cognitive testing of children, and in discussions on the classification of students and the notion of abnormality. As institutions charged with the care, education, health and well-being of children, both engaged in the discourse of puericulture, or child-rearing and the care of pregnant mothers. Papers from the first Congress of the Child, held in Mexico City in 1921, reveal the prominence of puericulture in these debates, as well as its ties to eugenics, a topic that featured its own section at the Congress.[23] The Sociedad Mexicana de Eugenesia para el Mejoramiento de la Raza [Mexican Eugenics Society for the Improvement of the Race], founded in 1931 by Dr. Alfredo M. Saavedra, traced some of its membership and its theories from the 1921 conference, thus showing clear continuity between projects in childhood health and education and the movement for "racial improvement," and between soft and hard eugenics.[24]

Disability, and the projects of eugenics and hygiene through which it often emerges, are not confined to these areas of state jurisdiction. In addition, they appear in a variety of literary works to be discussed in this book—some penned by physicians, educators, or technical experts—gesturing toward the dilemmas of futurity and national history, as well as the overarching problem of contingency, through which human differences and identities may be uncertainly suspended as the outcomes of external conditions, or the unfolding of pasts and futures. This temporal suspension partially echoes Eunjung Kim's concept of "folded time," in which the present time of the disabled body is subsumed by attention to nostalgia for the past and hope for the future (227). In the readings to come, such differences may also suspend or disrupt the progression of time, impacting and reshaping the way we might read or otherwise witness the text and the world. The encounter with these stories is itself a process marked by chance and uncertainty, regardless of the rigor of one's research methods. It is a witnessing of an always incomplete body of text, a potential and unfinished disability genealogy.

Chapters

Each chapter in this book centers on a mode of contingency—a dynamic through which difference may be placed in brackets, subsumed to its purported cause, or in which disability acts to rearrange the reader's perceptions and expectations. Chapter 1, Eugenic Itineraries, centers on the evolution of transnational discourses of eugenics and their impact in Mexico, with attention to the work of the Cuban-born Yucatec physician, Eduardo Urzaiz. Urzaiz has received critical attention for his 1919 science fiction novel, *Eugenia*, which depicts a futuristic world of state-controlled reproduction for the improvement of the population. In addition, as an obstetrician and psychiatrist influenced by his Cuban background and by a medical residency in New York, he wrote extensively for both professional and popular audiences, illustrated his work with sketches, and advocated for eugenics through selective sterilization as a means to improve the health of the population. Nonetheless, a combined reading of Urzaiz's medical and literary writing suggests some moments of ambivalence regarding disability, at times marked for elimination, but elsewhere an object of fascination and a mode of critical self-reflexivity.

Urzaiz's work, in dialogue with the diverse figures he admired, from Jean-Martin Charcot to José Martí, allows for an approach to eugenics and disability in twentieth-century Mexico as inseparable from evolving international contexts, and from the problem of the migratory point of view, one that approaches its subject matter from elsewhere, and is conditioned by the visual metaphors and practices of this perspective. In this chapter, the categories of race and disability emerge through eugenic discourse, through practices of looking and visual representations of corporeal difference. Visual forms of eugenics here take on the dual sense of a biological and an aesthetic project, as evidenced by Urzaiz's interest in sketching for both scientific and artistic purposes, an emphasis that further links him to the nineteenth-century French neurologist, Charcot. I argue that eugenics itself can be understood as a process of visual observation, and I ask the reader to consider his or her own situated viewpoint and line of sight as part of the dynamic that these texts make possible, within and beyond Mexican national spaces.

Chapter 2, Corporeal Causalities, discusses the temporal contingency of disability in reference to anti-alcohol campaigns of the 1920s and '30s, and the work of José Vasconcelos, including his 1932 text *Ética*. As in the previous chapter, disability appears through a complex and partial alignment with racial difference and is conditioned by an emphasis on visual representation. Here, however, the primary focus is on discourses of causality and temporality underpinning approaches to eugenics and hygiene during this period; specifically, disability often appears as potentially caused by moral or environmental ills (such as alcohol consumption) in the past, or such ills are projected as possibly leading to future disability. I link this reading of disability through time and causality to a contemporary critical framework in which the notion of a desirable disability of the future is postulated against eugenic pasts, and also against mainstream notions that promote prevention of disability for a "healthier" future. One of the aims of this chapter is thus to recognize the impetus to either congeal or tease out the relationship between bodies and the causality that may shape them. Another is to consider the discursive violence that potentially underpins readings of disability as defined by cause and effect.

My analysis focuses on anti-alcohol campaign materials published by the Ministries of Public Health and Public Education, and on a sketch by Diego Rivera published in the periodical *El sembrador* as part of a rural anti-alcohol campaign, depicting the effects of alcohol as tied to capitalist exploitation, and as counter to the liberatory aims of the Mexican revolution. At stake in these texts is the degree to which the negatively charged "difference" of disability can be separated from the body or population depicted, or in other words, whether or not the causality of disability appears as an intrinsic part of the bodies in question. In a parallel sense, Vasconcelos's writing activates the dilemma of contingency through the author's approach to embodied differences and spiritual transcendence, hovering between the rejection and the incorporation of human diversity in his aesthetic vision.

Chapter 3, Psychopedagogy and the Cityscape, considers the role of the built environment in creating and delimiting space for the expressions of human bodies and differences. This chapter places specific emphasis on architect Juan O'Gorman's 1930s project of "hygienic" primary schools for working-class Mexican children, sponsored by the Ministry of Public Education, in relation to O'Gorman's pessimistic vision of an urbanized future. The chapter pays attention to O'Gorman's rhetoric in his discussions of functionalist architecture, but also examines the role of the Department of School Hygiene in the same period. School physicians were responsible for examining and testing the bodies of students, and for assessing the hygienic properties of school buildings, as extensive archival documentation attests. I examine archived physicians' reports of visits to Mexico City schools, along with O'Gorman's work, to show how school hygiene practices and discourse transfer notions of health between human bodies and the buildings they inhabit.

The dilemma of human and architectural hygiene, as displayed in these texts, stems from an insistence on perfect efficiency that becomes self-reflexive, attempting to solve urban problems of public health and social inequality through quantifiable solutions that specifically and economically express the problem at hand. Architectural hygienic solutions link human bodies to their built environments through a logic of symbiosis. The result is both that biological, mechanical, and economic forms of health and functionality appear to mirror one another, and that bodies and buildings work to service the operation of an overarching system. In this sense, measurements of illness or disability in children, or of structural inadequacies in buildings, reveal a fraught and unsettled discourse of hygiene, hovering between specific physical expressions of social inequality and the goal of perfecting the vast workings of both revolutionary state and capitalist enterprise.

Chapter 4, Biotypology and Perception—The Prose of Statistics, looks at the use of statistics in population studies as a mode of defining a Mexican "character," particularly during the 1940s, with attention to the research of psychiatrist Dr. José Gómez Robleda, and to his brief works of fiction. In this chapter I consider eugenicists' and biotypologists' enthusiastic adoption of methods of probability and statistics in their approaches to the classification of schoolchildren, indigenous populations, and other groups under study. In these works, numerical data acquire liveliness in contact with diverse bodies and with the passion of the researcher, even as reliance on statistical measurement would seem to dehumanize the human objects of study. Disability, measured in bodily symptoms, thus helps to produce a relationship between bodies and numbers, and sets a story in motion.

In these texts, the relationship between eugenics and statistics produces a form of disability contingency through which human traits are calculated through numerical projections and framed through the uncertainty of external observation. At the same time, disability and racialized differences emerge here through mutual cross-referencing. If both disability and race tend to signify exclusion and disqualification here, these categories also operate in relation to signposted historical processes and intersubjective exchanges, or in other cases in relation to projected numerical data. Their negative charge works in an ambivalent sense, intermittently merged with or separate from the human subjects that these categories describe. In some cases, however, the perceptual framework of difference becomes virtually inseparable from the subject in question, as when Gómez Robleda emphasizes the skin itself as both sense organ and external marker of difference.

Chapter 5, Asymmetries—Injury, History, and Revolution, focuses on the work and reception of Rafael F. Muñoz, particularly his novels ¡*Vámonos con Pancho Villa*! (and the popular film based on the novel) and *Se llevaron el cañón para Bachimba*, paying attention to the relationship between pedagogical processes of individual transformation through the revolution, and corporeal markings of illness and disability. This chapter focuses less on archival sources and more on classic literary texts and their critical and popular reception. Yet like the earlier chapters, this chapter also centers on questions of pedagogy, in this case considering how characters and readers are framed as bodies that both enact and receive the effects of historical change.

While in previous chapters, I have primarily discussed forms of contingency in which disability appears as bracketed or mediated by causal, perceptual, or temporal frameworks, here I turn as well to a reverse phenomenon. Experiences of wounding in these narratives disrupt the sense of temporal and historical progression structuring the literary discourse of the revolution, resulting in an aesthetics of asymmetry that mediates the pedagogical project of the texts. At stake in these works is the unresolved question of allegiance to a national and political cause, and the possible embodiment of that allegiance as always conditioning—and conditioned by—a temporality of war. The literary aesthetics of the experience of wounding, as irreducible to the process of death, shapes the repeated forms of allegiance, as language becomes inseparable from lived corporeal history and marks proliferating sites of injustice, but also makes possible other forms of witnessing and denunciation.

Contingent Disabilities

I began this introduction in a somewhat guarded, confessional tone, as an approach to the topics of diagnosis and pedagogy that figure throughout this book, but also as a way to navigate the dilemma of contingency, through a story that is necessarily partial, potentially arbitrary, and subject to evolution over time, and, one might say, that is mine but does not define me in an absolute way. The structure of contingency through which disability appears in this book suggests that, in these readings of the early Mexican post-revolutionary period, diverse perspectives, causal circumstances, and uncertain pasts and futures bracket and mediate human differences. At the same time, disability and changes to the body in turn shape the narratives and the temporal progression of which they form a part.

In the contexts of the Mexican cultural production analyzed here, disability rarely occupies fixed sites, but instead hovers between distinct potentialities, at times defining a particular group or identity, but frequently remaining external, offering evidence of causes, warnings, fear, or desire—a judgment, a possible past, a future still to come. Unlike in the contexts of eugenics movements in the US, Canada, or parts of Europe, disability here does not tend in general to define conditions of absolute exclusion. Similarly, the figure of the mestizo, as I have discussed, provides instances of the more ambivalent status of unwanted difference, as at once linked to national selfhood yet potentially overcome, avoided, removed, or explained as the outcome of particular circumstances; in other cases, indigeneity fulfills a comparable role. The uncertain movement of disability, through causal perspectives that tend to partially separate it from particular bodies, whether of groups or individuals, nonetheless still implies forms of violence. This is the case, for example, when causal logic insists on disability as negative outcome or effect to be avoided, rather than accounting for the ways in which we have come to take both the causality and the undesirability for granted.[25] Eunjung Kim's reading of disability as "frozen in the moment of its creation" (19) and hence bound to a negative causal framework is instructive here. Or, in another sense, a partial separation between an individual or group and a pejoratively viewed difference may dehumanize the difference, leaving the individual body suspended between an ostensibly redeemed human status and a devalued mark or remainder that is still not quite erased, as occurs in Fanon's phenomenological reading of the racialized perception of self as other.[26] As I have noted, these structures find echoes in the evolution of disability studies, and in the diverse and shifting meanings of disability in our contemporary world. Such echoes might remind us that the witnessing of disability history as embodied archive, with the risks of misreading and appropriation this process implies, offers more than a record of a fascinating or troubling past. It is at once an encounter that shapes the conditions through which we unravel and reimagine our own disability genealogies, tracing out both marks of violence and their retellings, asymmetries of pasts and futures.

One

Eugenic Itineraries

Eugenic Observations

What if eugenics itself could take place through the act of looking? In one of the more remarkable scenes in Eduardo Urzaiz's 1919 science fiction novel, *Eugenia*, the reader witnesses an encounter between the president of the eugenics bureau of Villautopía, Doctor don Remigio Pérez Serrato, and two African physicians who have come to visit and learn about the advanced science of eugenics for the improvement of the human race and its societies. The novel, written in Mérida by the Cuban-born Yucatec physician-writer, depicts a futuristic society in the year 2218, distinguished by complex technologies of hygiene and transportation, but most importantly, by a modernized system of human reproduction, known specifically as "*eugenética*" [eugenics or eugenetics]. In Villautopía, which may be identified, through references to flora and architecture, as a futuristic Mérida, physically ideal adolescents are selected to be official reproducers, while all others are sterilized. Moreover, while conception takes place through sexual reproduction, pregnancies are carried to term through a more complex process, in which the embryo is extracted from the uterus and implanted into the body of a male. Again, a select group of surgically altered men is chosen for the task of gestation, all births are Caesarean, and children are raised in large groups by female employees of the state.

Declaring itself explicitly a novel of eugenics, Urzaiz's text was published more than a decade before eugenics would appear as a defined movement with its own organization in Mexico, the Sociedad Eugénica Mexicana para el Mejoramiento de la Raza, founded in 1931. However, notions of eugenics were already present in political and medical discourse of the early postrevolutionary period, as were the related tendencies of *puericultura, homi-*

cultura, and hygiene more generally, suggesting that the fictional project of improving the population through focus on reproduction might certainly have resonated with Urzaiz's contemporaries.[1] Moreover, theories of eugenics had risen to social prominence in Cuba by 1914, and Urzaiz would have encountered elements of such theories during his 1905 medical residency at psychiatric facilities in New York.[2] Urzaiz's Cuban origins, his interest in histories of Cuban-Yucatec migration, his time in the US, and certain details of this particular scene, to be discussed further, underscore the need for a geopolitically expanded perspective on the novel. In this text, eugenics becomes a transnational and volatile phenomenon, as well as an occasion for the detailed observation of human bodies, and the elaboration of a combined aesthetic and medical discourse in which human differences are categorized but never fully contained. The act of observation itself, in this broader context and within Urzaiz's novel, becomes crucial to the manifestation of eugenics as an artistic and biological phenomenon. Let us imagine, at least for a moment, that eugenics itself is produced and contained through such moments of observation.

Urzaiz's unique status as a transnational and regional figure means that his work resonates in specifically Caribbean and Yucatec contexts, as well as in a nationally defined Mexican post-revolutionary cultural scene. The familiar centrality of Mexico City, typically key to the production of national culture in this period and beyond, is thus displaced in Urzaiz's novel. By choosing Urzaiz and his work as an entry point into an exploration of disability and eugenics in Mexico, I purposefully shift the discursive terrain toward alternative configurations of Mexican nationalism, based not only on particular locales, but on a series of relations between them. The specificity of Urzaiz's personal and professional trajectory, as well as the political conditions informing his career, necessarily shape the project of eugenics that emerges in the novel, and in Urzaiz's other writing. At the same time, the place of this work, situated at a volatile and uniquely national, regional, and transnational juncture, allows for a mode of eugenic discourse in which narrative point of view must be obliquely conjectured through calculations of movement and relative distances between geopolitical sites and historical referents.

To arrive at the scene of Urzaiz's *Eugenia*, and by extension, at the eugenic project of early-twentieth-century Mérida, is necessarily to arrive, as did Urzaiz himself, from elsewhere. As a late-nineteenth-century immigrant from Cuba, and later an established physician in Mérida following his medical training in New York, Urzaiz offers the reader a complex series of observations on eugenics, reproduction, racial difference, and perhaps most importantly, on the problem of looking itself. Urzaiz's itinerary, and that of his work, places them in a constellation of shifting figures that link Mexico to Cuba and to the United States, in the company of other discursive and literal travelers such as José Martí, Fernando Ortiz, and—even further afield—Jean-Martin Charcot.[3] *Eugenia*, a strange and unique novel in the context of early post-revolutionary Mexico, has been briefly taken up by Mexican historians of science such as Beatriz Urías Horcasitas and Laura Suárez y López Guazo as an anecdotal focal point for understanding Mexico's eugenicist history. My own encounter with Urzaiz's work at the start of this book is intended to place Mexican eugenics in its transnational context, but also to situate the reader at a consciously calculated distance from the texts and their geographies, so as to make palpable the problem of relative positionalities. I ask the reader to observe eugenics and disability, up close and at a distance, as both objects and actions, to see herself and to see others seeing.[4] This approach-as-arrival—a eugenic itinerary—begins to define my reading of disability here and in the chapters to come. While focused on a particular writer and his work, the reading explodes outward to take on not only the question of historical context, but the farther-reaching resonance of disability and of eugenic discourse across time and space.

The scene in question is striking for its brief but exaggerated and visceral physical descriptions of the characters involved, specifically the Africans (referred to as "*médicos hotentotes*" [Hottentot doctors]), the physician whose narrative dominates the chapter, and the young Ernesto, male protagonist of the novel and recently designated "official reproducer of the species." Although the novel has only recently begun to receive significant critical attention, two of the scholarly texts that do treat it at length come to diametrically opposed conclusions regarding both the discourse of race in this scene in particular, and the author's own view of the eugenic utopia he proposes. The fact that the issues of race and racism come to the fore in this scene, and in the critical work that the novel has inspired, is significant in the sense that—although the history of eugenic thinking is of necessity also a history of racism and racialization—within the novel itself, eugenics functions to erase negatively perceived physical and psychological conditions from a population represented as racially homogeneous. In other words, the question of racial admixture or *mestizaje* is largely absent from the novel overall; in fact, it appears explicitly only once in a brief comment by one of the African visitors regarding the desirability and difficulty of "cross-breeding" with "superior races" (59).

In this chapter, I take as my starting point this strange, partial separation between the project of eugenics and the discourse of race through *mestizaje*[5]—a discourse commonly perceived as a central fixture in Mexican debates on human reproduction in this period. I wish to establish, first, what it is that the eugenic project of Villautopía seeks to improve on, or erase. By reading the project of eugenics in the novel in the context of both the transnational proliferation of eugenic campaigns in the early twentieth century and disability studies scholarship on eugenics in history, I argue that eugenics in this novel operates through an ambivalent engagement with disability—or human characteristics that the text depicts as signs of abnormality and imperfection. Second, I consider how the semi-elided dilemma of race in the novel works to filter the project of reproductive improvement, or in other terms, how race and disability operate through representations that are paradoxically separated yet interdependent. Finally, taking into account this ambivalent duality of race and disability, and the transnational context of eugenics through which it emerges, I engage with the complex dynamic of visual observation that structures the novel's depiction of corporeal differences. I borrow here from Irene Tucker's study of racial difference in history, in which she focuses on the role of the direct observation of the skin as crucial to the history of racialization from the Enlightenment to the present. While the history of pathology plays a significant role in Tucker's work, particularly regarding the late-eighteenth-century era of anatomical medicine, the concept of race as such is the central focus of her project. In my reading of Urzaiz's novel and its broader eugenicist context, I pay specific attention to a mode of eugenic observation in which both race and disability participate in an uncertain dynamic of seeing and being seen.[6]

I consider the ambivalence of disability here—and of acts of observation more generally—as partially shaped by an erotics of looking. Through these processes, desire is paradoxically mediated by multiple drives: to approach an ideal form, to erase differences and to see and retain those differences, and again, to see oneself seeing. A certain queerness of this erotics becomes palpable at some points, not simply because of the centrality of the male body as recipient of the male gaze, but more significantly because of how the structure of observation tends to undermine the grounding of fixed identities or positions. Eve Sedgwick's etymological reference to the word "queer" gives the term a paradoxical specificity in the context of this chapter. As she writes: "The word 'queer' itself means *across*—it comes from the Indo-European root—*twerkw*, which also yields the German *quer* (transverse), Latin *torquere* (to twist), English *athwart*" (viii). As eugenics and practices of visual observation traverse time and space in Urzaiz's transnational itineraries and his science fiction novel, they engage at times in a queer modality, marked by a shifting sexual imaginary and by unresolved or unexpected movement.

Before engaging further with the structures of eugenics in Urzaiz's work, I first offer a brief map of the novel itself. The futuristic story concerns Ernesto, a young and physically ideal male, and his older, intellectually gifted partner and former teacher, Celiana. Toward the beginning of the novel, Ernesto, thanks to his physical endowments, is selected by the state to be an official reproducer of the species, meaning that he will be required to work for at least one year, and to father at least twenty children. Reproduction takes place through conventional intercourse, followed by extraction of the fetus from the woman, and its implantation into a separately selected male gestator. Through his reproductive activities, Ernesto meets and falls in love with the young and beautiful Eugenia, also an official reproducer, and will ultimately father a child with her. Celiana, who is renowned for her intellect and beauty, but has nonetheless been sterilized at a young age due to cerebral and physical imperfections, is now abandoned and embittered. The novel concludes with her slide into drug addiction and decadence, in sharp contrast to the idyllic future projected through the entwined figures of Ernesto and Eugenia and the reproductive horizon they anticipate.

The foregrounded romantic plot and its eugenic project work in tandem with a political backdrop in which Villautopía and the world find themselves on the brink of a potential trade war, due to disagreements regarding the price of sugar.[7] In the novel's futuristic world, global politics have evolved alongside reproductive policies and practices. Broad international federations have taken the place of nation states, working for the collective good rather than for personal interest or patriotism. Personal economic interest has also disappeared, as societies now ensure the well-being of all, making the concepts of economic inheritance or savings unnecessary. In this socialist future, reproductive, economic, and political interests mirror one another. Artificial reproductive selection has led to increased equality of physical and mental aptitudes, along with a collective vision of the common good, according to one narrator, and similarly, the disappearance of political and economic interests has created a world in which selfish individual or small-scale competition has been replaced by harmonious collaboration. However, just as physical and mental imperfections and selfish interest persist in Villautopía, so do other forms of inequality. Whether these partial failures mean that the novel should be read as a dystopic critique of eugenics and of socialist projects, or whether such imperfections instead reflect Urzaiz's complex and more optimistic engagement with the political and scientific debates of his day, is a question that has been taken up by some prior critics of the novel (Abbondanza; Dziubinskyj). At stake, of course, is whether we might read Urzaiz as a strong advocate of eugenics, and hence take his futuristic proposal in a more or less literal fashion. To do so would mean encountering in the novel—and hence in early post-revolutionary Mexico, via Cuba and the United States—a bold advocacy for the elimination of disabled people combined with a form of unabashed racism. I will address this issue further; however, I wish to argue that regardless of the side of the argument one adopts, this dilemma itself provides a fruitful vantage point from which to consider eugenics and disability as informed by relative positionalities and acts of observation.[8]

While other scholars have addressed the question of how literally one should read Urzaiz's futuristic and eugenic vision in the novel, and of how the racist depiction of the African doctors impacts the work, it is worth noting that the role of disability as such in Urzaiz's work has not received sustained and extended consideration. By disability, I refer here not only to the specific conditions mentioned in the novel, such as "madness" or imperfections of vision, but to the social and aesthetic roles of these conditions in the novel, and over time. A disability studies approach, in this case, would seek to unsettle the stability of these categories, and to interrogate the aesthetic and political effects of corporeal, cognitive, and psychosocial difference in the narrative. In focusing on disability, the reader might ask herself what the delimitation of differences as undesirable can tell us about the prevalent notions of human worth, both at the time of the novel's publication and in the present day. For Tobin Siebers, "[human] disqualification is justified through the accusation of mental or physical inferiority based on aesthetic principles" (24). To the extent that such disqualification takes place in the novel, my goal is not to condemn the writer or the work, but rather to take seriously the process of a narrative engagement with discriminatory violence, and the stakes of the reader's positionality vis-à-vis this aesthetic and scientific project. In other words, I ask how the novel's aesthetics—and aesthetic ambivalence—in particular pertaining to human embodiment, situate us both affectively and politically, and what kind of work this embodiment and aesthetics performs.

Aesthetic Ambivalence

Urzaiz provides some clues to the question of what the eugenic project seeks to erase in his prologue to the text, where he notes that some readers may respond to the novel by exclaiming: "¡Pero esta es la obra de un loco!" (11) [But this is the work of a madman! (4).] Urzaiz continues with the following explanation:

Médico soy de locos, y nada tendría de extraño que, en los catorce largos años que llevo tratando a diario con ellos, algo se me hubiese pegado de sus delirios y manías. Yo, como es natural, me tengo por sano y cuerdo; y como, por otra parte, he conocido y conozco enajenados que escriben muy bella y razonadamente, ni me asombro ni me ofendo porque mi obra sea calificada de tal manera. Después de todo, hasta los mismos conceptos de cuerdo y loco son relativos, pues dependen del lado en que se coloque el que juzgue o califica. (11)

[I am a doctor of madmen, and it would not seem strange that, in the fourteen long years that I have dealt with them on a daily basis, something of their deliriums and habits would have been passed on to me. Naturally I believe myself to be sane and in my right mind. And in addition, I have known and still know insane people who write with such beauty and reason, that I would be neither surprised nor offended if my work were classified as such. After all, the very concepts of "sane" and "insane" are relative, since they depend on which side of the fence the one who judges or classifies them is standing.] (4)

Madness here is a relative category, yet it is not an inoffensive one, and comes with certain risks, as the author underscores in the concluding line of his prologue: "me queda el recurso—y a él me acojo desde luego—de aplicarte la misma vara que emplees para medirme" (11). [I am left with the option— and naturally take refuge in it—of using the same yardstick on you that you use to measure me (4)]. To be judged as mad would mean, beyond the frame of the novel, to risk becoming a mental patient of the novelist-psychiatrist. Within the novel, on the other hand, those who lack perfect, balanced health are sterilized, to avoid the transmission of imperfection. Madness is not the only category at work in the novel, however, for other forms of "imbalance" also justify sterilization. One character has "una sed insaciable y casi morbosa de adquirir conocimientos" (24), [an insatiable and almost morbid thirst for knowledge (13)]; another "era de una fealdad simpática y atrayente como la de ciertos animales raros" (27), [was of a kind and attractive ugliness, like that of certain strange animals (16)]. This character, it may be noted, also reminds the narrator of Voltaire, while another, the above-mentioned Dr. Pérez Serrato, has a round, pale face, with "bovine" eyes, and is compared to Charcot, the nineteenth-century French neurologist. In addition, some characters are described as having imperfect vision, either because of "estrabismo" [squinting] or being "tuerto" [blind in one eye]. In the futuristic world of Villautopía, any departure from a notion of perfect health, or from an aesthetic ideal referring primarily to physical beauty, but also encompassing mental stability and balance, is marked for erasure through sterilization. The novel suggests an aesthetic paradox, however, by combining this projected erasure with the detailed inclusion of such characters, and a narrative that lingers over descriptions of their unique bodies and behaviors. Comparisons to figures of "antiquity" (i.e., the eighteenth and nineteenth centuries) such as Voltaire and Charcot, although vaguely caricaturesque, seem to place them in a positive light, while the details of their imperfections add a kind of self-conscious pleasure to the reading. The female protagonist, Celiana, who writes of the decadent aesthetics of two or three centuries prior, clarifies the contrast between this previous aesthetics and the current privileging of harmony and balance: "Lo bello no se veía entonces en la armónica fuerza de la vida; sino en lo raro y extravagante, en lo anormal y morboso" (99); [Beauty was not seen in the harmonic force of life but rather in the strange and extravagant, abnormal and morbid (71).][9] But in describing Celiana herself as a character and a body in decadence (due to age, a mild squint, and intellectual excesses), the narrator participates in this "prior" aesthetics, and thus extends the paradox of projecting its erasure.

The lines used by Celiana to describe the aesthetics of a prior age here offer a clue to the novel's place in relation to Urzaiz's thinking, and to the larger trajectory of his professional development. In 1902 Urzaiz presented his undergraduate thesis to the Facultad de Medicina y Cirugía de Yucatán, with the title, "El desequilibrio mental." A number of concepts from the novel, written seventeen years later, emerge in this earlier work, offering a stunning link between the author's medical career and his novelistic aesthetics. In the final chapter of the thesis, devoted specifically to the roles of art, religion, and pedagogy in relation to the risks and prevention of mental instability [*desequilibrio mental*], Urzaiz offers the following reflection, which is worth quoting at length:

> Este hálito glacial de indiferencia y escepticismo que seca en la generación actual la fuente del sentimiento religioso, extendiéndose a todas las manifestaciones del pensamiento, ha modificado en su esencia el concepto de la belleza y ha impreso su sello en todas las artes, que no son ni pueden ser más que los medios que tiene el hombre de exteriorizar este concepto. Ya no se busca la belleza en la armonía, en la fuerza, en la vida: hoy se le ve en lo raro y extravagante, en lo anor-

mal y morboso. La música no trata ya de reproducir aquella armonía
eterna que vaga en el seno de la creación y en el fondo de nuestras
almas, sino de crear ritmos extraños y nunca oídos que haga vibrar los
nervios como cuerdas próximas a romperse. Las artes de la forma y el
color, despreciando el modelo inimitable, amalgaman los reinos de la
naturaleza, dando a la figura humana las líneas indecisas del molusco
o las ramificaciones del vegetal, y a sus producciones todas, los tintes y
contornos de esos seres que crea la mente que delira. La poesía idealiza
los extravíos de la razón, los horrores de la duda, las alucinaciones de la
embriaguez, el desorden, la neurosis, la degeneración. En la expresión,
huye de la claridad como de un vicio y busca pueriles combinaciones
de extraña cadencia y enigmático sentido. (39–40)

[A cold breeze of skepticism dries up the fountain of ideals for
the present generation and, moving into the realm of thought, has
changed at its very essence the concept of beauty and has placed its
stamp on the arts, which are nothing more than the means by which
man articulates this concept. Beauty is not seen in the harmonic force
of life but rather in the strange and extravagant, abnormal and morbid.
Music does not strive to reproduce that eternal harmony that wanders
in the depths of creation and our souls. Instead it creates strange and
unheard rhythms that make one's nerves vibrate like strings about to
snap. The visual arts, of form and color, spurning nature's eternal and
unique model, lump together different natural domains, giving the
uncertain lines of a mollusk or vegetative foliage to the human figure
and to all work produced in this medium, the tinges and contours of
beings created by the mind in a state of delirium. Poetry idealizes the
straying of reason, the horrors of doubt and hallucinations of drunkenness, disorder, neurosis, degeneration. Poetic form runs from clarity
as though it were a vice, seeking out combinations of weird cadence
and enigmatic meaning]

An older Urzaiz would reproduce the entire passage in his novel, *Eugenia*,
with the only difference that the narrator, Celiana, speaking from the twenty-
first century, is referring to a past aesthetics, while the younger Urzaiz, in
1902, is describing his own view of general attitudes toward art and aesthetics
among his contemporaries.[10] Whether Urzaiz's views on artistic production
and aesthetics had changed in the lapse between his thesis defense and the
writing of his novel is not entirely obvious here, for indeed it could be that

an older Urzaiz had come to appreciate aspects of the "strange, extravagant" or "abnormal and morbid" that his younger self critiqued as symptomatic of a society prone to mental instability. More importantly, the fact of encountering these lines within the text of a novel changes their sense entirely, opening an array of possibilities. Just as an aging Celiana reflects on the strange aesthetics of a more distant historical past, so does an older Urzaiz call forth a text of his younger self, one that also described the problem of strangeness and extravagance in the arts. For Urzaiz, of course, the past refers to his own earlier writing and hence is not so distant; the aesthetic problem persists in the present. Nonetheless, we may imagine Celiana as a kind of projected, authorial Urzaiz, whose slightly squint perspective simultaneously enacts a futuristic vision and a collapsing of past and present.

At the same time, the lengthy citation from the thesis serves as a clear reminder that Urzaiz's eugenic fiction is derived directly from his medical and psychiatric training. Moreover, this textual moment underscores the extent to which notions of aesthetics pertaining to the world of artistic production are present even at the early stages of Urzaiz's psychiatric training and impact his concepts of health and illness. And the novel makes clear at this juncture that an aesthetics rooted in the "strange and extravagant" provides the ground from which mental "abnormality" (or "instability") may flourish. Of course, without such elements of difference or strangeness, as in descriptions of Celiana's features, the novel would lack narrative interest.

The elements tracing this ambivalence between exquisite narrative detail and the mark of projected erasure may be termed disabilities in the sense that they suggest departures from both the ideal and the norm. The notion of the ideal fits the narrative context given that the proposed aesthetics of Villautopía is imitative of Greco-Roman models of human strength, symmetry, and beauty, as suggested in the physical descriptions of "perfect" bodies, in clothing styles evocative of classical antiquity, and in one of the sketches of characters drawn by the author. Normality, or normalcy, on the other hand, emerges far later, between the eighteenth and nineteenth centuries, as Lennard Davis and others have argued, and eventually correlates with the rise of modern statistics and eugenics.[11] In the context of the novel, disabilities appear through a framework that is simultaneously medical and aesthetic; they require surgical intervention in the form of sterilization and interrupt the physical and social perfection to which the futuristic world of Villautopía aspires. At the same time, these elements of difference sustain narrative interest, not only in the sense of a narrative prosthesis,[12] but also by offering a unique tension between aesthetic decadence and eugenic symmetry.

Fig. 2. Eduardo Urzaiz included a number of his own drawings in his novel *Eugenia*, including this image representing inhabitants of a utopic, futuristic society, with clothing styles and idealized physiques suggestive of classical antiquity. Eduardo Urzaiz. *Eugenia. (Esbozo novelesco de costumbres futuras)*. Mérida, Yucatán: Talleres Gráficos A. Manzanilla, 1919, p. 39.

At the time of Urzaiz's writing, debates on the practice of sterilization to which the author refers in his fictional world were part of an international eugenic landscape, although sterilization laws and the actual practice of sterilization were not yet widespread.[13] In a 1921 article, delivered as a lecture to medical students, Urzaiz himself describes techniques of sterilization by tubal ligation or radiation, and writes, "Es perfectamente factible esterilizar por este medio y con fines eugenéticos, a los criminales natos, a los epilépticos y a los degenerados en general, cosa que ya, en el caso particular de los criminales, se practica en algunos estados de la Unión Americana" (10). [It is perfectly feasible to sterilize born criminals, epileptics, and degenerates in general in this way and for eugenic purposes, as is already being done in some states of the American Union.] These lines, as one example of Urzaiz's eugenicist writing in his professional work, leave little doubt that the author was indeed a strong advocate for a form of radical, negative eugenics, in Esposito's terms, "one designed to impede the diffusion of dsygenic exemplars" (128).[14] Perhaps more surprisingly, in the same article, Urzaiz mentions his own recently published novel, and its discussion of a new method of human reproduction, in which embryos are implanted into selected males following a process of hormonal manipulation. As Urzaiz notes here, recent experiments with the hormonal injection of guinea pigs, and observations of the human embryo's capacity to develop outside the uterus, suggest that the novel's vision of future human reproduction is in fact not so far-fetched (17). He concludes his paper with a note of encouragement to his audience of youthful medical students: "Las glándulas sexuales y sus *hormones* os brindan un vasto campo para investigaciones y descubrimientos capaces de transformar por completo la faz del mundo y la organización social de los presentes tiempos" (18). [The sex glands and their *hormones* offer you a vast field for research and discovery, capable of completely transforming the face of the earth and the social organization of our present day.] The dream of changing the world and its rhetorical use situates these lines in a broad and familiar tradition of motivational discourse aimed at younger interlocutors, today perhaps reminiscent of graduation speeches. Yet here in addition, Urzaiz offers an explicit bridge between science's capacity to change the world, and an interest in radically changing the social organization of his time. Just as his brief discussion of his novel in relation to recent experiments with animals collapses the distinction between futuristic fantasy and achievable science, the concluding remarks similarly aim to link present and future, while at once underscoring the social application of medical science. Perhaps it is only a matter of a minor rhetorical shift for future to become present, and fiction science, just as in Urzaiz's terms, the implantation of an embryo into a male gestator is a delicate but simple process of extraction and reinsertion. Through such medical and discursive operations, temporality collapses into a singular instant, and surgical technique reshapes human society through its reproductive tissue. The slippage between medical technique and the aesthetic engineering of future humanity suggests that the work of the physician may also be akin to that of the artist.

In his critical analysis of male pregnancy, Michael Davidson describes a trajectory of the trope of the pregnant man that extends from antiquity through literary modernism to present-day popular culture, noting that in early modern narratives such as the work of Cervantes, male pregnancy serves as a metaphor for masculine aesthetic creativity (126–27).[15] Urzaiz's message in his lecture to his young interlocutors similarly appears to foreground the continuity of his own (male) legacy through reference to both his creative work and to a radical new reproductive science. In the modernist era with which Davidson is primarily occupied, however, male pregnancy becomes the site of biopolitical and eugenic fears and fantasies. In Urzaiz's novel too, male pregnancy occupies an ambivalent position, as both the reproductive mechanism of eugenic futurity, and as a manifestation of disability, that, in Davidson's terms, "lay[s] bare the artifice of bodily normality by imagining biological reproduction as an unnatural act performed through an unnatural body" (131).

By the early twentieth century methods of classification had been developed to identify those unfit to reproduce, or those unwelcome as new immigrants at national borders (Suárez y López Guazo, "Evolucionismo y eugenesia en México," Mitchell and Snyder, "Eugenic Atlantic"; Dolmage; Abbondanza). Disability, then, is the mark of both future erasure and present fascination in the novel, while in the heyday of eugenics, and arguably in the present day as well, disability works as "the master trope of human disqualification" (Mitchell and Snyder, "Eugenic Atlantic"). As Tobin Siebers describes, disability was used in the nineteenth and early twentieth centuries to disqualify groups of people based on gender, class, and race; but as he notes, "Beneath the troping of blackness as inbuilt inferiority, for example, lies the troping of disability as inferior . . . the mental and physical properties of bodies become the natural symbols of inferiority via a process of disqualification that seems biological, not cultural—which is why disability discrimination seems to be a medical rather than a social problem" (24–25). This observation points to the ongoing and historical intertwining of racism and ableism, along with other discriminatory categories, as forms of human disqualification. Returning to the text of Urzaiz's novel here with this in

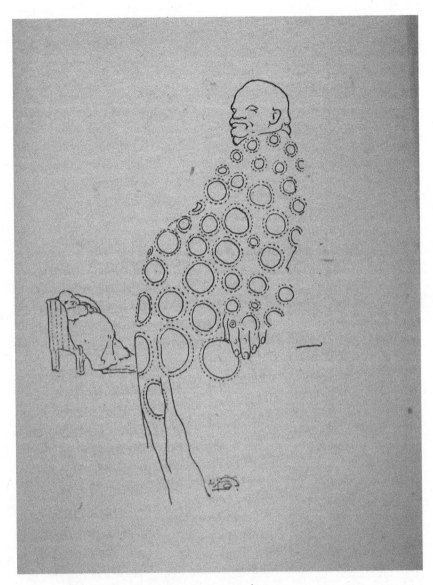

Fig. 3. Another of Urzaiz's drawings in *Eugenia* depicts a pregnant man, part of a eugenic, state-controlled system of reproduction in the fictional society of Villautopía. Eduardo Urzaiz. *Eugenia. (Esbozo novelesco de costumbres futuras).* Mérida, Yucatán: Talleres Gráficos A. Manzanilla, 1919, p. 66.

mind, we must wonder why the question of racial difference, emblematized in only one scene through the briefly mentioned figures of the African visitors, appears to be both central to the eugenic debate at hand, and yet carefully cordoned off from the main story line of the novel. Although the text itself leaves this question in suspension, its enactment of a partial separation between figures of race and those of pathology allows the reader to visualize the parallel processes by which these figures come into focus. Similarly, by attempting to keep the issue of race separate from that of the pathologization of physical and cognitive differences, the text effectively creates an imaginary lens through which each figure may observe the other at a distance.

Critical Distances

There is a degree of undecidability at work in Urzaiz's view of the categorization of human differences. Here we may recall his reflection on the category of madness in his prologue to the novel. By taking a virtual step back from the scene of observation, the author is able to conclude that the definition of madness simply depends on the position occupied by the observer. Taking this notion further, writing influenced by madness might actually be of high quality: "beautiful" and "well-reasoned," as he puts it. Reading *Eugenia* in the spirit of this observation, one might, in theory, find that the negative traits that justify human sterilization within the novel were offered with a similarly impartial intention, inviting us to step back, like the "author" of the prologue, and remember that negative difference is in the eye of the beholder. However, as I have suggested, this apparent impartiality does not represent a comfortable or decided position, but rather a nervous hovering. Moreover, contextualization of the novel in relation to Urzaiz's professional work suggests that the author's actual views on human differences as justification for sterilization were clear and precise. A similar structure occurs with the question of the racial difference that appears in the scene described above. The depiction of racial stereotypes is so blunt that Aaron Dziubinskyj, in a 2007 article on the novel, would conclude that the narration was offered as a satirical critique of both racism and eugenics.[16] Yet another critic, Ermanno Abbondanza, reaches the opposite conclusion regarding the novel's depiction of race, suggesting instead that the racism can be taken more or less at face value.[17]

The juxtaposition of the two readings, one that sees elements of a dystopic critique of eugenics in the novel, and the other that takes its projection of racist eugenics fairly literally, that is, as congruous with Urzaiz's worldview, allows us to consider how textual interpretation in this novel of eugenics comes to hinge on a question that is simultaneously crucial and apparently undecidable. In asking whether the novel celebrates or critiques aspects of the racist and eugenic future society it represents, the reader must also navigate the dynamic of intercorporeal (and racialized) observation and aesthetics, through which the characters size one another up. The textual operation that allows space for such distinct critical perspectives also reveals how race and other categories of difference emerge and speak to one another.

Aaron Dziubinskyj, author of an article about *Eugenia* published in the journal *Science Fiction Studies*, situates Urzaiz alongside British and US science fiction writers of the late nineteenth and early twentieth centuries who work with the eugenic theme. His theory that Urzaiz's novel is a dystopic satire is based in part on his reading of the novel's conclusion, in which the young reproducing couple, Ernesto and Eugenia, retreats to a chalet outside Villautopía, escaping to nature from the overly controlling context of the scientifically perfect city. Yet he also bases his argument on the above-mentioned scene of the African visitors, and the following description: "los negros al sonreír descubrieron el teclado de sus formidables dentaduras de caníbales. Joven el uno y viejo el otro, los dos eran feos y bembones y tenían un aire muy cómico de asustada curiosidad; se expresaban correctamente en inglés y sus ademanes eran afectados . . . el viejo, con su collar de barba blanca, parecía un chimpancé domesticado" (42). [Smiling, the Africans displayed their pearly rows of formidable cannibal-like teeth. One young and the other old, they both were ugly, thick-lipped, and had a comical air of frightened curiosity about them. They spoke perfect English and their gestures were animated (. . .) The elder with his long white beard, looked like a domesticated chimpanzee (27–28).] For Dziubinskyj in his 2007 reading, this narration revealed a satire of the politics of the Bureau of Eugenics, and a critique of the racism of eugenics itself.[18]

Perhaps the passage expresses Ernesto's inner thoughts as he visits the Bureau of Eugenics, as Dziubinskyj suggests. Narrative contrasts between the young, white, idealized reproducer and the African physicians he meets underscore the stereotypical and racist qualities of the description, while at once implying that racialized difference emerges at this moment of visual encounter. Use of Ernesto's mediating perspective allows the extreme description to appear as specific to his experience, but still lets the reader partake vicariously in the exchange. Through this framework, racial otherness is visualized simultaneously as both definitive and contingent on point of view, sustaining the viewer in a dizzying double focus. If a critique is at work in this process, it appears to rely on an ambivalent structure of the racialized visual encounter, in which the reader perceives through a more racist proxy, as intermittently separate from and part of the action.

In addition, it should be noted that the description of the Africans appears in contrast to that of the doctor who receives them at the Bureau: "Como de sesenta años, alto y grueso, el doctor Pérez Serrato usaba la bata blanca y lacia caballera larga y peinada hacia atrás. Su cara redonda y pálida, totalmente afeitada, sus cejas negras y muy espesas sobre unos ojos bovinos, le hacían parecerse bastante a otro médico ilustre de la antigüedad, al célebre Charcot" (42). [About sixty years of age, tall and stout, Doctor Pérez Serrato wore his long, straight white hair combed back. His round pale face, cleanly shaven, his thick black eyebrows above bovine eyes, made him closely resemble another illustrated doctor of antiquity, the celebrated Charcot (28).]

I will return later to this literary re-embodiment of Jean-Martin Charcot, the nineteenth-century French neurologist, who, along with his teacher, Guillaume-Benjamin Duchenne de Boulogne, influenced the development of psychiatry as a field.[19] Charcot's work on the visual signs of pathology as archetypes, and his use of drawing and photography to exemplify the logic of links between inner condition and external manifestation, could tell us much about Urzaiz's clinical literary techniques and the dilemmas of physical observation that his work confronts. For the moment, it is worth noting that the narrative suggests a sharp contrast between the appearance of the Africans and that of the Yucatec physician, "de cara redonda y pálida" [with a round and pale face], one so extreme that Dziubinskyj would read it, in his 2007 article, as a satire of racism, although in his more recent work, coauthored with Kachaluba, the position is revised.

Leaving Charcot in brackets for the time being, I now turn briefly to another interpretation of the novel *Eugenia*, and of this scene in particular, by the historian Ermanno Abbondanza. For Abbondanza, the inclusion of the two English-speaking African doctors—who, it might be added, are named Booker T. Kuzubé and Lincoln Mandínguez—points to the fraught political climate of Cuba, the novelist's birthplace, and polarized debates on the threat of the US political, economic and linguistic presence and on the racial identity of the island and its future. The rich historical and political contextualization that Abbondanza provides does not reduce the caricaturistic effect of the description of the African doctors, whose names crudely evoke fears of black political mobilization in the Americas. It does, however, resituate the caricature in a more dynamic and ambivalent geopolitical context, in which the African doctors may or may not hail from the Cuba of Urzaiz's not-so-distant origins. Abbondanza reads the "Africans" as evocative of Cuba not simply because of race, but because the way one of them describes the particular challenges their country faces in attempting racial improvement via immigration is reflective of the racial politics of Cuba at the time. Through this added nuance, and the additional background that Abbondanza provides on Urzaiz's contact with the eugenics movement via his medical residency in New York in 1905, the critic portrays the physician-novelist as a dedicated eugenicist, whose perspectives, expressed within and beyond the text of the novel, were complicit with the racism of the cited passage. The US presence in the novel thus appears from several angles. The author's US-based medical specialization shaped his career, at a key moment in the establishment of the eugenics movement in that country (Abbondanza). At the same time, references to Cuba, inflected through debates on race and language, immediately place the island in the looming shadow of the United States and its economic and political influence. The incorporation of the names Booker T. and Lincoln further underscores the US role here, both via its projection into the Cuban sphere and as a more direct reference to the history of US racial politics regarding emancipation and socioeconomic mobility. In this reading, the visualization of racial difference depends less on the individual character's point of view, as was the case for Dziubinskyj, and instead emerges through the superposition of a fraught political landscape, in which racialized embodiment and language gesture toward their potential geographic origins. Abbondanza's reading thus pushes the scene of cross-racial encounter into the realm of a more specific transnational framework. The futuristic scene manages to maintain a racist depiction along with projections of ongoing linguistic and geopolitical uncertainty in which exaggerations and extremes are all too close to home. For the expatriate novelist, the full political implications of the scenario are perhaps by definition, unresolved.

Urzaiz's nonfiction publications, from his undergraduate thesis to clinical articles and other books, clearly support the view that the author looked favorably on eugenic practices, including selective sterilizations, with the goal of improving human society. And the racism of the depiction of the African physicians in the work of fiction is commensurate with eugenicist thinking of the day.[20] Yet potential for a satirical and critical interpretation of racism and eugenics, as suggested in Dziubinskyj's earlier article, could be said to emerge through the ambivalent aesthetics governing Urzaiz's approach to human corporeality throughout the novel, and in this scene especially, through the positionality of the characters. One might imagine a debate on whether Urzaiz could be claimed (along with Huxley and Orwell) to be a progressive science fiction writer who warned of the dangers of the future (racism and an excessively mechanized lifestyle), or whether instead we might see his work as largely interwoven with the writer's contextually specific eugenic and racist hopes, perpetually projected into the future. The second position withstands greater scrutiny but does not exhaust the critical possibilities of the work and its geopolitical configurations.

From the perspective of a contemporary critical context that includes Urzaiz's other writing, scholarship on the novel, and the early-twentieth-century geopolitics of eugenics in the region, the text articulates an unmistakable racist and eugenicist project. Yet as the juxtaposition of these contextual elements suggests, the ambivalence and uncertainty governing the visualization of corporeal difference allow for the emergence of a broad interpretive landscape, complicating and raising the stakes of any critical position. Positionality itself, in these scenes, tends to emerge through multiple superimposed and self-reflexive viewpoints, in part because eugenics itself operates through both the practice and representation of looking.

Urzaiz's Cuba-Mexico–New York itinerary, and the complex allegiances and affinities it suggests, along with debates regarding the author's position on eugenics and racial difference, might remind readers of a similarly ideological debate regarding a more famous Cuban figure, who also traveled, though more briefly, to Mexico, namely José Martí. The link to Martí is in fact more than speculative, for Urzaiz's fascination with his compatriot inspired him to write the book, *La familia, cruz del apóstol. Ensayo psicoanalítico sobre José Martí*. The book's introduction, coauthored by Urzaiz's grandnephew, Carlos Bojórquez Urzaiz, affirms Urzaiz's strong affinity for Martí and the cause of Cuban independence, noting that Urzaiz became a member of the Club Patriótico Yucatán y Cuba, founded by Martí (Bojórquez 23). Urzaiz's reading of Martí, as his title suggests, centers on the role of family and love as encumbrances to the leader's true revolutionary cause. As Urzaiz states, "Si él hubiera sido casto, fuera tan grande como San Pablo [. . .] ¿Mas cómo puede ser casto quien nació bajo el ardiente sol de Cuba y además nació poeta?" (36). [If he had been chaste, he would have been as great as St. Paul [. . .] but how could anyone born under the burning Cuban sun, and moreover born a poet, be chaste?]

Urzaiz's fascination with Martí emerges from a different angle in his *Nociones de antropología* (originally published in 1918), particularly in a chapter describing "morphology of human types." Urzaiz refers to four general types: respiratory, digestive, muscular, and cerebral, a taxonomy borrowed from the early-twentieth-century work of C. Sigaud. José Martí himself serves as Urzaiz's example of the cerebral type, described, in part, as follows:

"En la cara del tipo cerebral, se nota desde luego el predominio del departamento superior o frontal; la frente es alta y ancha y el cráneo grande" (202). [In the face of the cerebral type one immediately notes the predominance of the superior and frontal area; the forehead is high and wide, and the cranium is large.]

As in the case of each of the four types discussed, Urzaiz includes here a drawn portrait of his example, possibly his own artistic rendering. Beside the image of Martí's face, we read: "Los ejemplares puros de este tipo constituyen la aristocracia del talento: al tipo cerebral pertenecen los grandes pensadores y filósofos, los hombres de ciencia, los literatos, inventores y reformadores. Mal adaptados o educados impropiamente, los sujetos cerebrales resultan soñadores, misántropos, eróticos o grandes viciosos" (203). [The pure examples of this type constitute the aristocracy of talent: great thinkers and philosophers, men of science and of literature, inventors and reformers belong to the cerebral type. If they are poorly adapted or improperly educated, cerebral subjects turn out to be dreamers, misanthropes, promiscuous or depraved.]

As Bojórquez Urzaiz would note elsewhere, his great-uncle, Eduardo Urzaiz, was the primary promoter of the study of Martí in the Yucatán, and this strong affinity is reflected in a number of Urzaiz's works, as well as those of Bojórquez (Bojórquez, *Entre mayas y patriotas* 10). Yet the above-cited text and image on morphology suggest something further, a fascination that transcends the strictly intellectual sphere, or through which intellect itself becomes a visibly manifested corporeal property. In contrast to the exemplary figure of Martí, Urzaiz references the Spanish king Fernando VII as an illustration of the digestive type, describing him as "uno de los más ineptos reyes de España" (201); (one of the most inept kings of Spain). He notes that the digestive type is generally predisposed to a sedentary lifestyle and produces excellent watchmakers, metalworkers, painters, and sculptors (201). Emphasis on the visible qualities of hierarchically conceived human types suggests echoes of Urzaiz's characterization of human traits in *Eugenia*; the visualization process also underscores the dilemma of intellectual affinity as a potentially shared point of view. For if Urzaiz's admiration for Martí leads the author of *Eugenia* to see (or imagine) the world through the eyes of the Cuban apostle, his morphological sketch depicts a gaze that sees itself seeing. In other words, this view implies that Martí, too, shares in the logic of typology that Urzaiz seeks to illustrate, through physical features that mirror and uphold ideology as well as intellectual and moral value. The argument is not that a ghostly Martí might approve of Urzaiz's portraiture or his typology, but rather that Urzaiz's Cuban and transnational affinity for

Fig. 4. A drawing of José Martí from Urzaiz's book, *Nociones de antropología pedagógica*. In his discussion of human morphology, Urzaiz offers Martí as an example of "the cerebral type." *Nociones de antropología pedagógica*. Prologue by Rodolfo Menéndez. Talleres gráficos manzanilla, 1918, p. 136, fig. 106. Private collection of Carlos Bojórquez Urzaiz.

his (ex)-compatriot allows him to reinvent a Martían body and viewpoint as his own, projected through the interlinked angles of human value and visual positionality. The desire implied in Urzaiz's gaze moves between corporeal and cerebral characteristics, as between self and other. The erotic effect of this movement emerges through the space between the author and his compatriot as it tightens but never fully closes—a queer encounter for its suspension of defined selves and positions.

As a towering literary and intellectual figure, with his own geopolitical itineraries that also included Cuba, Mexico, and New York, Martí invites divergent critical claims regarding his ideological position. As in the case of the above-referenced and similarly divided debate on Urzaiz, the question of Martí's position includes reference to his views on eugenics and racial and ethnic difference, particularly regarding immigration. In addition, the problem of viewpoint emerges specifically through a dynamic of migratory movement, one that situates the writer with respect to those he encounters in diverse locales, those who receive or follow his gaze, and those through whom he speaks, or appears to speak, whether or not the words are also his own. In this sense, Martí becomes a key, like-minded interlocutor in Urzaiz's transnational and eugenicist landscape, as well as a fellow traveler. The role of eugenics in this geopolitical and literary landscape emerges through a series of shifting, overlapping and self-reflexive lines of sight. Urzaiz and Martí, in their oblique Mexican and pan-American dialogue, thus participate in a specifically visual engagement with disability and racial difference, situating the reader as viewer in a broad terrain of potentially conflicting positions.

I engage Martí only briefly here, and in the context of particular links to Urzaiz and to eugenics in the Americas, yet the eugenicist aspect of his work has been amply addressed elsewhere. In his 2014 monumental study of Martí, Francisco Morán emphasizes strong connections between Martí's writings, particularly his essays on immigration from the early 1880s, and the work of Francis Galton, the father of eugenics.[21] As one example, he cites the following from Martí's 1883 text, "Inmigración Italiana": "Como no se tiene derecho para ser criminal, no se tiene derecho para ser perezoso. Ni indirectamente debe la sociedad humana alimentar a quien no trabaja directamente en ella" (379, ctd. en Morán, 577). [Just as no one has the right to be a criminal, no one has the right to be lazy. Society should not even indirectly support those who do not work directly within it.] Martí's frequent references to immigrants, foreigners, and workers, through metaphors of insects and worms (as Morán notes), reveals the writer's discomfort with categories of humanity that he demarcates by race and class. The eugenicist Martí that Morán reveals launches epithets against European immigrants in Washington, DC: "judío ruso que no sabes leer . . . zíngaro raquítico . . . . extranjero!" (EEU 1138–39, ctd. en Morán 587). [Russian Jew who can't read. . . . rickety gypsy . . . foreigner!] The fraught dilemma of claiming or rejecting Martí, the full arguments of which are beyond the scope of this book, seems to surface in scenes like this one. The racialized attacks are particularly blatant here, yet it is precisely in such moments of oblique and racially charged encounter, nuanced by the writer's transnational position, that voice and line of sight may appear to shatter, as the reader could imagine that Martí is critically citing from the discourse of another, cruder observer, conjured by his text, rather than speaking in his own voice. Such troubling scenes, and the uncertain cohesion they suggest between voice and body, through a kind of potential ventriloquism, require the reader to consider more closely the complex dynamic of relative distances through which intercorporeal perception and judgment take place. Here again, readers may ask to what extent we should take Martí's words "at face value," or whether the writer's virtual movement between national and foreign space impacts the possibility of an explicitly determined position. The question points toward the dilemma of defining and situating the writer's body in relation to both his textual voice and the explicitly identified bodies of the "foreigners" in this immigration scene. The point here is not to minimize Martí's racism and eugenicist sympathies, which Morán effectively documents in many of his texts. Instead, the juxtaposition of this scene with the interpretation of Urzaiz's *Eugenia* reveals how the volatile, transnational movement of eugenicist perspectives appears to complicate their positionality, while at once making clear that such perspectives, when emerging from the depiction of a face-to-face encounter, are necessarily both fleeting and dependent on a visible or otherwise tangible embodiment. Moreover, as noted above, Martí, like Urzaiz, occupies an ambivalent transnational space, for both figures traveled at different times between Cuba, Mexico, and the United States. In part because of this, critical approaches to both writers depend on the reader's national orientation, which in turn virtually situates the writer's body and gaze vis-à-vis the map he traverses. The question is not only the writer's national origin and identity, but where he physically stands at a given moment, and in which direction he projects his textual voice and line of sight. For this reason, Urzaiz's evocation of Martí himself as a fleshly example of the "cerebral type" suggests more than the Yucatec-Cuban's ideological affinity for his predecessor. The evocation also depends on the tracing of geographic movement, whereby Urzaiz's queerly itinerant gaze encounters Martí's trajectory and makes it his own.

As Morán emphasizes, Martí's eugenicist leanings emerge in particular through the question of immigration in the Americas, and as a warning to Latin American countries of the dangers posed to them by immigration (568). Racialization in Urzaiz's *Eugenia* also occurs through reference to migratory movement, as we have seen with the sole explicit appearance of racial difference embodied in the African visitors, dually marked by distinct physical characteristics and by the fact of having traveled to Villautopía from afar to learn about eugenic practices. The diverse geographic locales featured in the trajectories followed by Martí and Urzaiz mirror an account of racial history through which bodies are marked and appraised, and hence acquire their differences. The appearance of the African physicians in the text offers a more explicit rendering of this history, compounding and underscoring the fact that human movement through geographic space creates and defines racial difference, eventually becoming inseparable from this difference.

Migration, then, is a central component and motor of eugenic thinking, even when concepts and policies refer to a single location or community. And as we have seen, Martí's and Urzaiz's literary eugenics offer a certain logic of racial difference founded on geographic distance and fear of immigration. Yet at the same time, eugenics, from its origins, is founded on a tightly knit relationship between the community and what it seeks to expel from within. This is Esposito's rendering of a Nazi "homeopathic tonality" (137), whereby life marked as death continually threatens to contaminate the people as a whole, and hence must be subjected to a purifying death. Mexican eugenics fails to assume this destructive tonality on a massive scale, yet it does repeatedly offer the racial conundrum of the mestizo as both the overarching emblem of a perfected people and an internally ambiguous source of potential contamination, hence perpetuating an intimate and violent structure of self-referential immunity and contagion. Hygiene works as the preferred antidote to disability in this framework, simultaneously promoting both a positive eugenics through emphasis on cleanliness, strength, and moral and physical health, and a negative eugenics through the elimination of traits considered mutually associating, including criminality, immorality, epilepsy, and "mental weakness." That these "positive" and "negative" forms operate as necessary complements to one another, producing an inextricable whole, enhances the sense of tight enclosure defining the primary eugenic operation.

The simultaneous association of eugenics with both potentially vast migratory distances and a fear of close proximity, collapsed into self-referentiality, suggests a unique tension at work in this concept, shifting between the opening and collapsing of geopolitical and interpersonal spaces and distances. Rather than reading these forms of eugenics as contradictory, or simply as separate, diverse manifestations of racist and ableist practices, I approach the dilemma of ambivalent spatial distribution itself as key to the operation of local and transnational eugenics. In the literary context exemplified here in works by Martí and Urzaiz, the eugenic itinerary is at once a migratory pathway linking those who traverse it over time and space, and a more intimate—at times erotic—process of encounter at close quarters, primarily through acts of visual observation. The dynamic of seeing others, and of implicitly seeing oneself seeing, implies the projection into the scene of distance traversed, as in the case of Martí's depictions of immigrants who arrive from elsewhere. Yet seeing also happens at close range, requires corporeal proximity, and carries the risk of receiving an other's unexpected gaze, or indeed of becoming the subject of one's own observations. The visual encounter is in many ways emblematic of a larger dilemma of eugenics, ambivalently stranded between the distant and the intimate. In slightly different terms, the viewer is compelled to navigate a simultaneous and impossible expulsion of difference and preservation of the self, even as these terms define one another at increasingly close range.

Clinical Scenes

Returning here to the originally cited scene from Urzaiz's novel, and with this dynamic of corporeal observation in mind, it is worth noting that the reader learns most of the details of futuristic human reproduction in Villautopía in a single chapter, through the voice of the above-mentioned doctor and president of the Eugenics Bureau, as he guides his visitors, the two unnamed "Hotentotes" and Ernesto, an official reproducer, on a tour of the institution. In this sense, the reader's understanding of the eugenic reproductive process is mediated by the combined perspectives of the lead physician, who has been compared to Charcot, the two African visitors, whose racialized physical features are a key element of the scene, and Ernesto, the young, ideal reproducer at the point of initiation into his new role. Throughout the visit, visibly specific racialized difference is the mediating factor through which eugenics is perceived and explained.

The reader accompanies the group, observing, along with Ernesto, the physiognomy of the Africans, and that of the head doctor. This perspective becomes apparent at various points, such as in the following description: "Por la cúpula de cristal que hacía de techo, entraba la luz a raudales, haciendo relucir las barras niqueladas de las mesas de operaciones, que a Ernesto, como a todo extraño a la profesión médica, se le antojaban máquinas infernales de tortura" (48). [Light flooded in through the crystal dome of the ceiling, causing the nickel bars of the operating tables to shine, which for Ernesto, as for all those outside of the medical profession, gave the appearance of infernal torture machines (33).]

Of course, all of the other characters in this scene, as well as the author of the novel, are medical doctors, and so through such language the narrative perspective begins to diffract like the glittering light, suggesting a gaze that is simultaneously of the medical specialist and of the curious yet frightened layperson. The fragmentation of perspective operates similarly with regard to the question of racialized physical features. The doctor, we may recall, is identified with the French neurologist, Charcot, through physical similarity, a curious detail since Charcot himself relied extensively on visual cues documented through sketches or photography for the diagnosis of patients. Charcot referred to the importance of the study of archetypes in the identification of diseases, and noted in one case on his medical techniques, "I only observe, nothing more . . . I am a photographer" (Goetz 425). Viewed in this light, the physical description of Dr. Pérez Serrato, "su cara redonda y pálida . . . ojos bovinos" [his round, pale face . . . his bovine eyes], etc., as justification for the comparison to Charcot creates the effect of a strangely inverted gaze. Whether or not the doctor looks like Charcot is of course beside the point; more significant is that the description reveals how, and through what process, he sees himself and others. As in the case of Urzaiz's reading of Martí's physical traits as exemplary of a physical type, referenced above, here too the physical description offers a model for the act of looking. Rather than only seeing Martí, Dr. Pérez Serrato, or Charcot, Urzaiz also sees with them, sharing in the visual techniques that he gleans from or projects on his real and imaginary interlocutors.

This self-reflexive physiognomic technique is immediately applied to the two Africans, whose physical features complement and complete the scene. In the conclusion to the physical description of Dr. Pérez Serrato, we find: "Sobre el pecho ostentaba el tradicional botón rojo de la Legión de Honor, insignia que, por no ser menos seguramente, lucían también los africanos en la solapa de sus respectivos levitones" (42). [On his chest he boasted the traditional red button of the Legion of Honor, an insignia that, without a doubt, the Africans also flaunted on the lapels of their respective coats (28).] The visual symbol of membership in the French national order acquires a tinge of ridicule here, which extends surreptitiously between the white and the black wearer, as both are revealed and disguised by these outer trappings that seem to repeat the question, who is looking at whom? To be sure, the text does not depict a relationship of equals, but rather a racially determined hierarchy in which both white and black participants appear ridiculous by virtue of their engagement with the other, and with an implied logic of social value that accrues through the face-to-face encounter. The reference to the French Legion of Honour badge should not be taken as gratuitous, in particular considering that Charcot himself wore the same badge. Most visual depictions of the late-nineteenth-century physician reveal the conspicuous badge, including a famous 1887 painting by André Brouillet, *Une leçon clinique à la Salpêtrière*, featuring Charcot giving a clinical demonstration on the effects of hysteria, using a female patient as his example.[22] The detail of the badge thus solidifies the identification of the fictional Dr. Pérez Serrato with Charcot, while at the same time inscribing the African physicians into the same visual iconography, denigrating their wearing of the badge as an act of mimicry.

Urzaiz, it turns out, in addition to being a medical doctor with a specialty in psychiatry, a field on which Charcot had great impact, was also, like

Fig. 5: In this 1887 painting by André Brouillet, *Une leçon clinique à la Salpêtrière*, Charcot gives a clinical demonstration on the effects of hysteria. Wikimedia Commons.

Charcot, a practitioner of visual arts, primarily sketches, which the reader can appreciate at various points throughout the text of *Eugenia*. While Charcot made frequent sketches of his patients—in addition to his famous catalog of photographed patients—to study their features and conditions, Urzaiz uses his drawings in the novel to highlight plot features or human traits. The partial and momentary continuity that the text suggests here between Urzaiz (the author), Dr. Pérez Serrato (the physician character in the novel), and Charcot (the nineteenth-century neurologist) suggests that writing, medical practice, and the eugenic enterprise congeal through the process and instance of looking. The scene of observation is necessarily a dynamic one, because for Charcot and his contemporaries, expression and the physiology of affect tend to emerge at the moment of encounter between the observer and the subject being observed.

Racial difference, too, takes place within this phenomenon of interactive surfaces, as a series of perceived expressions, bounded by the temporal constraints of human exchange. The fluidity of the interaction, which even allows for moments of cross-racial identification, as when the younger African doctor bursts out laughing at the sight of pregnant men, and Ernesto (the white protagonist) can barely restrain his own laughter, does not mitigate the racism of this depiction. Instead, the structure of the scene suggests that the work of race and eugenics, defined by a continual movement that keeps the reader-viewer suspended between here and there, then and now, undermines the logic of fixed positions, and leaves little in the way of solid ground. The act of looking, as we have seen in both Martí and Urzaiz, is itself a form of movement, repeating and attempting to contain the migratory processes through which racialized and corporeal differences emerge and take place. In this scene, the figure of the pregnant man also becomes the occasion for a momentarily queer exchange, as fear, curiosity, and humor tentatively bridge the divides of age, language, and race between the men, while male pregnancy itself posits a radical reconfiguration of sexuality and reproduction.

The awkward giddiness of these scenes shows that the representation of racial difference both sustains a racist narrative and offers a unique lens through which to perceive or project images of pathologized human variety. The "abnormality" that the scenes suggest is projected onto the (absent) bodies of the population deemed unworthy of reproduction and hence destined for sterilization on the displayed operating tables. Yet from the perspective of the visitors, the pregnant male in particular functions as visible evidence of aberration, and the laughter of the younger African doctor suggests a nervous instability underpinning the eugenic project. Here, the attempt to perfect human reproduction on a universal scale has led to discomfort with the corporeal aesthetics that the eugenic project has produced (as a kind of side effect). At the same time, the narrative insistence on the Africans' varied expressions and reactions to the tour of the facility works to emphasize the instantaneous quality of the process by which differences are perceived. These instances of cross-racial interaction, recognition, judgment, and identification underscore the supposed universal quality of the eugenic project, but also the subjective immediacy and potential erotics of its aesthetics. Within this process, the constructs of racial difference and human aberration define one another through the subjective yet familiar and codified act of looking. Male pregnancy, as noted previously, functions here as a particular marker of the ambivalence underpinning the eugenic project in the novel. It is offered as a modern, state-controlled means of human reproduction in the future eugenic age, but at the same time subverts conventional notions of normalcy and fails to comply with the idealized corporeality featured in the novel's depictions of perfected humanity.

In these scenes from *Eugenia*, and in the neurological project of Jean-Martin Charcot, discussed briefly above, the act and instant of observation itself is crucial to the processes of judgment and diagnosis that project notions of racial difference and pathology. Irene Tucker's analysis of the racial sign and its connection to observed pathologies of the skin is useful here in revealing how, in Urzaiz's novel (and elsewhere), scenes of racial difference work to create a universalizing context for the eugenic utopia, while at the same time framing it with ongoing subjective particularity. In addition, Tucker's work merits referencing in some detail, as it provides further context to the processes through which the temporality of the visual encounter underpins the contingency of corporeal difference, in tension with a logic of human standardization.

Tucker grounds her analysis of the racial sign and its instantaneous legibility through Kant's 1788 essay, "On the Use of Teleological Principles in Philosophy," in which the philosopher posits his notion of originary "seeds" and "predispositions" existing universally in all humans, allowing them to potentially live in any climate or location. The appearance of different skin tones becomes evidence of past migrations and subsequent adaptations. As Tucker states, "Kant's racialized skin thus superimposes the likeness of the body to other bodies and the changeful, contingent particular history as qualities of a single seamless sign" (60). In this reading, differences of skin color thus work in a paradoxical fashion, upholding a notion of universal human sameness, observed and read through the manifestation of accidental changes that may have occurred sometime in the distant past.

Within the late-eighteenth-century paradigm of anatomical medicine and its standardized body, the concept of "Kant's racialized skin" at once allows Tucker to read the tension between likeness and difference, or between sick and dead bodies, as both comparable to one another for diagnosis, and necessarily distinct. The skin separates the living from the dead, by hiding the diseased organs that will be revealed and diagnosed only later, through autopsy. Racial difference, like the temporally contingent differences of pathology, following Kant's explanation, operates according to an uncertain separation between standard human qualities, and vulnerability to the contingency of change that may have produced differences over time. Yet because skin color is perceived and recognized in a single instant, in Tucker's reading the logic of visible race works to repair the breach between standardness and contingency, and in particular the inevitable vulnerabilities to pathology, accident, and death (60).

In one key instance the link between notions of racial difference and observations of pathology is derived directly from an early-nineteenth-century text on dermatology. Tucker discusses passages from Robert Willan's 1809 *On Cutaneous Diseases*, focusing on the description of a man covered with "an innumerable company of warts" (70). As Willan notes, the fact that the man has six children with the same "rugged covering" leads the dermatologist to speculate on how racial difference may in fact have been produced by some such now-forgotten "accidental cause" in the past. For Tucker, the point once again is that race, as a phenomenon of the skin, upholds a notion of the standardized body that is nonetheless individual, contingent on past events, and observable in the present moment. Racial difference may have been produced by an accident in the past, but crucially, the accident must be long forgotten, in other words, outside the reach of current observation, to uphold the difference as race. The fact of human observation in the present, in turn, continuously sustains a logic of recognition and standardized difference, marking out its distance from hypothetical, pathological causes. In this reading, the separation between racial difference and differences of pathology or accident is necessarily a matter of time.

The eugenics movement, initiating with Galton in 1883, does not coincide historically with the Enlightenment texts offered by Tucker as prime examples of racialized skin as key to the dilemma of the simultaneously standardized and contingent body. Nor, in fact, does Charcot, whose late-nineteenth-century work shaped the development of neuropsychology—he may be best known today for his major impact on Freud. We may nonetheless read Charcot and Urzaiz within the overall framework of post-Enlightenment thought.[23] The novel's scene does work quite explicitly through the dilemma of the standard and the contingent, with visual details of the Africans' appearance and perspective upholding a notion of universalized humanity through visible difference.

Yet additional contextualization will be useful for understanding the arrival of Charcot, and implicitly, his student Freud, at this depiction of the Yucatec-Cuban eugenicist fantasy. If Freud's development of psychoanalysis and the concept of the unconscious marks a crucial shift in the history of medicine and in theorizations of human subjectivity, they also influence the role of the visible in relation to clinical observation and scientific knowledge. Charcot's diagnostic work at La Salpêtrière, where he photographed examples of hysteria induced by hypnosis, and delivered lectures with clinical demonstrations of hysteria, offers a prior and foundational instance of what would become the Freudian transformation of the visible. Charcot's insistence on visual evidence of hysteria would be countered by critics who insisted in turn that the patients were faking their symptoms, responding to the desires and suggestions of the physician (Morlock 133). This disagreement underscores the erotic charge of the scenes of hysteria, fueled by the ambivalence of visual evidence in its relation to a powerful gaze. Charcot defended his argument through further recourse to the visual regime, copublishing a book on hysteria as exemplified in great works from the history of art. To some degree, Charcot faced a dilemma already common to the study of pathology and physiology; for, as Didi-Huberman notes in reference to Charcot's methods of "cerebral localization," "One cannot watch the brain as it functions, but one can locate the effects on the symptomatic body provoked by alterations, and thus prejudge its operation" (21). Charcot's method, as Didi-Huberman again describes, would be to repeat the observation of symptoms, followed by the study of cerebral lesions after the patients' deaths over a large number of cases, so as to eventually establish a correlation, through a process that "implicates a temporalization, as if paradoxical, of the clinical gaze" (21).

The problem of time lapse between the observation of living and dead bodies is one that we have seen previously, through Tucker's work in reference to eighteenth-century anatomical medicine and autopsies. Here, however, the symptoms in question are associated with the neuropsychological condition known as hysteria, and hence introduce further difficulties, for visual observation of the hysteric is ultimately not enough. As Freud would later suggest in his account of the talking cure for such cases, "the information I receive [from the patient] is never enough to let me see my way about the case" (16). In fact, these unseen and unknown elements point to the key role of the unconscious, and therefore to a new mode of opacity of the subject, and of the psychoanalytic cure. Moreover, and even in Charcot's work at the Salpêtrière, prior to Freud's writings on hysteria, repetition of hysteric symptoms through photographic images, as well as paintings and drawings, underscores the centrality of the image itself in the manifestation of the hysterical symptom. This symptom is always an image, and in this sense is always repeated, displaced, and duplicitous (Didi-Huberman 158–59). Hysteria, prior to Charcot's work, was generally understood as a capricious condition, a collection of unpredictable symptoms with the capacity to imitate those of other, more physiologically grounded illnesses (Morlock 132). In attempting to establish a specific physiology for hysteria, Charcot situates himself between two modes of clinical observation, one derived from adherence to the corporeality of visible evidence, and the other from insistence on what can never be seen entirely as itself. This dilemma is further shadowed by the suspicion that the condition behind the symptoms and images does not in fact exist at all.

Charcot's intrusion into Urzaiz's unusual scene of racial encounter thus underscores the complex and evolving status of the act of looking in medical history. While Freud's writings were fundamental in shaping Urzaiz's training and career in psychiatry, it is Charcot who emerges here as key to a transitional moment for the regime of the visual in medicine. By seeing with Charcot and Freud, between clinical images of the body, artistic renderings, and psychoanalysis, Urzaiz offers a mode of observation that insists on visible evidence, but still reverts continuously to a self-reflexive process of looking, in which the image suggests and reiterates movement between viewer and object. This migratory gaze mimics the literal migration of human subjects through geopolitical space, and counter-poses the physical evidence of clinical observation with the subjectivity of impressions, always returning to the viewer and to prior, absent referents.

The act of looking we can imagine, between Martí and Urzaiz, or Charcot and Freud, therefore involves both geographic and trans-historical movement. In addition, this looking as movement operates as a diagnostic gaze, in the context of the eugenicist discourse that implicitly asks the viewer to classify, rank, and select, but also—crucially—to situate him- or herself in relation to the scene of observation. Features and individuals marked for elimination are absent in Urzaiz's scene of racial encounter, as noted above, but referenced through the sterilization facilities. Absent too, are female gestators, and in this sense, the traditional source of hysteria, as Charcot's subject matter, is nowhere to be found, although the erotic ambivalence of the female hysteric has been displaced onto the pregnant male. Elsewhere in the novel, negatively charged features abound, and justify the denial of reproductive futures for those who bear them. The African doctors in this scene are ridiculed and dehumanized through physical description, yet as outsiders, they are beyond the scope of Villautopía's eugenicist project. Moreover, their role as visiting physicians defines them as potential proponents of eugenics rather than as its targets. In this way, disability emerges through a visually constructed aesthetic ambivalence, marked by and dependent on but never quite equivalent to the construction of racial and ethnic differences. Visible evidence is key to the demarcation of racial difference and eugenicist diagnosis, yet its standardized referents are partially undercut by the volatile and subjectively filtered repetition of images.

Picturing Difference

If the categories of race and disability may be said to counterpose one another in the texts discussed here, through an uncertain dynamic of seeing and being seen, further attention to artwork by both Charcot and Urzaiz reveals the juxtaposition of these categories in greater detail. Urzaiz's visual references to racial difference surface most explicitly in a book of local Yucatec scenes and customs, *Reconstrucción de hechos: Anécdotas Yucatecas Ilustradas*, which he wrote and illustrated under the pen name Claudio Meex. Each drawing in the book is accompanied by a one-page explanatory text, and the work covers a broad variety of topics, including local and national politics, baseball, medical innovations, and humorous neighborhood conversations. A particular area of interest for Urzaiz in the book is the question of Cuban politics and Cuban migration to Mérida. The representation of racial and ethnic difference also emerges quite frequently, at times in relation to such immigration, and in some cases in reference to linguistic encounters between Yucatec Mayan and Spanish speakers. In one instance, Urzaiz depicts the Yucatec artist Juan Gamboa Guzmán, painting a portrait of "*el negro Miguel, el butifarrero*" [black Miguel, the sausage-maker].

As the text describes, the model arrived for his second session, "bien bañado, pelado, afeitado y empolvado, por lo que el artista tuvo que esperar ocho días para que volviese a adquirir lustre y carácter" [well bathed, with a clean shaved head and face, and powdered, so that the artist had to wait eight days for him to re-acquire his look and character]. In this scene of visual misunderstanding, the black model, identified by both race and trade, prepares himself so as to appear attractive in the portrait. This is a source of frustration for the artist, who had hoped to depict him with "character," and a source of

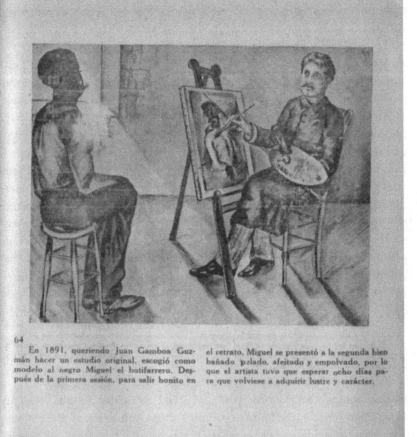

64

En 1891, queriendo Juan Gamboa Guzmán hacer un estudio original, escogió como modelo al negro Miguel el butifarrero. Después de la primera sesión, para salir bonito en el retrato, Miguel se presentó a la segunda bien bañado, pelado, afeitado y empolvado, por lo que el artista tuvo que esperar ocho días para que volviese a adquirir lustre y carácter.

Fig. 6. A drawing by Eduardo Urzaiz (under the pseudonym, Claudio Meex) depicting the painter, Juan Gamboa Guzmán creating a portrait of "el negro Miguel, el butifarrero" [the sausage-maker]. From Claudio Meex. *Reconstrucción de hechos: Anécdotas Yucatecas Ilustradas.* Mérida, Yucatán, 1943, p. 64. Biblioteca Nacional de México.

humor for the reader and viewer, who witnesses the dual interpretation of appropriate visual presentation. The artist in this case seeks to represent a category of racialized class difference in accordance with his own socially current point of view. The model, in contrast, sees the painting of his portrait as an occasion to transcend a pre-inscribed category, and to elevate himself as a work of art. The joke for the viewer occurs at the expense of the black model, who apparently believed that bathing and shaving would change his status, at least in the context of a visual representation. But as the artist and viewer understand, signifiers of race and class cannot be washed or shaven away, and attempts to do so merely create a comical artifice rather than the desired true-to-life portrait. Beyond the denigrating humor, this scene suggests the strangely troubled status of racial imagery. The artist attempts to fix a standardized relationship between race, class, and outward appearance, through the visual repetition of his social knowledge. Yet the model's actions point to the possible transformation of that relationship through a simple change of appearance. An unwashed and unshaven appearance does not signify disability but does suggest the social stigma associated with undesirable features. Moreover, the juxtaposition of ostensibly fixed racial difference—read as skin color—with more flexible corporeal markers contingent on status, class, individual action, and the passage of time echoes a similar relationship between racial difference and differences of pathology or accident, as observed in Tucker's reading of Kant.

Amending one's appearance through personal grooming allows for a marked contrast between the permanent and the malleable, but it is only a matter of time for the body to conform once again to social expectations. Although the model's attempts will not be successful, the artists' and writer's need to immediately thwart the change reveals the high stakes of racial classification and its visual coding, for if bodily presentation can be changed through such simple actions as bathing and shaving, perhaps racial differences, too, must be understood as nothing more than a matter of superficial appearance. In the scene from *Eugenia*, the fact that the African physicians wear the badge of the French Legion of Honour, in imitation of their white host, similarly points to the paradoxically uncertain nature of visual evidence, as both standardized and potentially untrustworthy.

In the work of Charcot, in contrast, sketches and photography generally have a precise diagnostic function and are not deployed for purely artistic or humoristic purposes. Yet Charcot does engage with the visible signifiers of ethnic difference on at least one occasion, and in doing so reveals a clear tension between standardized and contingent features. The drawing in question appears in Charcot's Morocco diary, and was sketched during his travels. Titled "Un juif de Tétouan atteint de maladie de Parkinson," the 1889 drawing features an elderly, bearded man wearing a long tunic, sandals, and a fez. The entire figure is framed by a horseshoe or keyhole arch, effectively situating the sitter in an Islamic architectural context. Charcot's creation and use of this drawing demonstrates the complex filtering of ethnic difference and pathology. The physician's notion of Jewishness as linked to inheritable pathologies is well documented and was common among his contemporaries (Gelfand 24). As Charcot notes in his journal regarding the Jews he observes in Morocco, "These people are all eczematous, arthritic, puffy, scrofulous" (75). Yet the same drawing appears as an example in Charcot's notes for his Tuesday lectures at the Salpêtrière, where he writes, "I have seen such patients everywhere, in Rome, Amsterdam, Spain, always the same picture" (qtd. in Goetz 423). Goetz describes this picture as an example of Charcot's insistent sketching of patients wherever he saw them, "on vacation or on foreign travel, neurological disease did not escape his eyes. For example, he sketched a North African with Parkinson's disease, capturing in his hasty strokes the hand posture, body attitude, joint deformities and masked facies typical of the disease" (422). Curiously here, both the critic (Goetz) and the neurologist-artist (Charcot) emphasize the "typical" aspects of the disease that would be the same anywhere: "always the same picture." Yet attention to the actual sketch shows that this is not the same picture that Charcot would probably have sketched in the other listed locations. The keyhole arch immediately identifies an Orientalist perspective, and the title of the drawing specifies the sitter's North African Jewish identity, while the accompanying text from Charcot's Morocco diary clearly notes the pathological characteristics that the physician artist generally associated with Jewishness. Back at La Salpêtrière, however, the framed image becomes a useful illustration of the universal qualities of a particular illness.[24] Indeed, it would seem that Charcot just happened to see the seated man as he peered through an archway during the course of his travels and discovered a familiar picture of illness that he could recognize from numerous examples he had observed elsewhere.

In the context of the Tuesday lectures at the hospital, the evidence of both disease and ethnic specificity, identified through recognizable features of clothing and architectural setting, appear in an instant, snapshot manner, and yet retain their distinct and separate status. This is what allows Charcot to point out that this disease presents as "always the same picture," presumably placing in brackets the cultural details that he nonetheless chose to include. The conundrum of picturing disease and ethnicity is not, in this case, based

UN JUIF DE TÉTOUAN, ATTEINT DE MALADIE DE PARKINSON

Croquis fait par CHARCOT,

au cours d'un voyage au Maroc, en 1889.

MASSON & Cie, Éditeurs.

Fig. 7. An 1889 drawing by Charcot from his Morocco diary. The caption reads, "Un juif de Tétouan atteint de maladie de Parkinson. Croquis fait par Charcot, au cours d'un voyage au Maroc, en 1889." Plate 58, between pages 504 and 505, Henry Meige, "Charcot Artiste," *Nouvelle Iconographie de la Salpêtrière*, vol. 11, F. Raymond, A. Joffroy, A. Fournier, Paul Richer, and Gilles de Tourette, eds. Masson et Cie, 1898, pp. 498–505. Bibliothèque Interuniversitaire de Santé, Paris.

on the notion that ethnic difference is a form of disease to be eradicated, but rather that physically visible difference works to prove that the traits of disease are the same everywhere, while at the same time depicting these traits within a specific and recognizable ethnic framework. When the image appears within the text of Charcot's diary, in contrast, racialized Jewishness and pathology are more closely intertwined via an obviously anti-Semitic perspective. As the image travels between Morocco and Paris, it cannot fail to retain elements of this rendering of exoticized pathological Jewishness, but at the same time ethnicity now serves a paradoxical, universalizing function, even while it insists on its own visibility as difference. The juxtaposition of these two modes of relating ethnicity and illness underscores the complexity of the artist's framing devices, for if ethnic markers allow the viewer to see pathology in a standard way, they may also work to blend into and become a feature of that pathology. As in the case of Urzaiz's depiction of "*Miguel, el negro butifarrero*," visible, physical characteristics of the body depend on the timing and strategy through which they are conveyed. In both cases, the images admit, in a sense, to relying on external, contingent signifiers (the keyhole arch, the fact of the artist waiting eight days before painting), in order to transmit the separation or fusion between racialized features and the markings of disease and dirt. In this way, the artists ultimately have it both ways, suggesting an alignment between racialized difference and the markings of disability or other stigmatized conditions, as separate but nonetheless mutually engaged and potentially interlocking.

As these examples suggest, race and disability emerge through the processes of looking, and literally or figuratively sketching the scene, allowing various modes of difference to align and, implicitly, to witness one another. In the episode of the African doctors from Urzaiz's novel, as they look curiously at the examples of eugenic improvement presented to them by the head physician at the Bureau, the text emphasizes both the caricaturesque racialized physical features of the visitors, and the uniformity of a medical gaze that they share with their white hosts. The goal of the "Hottentot" doctors is to apply eugenic techniques in their own country to avoid the "the evolutionary stagnation of their race" (27). The expressed desire indicates a clearly demarcated separation between the race of the Africans and that of Villautopía, while the project implies enough similarity between the two societies that the biological lessons in one might be applied in another. It is only in the next chapter of the novel that we learn that the Africans have also looked into the possibility of mixing with "superior races" (42). Racist stereotypes, based in physical description, are quite evident in this text, as is the assumption of white superiority, yet ultimately the African doctors' eugenic strategy will be to underscore the universal applicability of the methods from Villautopía. Racial or ethnic differences are not explicitly marked for eradication or assimilation in Urzaiz's novel, for the doctors have determined that mixing with whites will not be a sustainable eugenic option. Instead, desire for eugenic improvement is what unites the white and black physicians with a common purpose, while physical, racialized difference sustains the paradoxical fantasy that all humanity can share equally in this purpose.

If the racialized visitors in this novel offer readers a vision of utopic eugenics that is universal, transracial, and at the same time marked by the specificity of the subjective, racially marked gaze, the roles of disability and race in relation to one another here also complicate this scenario. By avoiding the straightforward equation of racial difference with disability or pathology that is typical of much eugenic discourse, the narrative instead posits these categories as distinct from one another, though potentially entangled, each one bracketed by the conditions of visibility that allow it to appear. Race and disability in Urzaiz's novel thus function as ways of seeing, embodying modes of human difference that observe one another and continually mark out their contingent and vulnerable positions.

Our arrival at the scene of this novel begins to establish the coordinates of an extended eugenic itinerary, in which the site of a futuristic Yucatec imaginary necessarily expands to include transoceanic histories and geopolitics. Urzaiz's individual career and migration are part of this story, linking Mexico to Cuba, to the United States, and to Europe, through both literal journeys and textual references. Beyond the particularity of this physician-artist and his unique early-twentieth-century novel, however, this reading allows us to consider the complexity of eugenics, in Mexico and elsewhere, as a mode of observation and migration, grounded in the movements and desires of bodies and eyes. The visual encounter, from Martí to Urzaiz, from Charcot to Freud, and between both fictional characters and historical figures, establishes the aesthetic conditions—and at times, queer potentiality—through which racial difference and disability come to be known, through a close but unstable proximity to one another. The intimacy of this encounter, as we have seen, occurs in tension with the geographic distances of migration, underscoring a structure of eugenics that perpetually marks off and excludes foreignness and difference as paradoxically both arriving from elsewhere and already too close to home.

Critical encounters with these eugenic scenes also demonstrate divergent responses, revealing the contingency of point of view itself as key to the aesthetics and politics of disability and racial difference within an evolving and transnational framework. The resulting ambivalence impacts the scenes and extends beyond them, toward the generation of further affective responses, extending to present and future readings. Within this incomplete field of eugenic observation, disability is not simply a list of conditions marked for elimination, but also becomes an active element in the processes of seeing and being seen. The ambivalent eugenic aesthetics displayed in these scenes participates in the violence of race and disability-based visual exploitation, and in this process also offers its readers, as witnesses, a potentially destabilizing mode of observation, through the embodiment of mutually dependent sites of vulnerability.

Two

Corporeal Causalities

Archival Encounter

In the early 1930s, the *Weekly Bulletin* of the Mexican Department of Public Health printed a series of messages to its readers, usually in large block letters on the back of the publication, where they might easily catch the eye. As we read in one instance, "Niños imbéciles, escrofulosos y epilépticos, o de instintos depravados, son con frecuencia hijos de alcohólicos." [Imbecilic, scurvied, and epileptic children or those of depraved instincts are frequently the offspring of alcoholics] (Boletín 1.17). A second issue of the same bulletin contained a slightly more graphic warning on the dangers of alcohol: "El alcohol es un buitre que arrancará lentamente las entrañas del bebedor. El bebedor está siempre atado en la roca del infortunio." [Alcohol is a vulture that slowly rips out the entrails of the drinker. The drinker is always tied to the rock of misfortune] (Boletín 1.19).

Coming across these carefully conserved bulletins in the Public Health archive, I notice the dramatic urgency of their message, tightly contained and quickly digested. The evoked images resonate and refuse to leave us quickly. Alcohol, we are told, grabs hold irrevocably, but works its damage with exquisitely painful slowness, over a time span that is both individual and intergenerational. The anti-alcohol campaign of this period, under the presidency of Emilio Portes Gil, was effective in mobilizing large sectors of the population, and operated through the work of several ministries, in particular those of Public Health and Public Education (Pierce 164–65); messages of this kind clearly were numerous and found an audience.[1] Yet especially striking is the way in which disability emerges here in relation to distinctive temporal frameworks. Disability, signified through conditions implying the lack of morality, health, or intelligence of particular children, functions as a warning or prediction of the future, or a form of speculation about the past. In the case of alcohol as an entrail-hungry vulture, in contrast, time becomes a lived, continuous, visceral present, an experience of endless pain brutally contained in a perpetual here and now.

In the previous chapter, my analysis of Mexican and transnational eugenic itineraries focused on a mode of visual encounter influencing the relative positions and movements of racialized and disabled bodies. Acts of observation and projections of desire in literary, scientific, and visual texts, enacted at close range or imagined over vast geographic distances, shape eugenic thinking and mold the landscape through which figures such as Urzaiz and Martí continue to circulate in an evolving critical geography. In this sense, as I have suggested, our own reading practices and desires participate in a geopolitically rendered framework linked to these eugenic itineraries. In the pages to follow, the visual transmission of corporeal difference will remain crucial to the eugenic project and the demarcation of exclusions. However, analysis in the present chapter also considers disability as inseparable from a negotiation of time, and hence from the complex and volatile ways in which history and temporality may be imagined and experienced. When it comes to the causality that ostensibly leads between alcohol and the drinker's offspring, it seems that time only perhaps will have told, for any resulting proof is speculative rather than definitive.

In this chapter, focused on the work of disability and causality in the anti-alcohol and other hygiene campaigns of the late 1920s and early 1930s, and on José Vasconcelos's work of the same period, I pay attention to how the contingency of disability becomes central to the construction of collective pasts and future, in this case in a specifically national, Mexican context. Disability, in conjunction with racialized forms of difference, does not generally define or situate excludable types in a definitive manner, but rather hovers over the temporal horizon as a kind of undefined warning. Alcoholism and the act of drinking, along with other practices considered unhygienic, come to signify possible past and future disability through a process marked by uncertain causality over time, while at the same time implying a form of perpetual, present condemnation. The two public-health slogans on the dangers of alcohol perfectly capture this dual model of disability through time, as either immediately defined present or projected, possible pasts and futures. In addition, my reading here emphasizes the dilemma of a partial or blurred separation between the identity of the disabled subject and the causes of his or her condition. In these texts, the question of whether particular characteristics ultimately adhere to and define particular human subjects is central to the role of disability as tied to the causal relations it evokes, and to the oppression or dehumanization with which it is frequently associated. This structure of causality and contingency is a familiar one in the context of twentieth-century Mexican philosophies of national identity and debates on the nature of Mexican culture, with roots in a range of disciplines.[2] An examination of the emergence of disability via the rhetorical framework of causality over time thus becomes highly pertinent to an understanding of the roles of dehumanization and difference in producing national culture; moreover, this analysis reveals archived public-health and education documents as key cultural texts through which disability circulates, manifesting its rhetorical and material effects. Archives themselves purport to congeal and maintain a particular chronology, suggesting that evidence follows order and that each document follows from its predecessor. As repositories of institutional history, the public-health and public-education archives thus rehearse the temporal causality through which their human subjects appear to emerge.

I conceive of my present-day encounter with these Mexican archival materials of disability in history as an embodied experience that is necessarily bound to twenty-first-century notions of disability, including key insights from disability studies, with the evident risks that such a juxtaposition implies. This reading practice offers a transhistorical approach to disability politics, and specifically to the dilemma of disability futurity in Mexican and global contexts—in other words, the question of how we might imagine and inhabit a disability to come. Projects for a hopeful, desirable disability present and future, as evoked by a number of voices in contemporary disability studies scholarship, must here account for the already complex negotiation of temporality and contingency evidenced in Mexican public-health history, and in particular, for the fraught horizons of cause and effect that appear to be closely tied to the body's origins and becomings.

In negotiating these readings, I consider as well the role of historical materialist approaches in contemporary disability studies, as in the compelling and influential research of scholars such as Nirmala Erevelles and Jasbir Puar. In their distinct critical projects, both Puar and Erevelles emphasize the causal processes whereby disability or debility emerges as the outcome of colonialism and global capitalist inequalities.[3] As Erevelles provocatively asks, for example, "How is disability celebrated if its very existence is inextricably linked to the violence of social/economic conditions of capitalism?" (*Disability and Difference* 17). This observation has important implications for the broader field of disability studies, and particularly for reading disability in contexts asymmetrically marked by globalized exploitation, as in the case of this book. In building on aspects of this scholarship, I pay attention to the ongoing dilemma of causality, and how the notion of disability as outcome gestures toward a genealogy of disability contingency, as represented, for example, in early-twentieth-century Mexican hygiene campaigns. If, as I will argue further, the emphasis on causality and hence the contingency of disability may entail a certain discursive violence in the Mexican post-revolutionary texts to be discussed here, a transhistorical reading might allow us to reframe our attention to contemporary uses of causality as well. My argument does not avoid or minimize the global conditions of exploitation and inequality that undoubtedly continue to structure lived experiences of disability and debility. Instead, by attending more specifically to the rhetorical uses of causality, their potential genealogy, and the violence they may encapsulate, I want to pressure the inevitability of their logic. Borrowing here from Tanya Titchkosky's reflexive approach to disability studies through a "politics of wonder," as she writes, "the activity of making uncertainty out of what is certain" (132), I project the problem of causality toward the question of *how* this structure shapes our perceptions or interpretations, and how we might perceive otherwise.[4]

This chapter first navigates the questions of disability contingency and causality in post-revolutionary Mexican archival texts as well as in contemporary mainstream and critical approaches to disability, exploring the complexity of discursive and material relations between disability and temporality. I then turn my attention to aspects of the history of eugenics and its implicit links to disability futurity, discussing key differences between Latin American and Northern European or Anglo-American eugenic models. Here I consider the paradoxical degree of fluidity in Mexican discourses of eugenics and hygiene, or "hard" and "soft" eugenics. Within this paradigm, I analyze an anti-alcoholism campaign document featuring a sketch by Diego Rivera, focusing on the slippage between notions of racial difference and corporeal marks of addiction and intoxication. The final section of the chapter shifts to the work of José Vasconcelos, the Mexican philosopher and statesman, juxtaposed with the public hygiene documents. Here, the question of temporally conditioned human differences expands toward a reflection on the reading of Mexican history and national identity, while scientific debates on hygiene and heredity extend toward the elaboration of cultural aesthetics.

The children of alcoholics, the "imbeciles, scurvied, epileptic, or those of depraved instincts," who emerge so vividly in the public-health text and many others like it, effectively capture the reader's imagination, and yet ultimately they are not real. They appear in a sense as imaginary composites of names and data that appear elsewhere in the Public Health and Public Education archival files. Schoolchildren's or patients' names are listed, often accompanied by IQ measurements, anthropometric data, or lists of illnesses and conditions; in some cases, physicians and educators apply categories of "normal," "abnormal," "educable," and "non-educable" in their creation of "homogeneous groups" (Santamarina, "La cuestión de los anormales"). Proper names do of course refer to real individuals, whether in the case of schoolchildren or teachers listed only once, or those of more prominent individuals, administrators in education and health, who reappear over the years, from file to file and from box to box. But disability, appearing through a repeating set of pathologizing terms, or at times through data and physical description, or through a rhetoric of hygiene exhorting the reader to avoid particular practices in order to produce favorable national and reproductive futures, is more difficult to locate in a precise manner. The experience of the archival encounter may at times blur distinctions between what count as historical facts as opposed to personal impressions. There are letters and reports that conjure up specific bodies, as in the case of a blind man, described as a beggar, who tried to escape from the School for the Blind by lowering himself from a window by a rope (Lavín). There are accounts of numbers of institutional inmates, including numbers of deaths and of released individuals ("Distribución de los mendigos"). And there are numerous letters and discussions on social and physical ills, through a range of terminology, their causes, prognosis, ways to avoid them, and techniques for their classification. Taken together, these records produce a notion of disability over time, variably conjoined with and severed from referenced names and bodies. The encounter with disability in history, and perhaps moreso in these cases of archival documents, and others that pose the question of collective and national futures, demands further reflection on the roles of present and future disability in Mexico and in the world. These archival sources cannot fail to resonate in relation to contemporary experiences and depictions of disability in Mexico and elsewhere. The moment of reading, then, points to further spaces of recognition, imagination, and embodiment of disability in the present and the future.

Causalities

As noted above, in the contemporary context of neoliberal globalization, disability is produced and proliferates through processes including labor exploitation, pollution, war, and border policing, disproportionately impacting regions of the Global South as well as racialized communities in the North

(Erevelles, *Thinking with*). The disability of our present day circulates through these familiar patterns of inequality and may remind us that the temporal horizon of disability, however conjectural, today as in post-revolutionary Mexico is perpetually conditioned by asymmetrically distributed material violence. In the more specific context of late-nineteenth- and early-twentieth-century Mexico, lack of access to adequate food, water, healthcare, and housing caused high rates of preventable illness, infant mortality, and precarious living conditions for large population sectors.[5] The archival documents from the public-health and public-education ministries tend to associate disability, including "mental weakness," "abnormality," and a range of health conditions, with the economically underprivileged, and with recipients of public welfare, and these were the groups specifically targeted by hygiene campaigns. Proceedings from the Fifth Pan-American Child Congress, held in Havana in 1927, note the participation of Dr. Rafael Santamarina, of the Department of Psychopedagogy and Hygiene, and are categorized by topics such as hygiene, child psychology, delinquency, child development, and schools for abnormal children. The concluding agreements of the Congress include the statement, "La pobreza es en gran parte una enfermedad social evitable. Las causas de la pobreza pueden en su generalidad vencerse por el ataque concertado de la sociedad." [Poverty is in large part an avoidable social illness. The causes of poverty can in general be defeated through a concerted attack by society.] ("Acta final"). Elsewhere, Dr. Santamarina would include poverty of the child's parents among the listed social causes of abnormality affecting the educability of children ("La cuestión de los anormales"). Other stated causes range from physical conditions, including illness, decreased visual or auditory acuity, and disturbance of intelligence (4).[6] If the work of psychopedagogy and hygiene included a tendency to categorize poorer populations as deficient or predominantly abnormal, it is also true here that a particular rhetoric of causality often situates disability, as in the case of developmental delays of schoolchildren, as the outcome of poverty that could be or could have been avoided.

Dr. Santamarina illustrates his argument on abnormality in school children with a classification chart listing the types of abnormality, organized by causes and recommended treatments. Causes begin with those of the psyche, divided into the resulting categories of "idiots," "imbeciles," and "mental weaklings." The list then proceeds to physical causes and includes a range of physical impairments. The next category covers causes from beyond the school setting, including poor living conditions and parental illiteracy, and the final category encompasses problems in the school setting, including

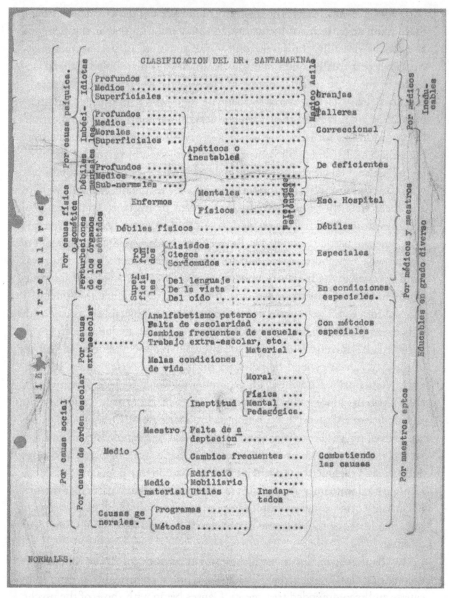

Fig. 8. A classification chart of abnormality in schoolchildren, created by Dr. Rafael Santamarina, featuring causes, types of abnormality, and proposed solutions. "Clasificación del Dr. Santamarina." Caja 35514, Ref. 139, exp 16, "Niños anormales y retardados" 1927, folio 20. Archivo General de la Nación.

inadequacies of the teacher, the curriculum, facilities, and materials. Brackets on the left side of the page indicate the causes of each condition, while those on the right suggest the appropriate response to be taken in each case, whether the children can be best taught through special methods, sent to farms or workshops, or in the case of the "uneducable," treated by physicians. In cases in which educational setting has been the problem, the response is to "combat the causes" of the abnormality ("Clasificación del Dr. Santamarina").

The causal framework evident here in Dr. Santamarina's writing offers a socially conservative structure designed to identify abnormality, remedy it when possible, and isolate it in cases deemed too extreme for education to tackle. It also attempts to depict children as at least partially separate from the causes of their presumed abnormalities. This approach undoubtedly differs in tone, intentionality, and scope from contemporary readings of the material production of global or local inequality as intrinsic to disability as injustice. Yet this framework serves as a reminder that contingent causality as a mode of persuasion persists with widely varied motivations and structures, in conjunction with disability and its material and social effects. If a model of disability as grounded primarily in the recognition and critique of globalized inequalities offers compelling evidence and crucially necessary tools for dismantling oppression, it nonetheless bears examination for the patterns of causality through which it may persuade us, and for its particular entanglements or parsing of bodies and contexts, causes and effects. Rather than abandoning the arguments of causality here, those that explain, for example, the connections between colonialism, capitalism, poverty, and disability, we might pause to consider how their logic has become undeniably compelling, and how it may continue to shape our perceptions and experiences of disability, even in unrecognized ways. It might then be possible to challenge the processes that produce inequality while disrupting the interpretive pathways that often determine bodies as causes and effects.[7]

More familiar, mainstream depictions of disability in contemporary media frequently invoke pathos and emphasize the need for a cure. In such representations, including popular literature, television, and film, charity campaigns, and daily interpersonal encounters, disability may be portrayed or read as the result of a "tragic" accident, a failure to maintain good health habits, a reproductive mishap, the unfortunate outcome of aging, or even as a unique opportunity to prove one's inner strength.[8] Through these explanatory patterns, disability takes its position along a temporal trajectory linking cause to effect, solving the conundrum of difference, and at times serving as a warning or lesson to nondisabled observers. As in the case of the anti-alcohol slogans of the early 1930s, numerous present-day examples reveal the extent to which mainstream encounters with disability involve a discourse of potential or actual causality, often with a message of how to best avoid a future disability.

Here we might consider a recent visual depiction of disability from the Mexican branch of the pharmaceutical corporation Eli Lilly. Their 2008 advertising campaign features a series of photographs, with the same subtitle in each case: "If you have diabetes, don't let the shadow of complications catch up with you" ("Sombras"). In one photo, we see a man sitting in a chair. The shadow of the chair, projected behind the man, has the form of a wheelchair, or more precisely, the international symbol for disability. In a second photo, with the same subtitle, a man walks down the street, and the shadow of a crutch appears behind his leg. In a third case, a woman, loaded with shopping bags, strides along the sidewalk; her shadow is in the form of a woman walking with a cane. The ads give the impression of being public service announcements, though closer inspection reveals that they are promoting Eli Lilly insulin and related products for diabetics. The visual rhetoric of Eli Lilly's campaign represents potential disability as a disturbing presence. In the ads, a dark shadow pursues—or lies in wait for—those with diabetes. The shadow can't be erased, but perhaps it can be overcome through appropriate public and private actions. The shadow, separate from the body in each image, insists on the difference between diabetes and its complications, evoked through recognizable disability symbols. But at the same time, it underscores a necessary causality between condition and prognosis. Shadow and body depend on one another, as inseparable but never quite equivalent.[9]

These shadowed images of disability as a future that may lie in wait, or may be avoided, circulate in contemporary media, and inevitably inflect my approach to the discourses of post-revolutionary hygiene and psychopedagogy. The causal rhetoric surrounding the emergence of disability in these carefully targeted contemporary advertisements serves to underscore the ongoing resonance of the anti-alcohol message and its particular mode of persuasion. These are messages that continue to speak, and in this sense gesture toward our possible responses. Given the violent inequalities that produce disability both historically and in contemporary contexts, and given the causal, temporal frameworks so frequently employed to explain disability or to conjure it away, the question of what conditions might allow us to effectively receive the disability of the future acquires particular urgency, although the issue is not a new one. The goal in this case is not to determine the "true" causes or definition of disability and its prognosis, as distinct from erroneous ideas, nor is it to separate disability or disabled people from all causal processes. Instead, my intention is to underscore the impetus to either congeal or tease out cause and effect, or context and body, and to recognize, too, that disability as discursive production and embodied experience exists within this fraught terrain, one that continues to shape our arguments and expectations.

The goal of prevention or avoidance of a negatively charged diagnosis generally passes as acceptable, unquestioned, and consistent over time, despite significant historical changes in medical practice and public opinion. As an example of this common horizon linking a contemporary readership to Mexican post-revolutionary medical standards, Andrés Ríos Molina notes in his 2016 book, *Cómo prevenir la locura, psiquiatría e higiene mental en México, 1934–1950*, that his readers may well wonder whether the labor of the psychiatrists who worked toward the prevention of "mental illnesses" was actually effective (14). The book does not posit an answer to this question, stating instead, "we do not know," and explaining that for the psychiatrists of the period in question, such prevention was both possible and necessary (14–15). Yet posing the question implicitly positions the notion of prevention as central to the temporal horizon extending from midcentury to the present day, through a logic that identifies madness [*locura*] and mental illnesses [*enfermedades mentales*] and binds them irrevocably to the goal of prevention.

The questions I imagine readers might pose here are different ones, though in a similar sense, they gesture toward the present-day and future, and similarly, I don't pretend to offer absolute answers. One could consider whether aspects of the disability we encounter in these documents, through descriptions, data, hygiene campaigns, and implied or explicit warnings, might be said to exist in a meaningful sense today, in Mexico or elsewhere. On encountering the reports, studies, letters, and programs for a more hygienic future, readers today might wonder how they and their actual or future offspring fit the classifications, and whether contemporary classifications of human difference reflect aspects of earlier practices. Do we find traces of the *tarjeta sanitaria* in children's school report cards? Do we inadvertently look for IQ scale evidence in their schoolwork?[10] Are my current nervousness and fatigue the result of staring too closely at these now-faded yellow pages, as some experts of the day suggested? And how does our contemporary evidence of disability exploitation, through inequality on a global scale, impact our readings of these earlier documents, in which disability is almost invariably associated with poverty, but also quite often with practices viewed as immoral or unhygienic?

One could ask as well how the disability that we know today, or think we know, might either reify or contest not only these earlier classifications, but the temporal horizon through which they emerge. Must disability always be a contingent past or future, a possible cause or a forthcoming effect? Or, as Eunjung Kim similarly asks, "Can one ever see a disabled body as it is, not as it was or as it should become?" (220). The ethical imperative behind this questioning is central to the disability studies–informed framework of this book, which interrogates the repeating tendencies to predict, explain, cure, prevent, or normalize disability, and critiques the historical and ongoing exploitation and exclusion of disabled people. To be sure, the purpose of this analysis is not to undermine the need for resources such as health care, clean water, or the prevention of alcohol abuse. Instead, by focusing on how human differences emerge as a function of time, and in turn produce a series of discursive and material effects, my aim is to reconsider the logic of this serial causality, while remaining attuned to the risks that specific rhetorics and notions of time and causality pose to disabled lives and to racialized bodies, both within and beyond Mexico.

Hard and Soft Eugenics

A number of works by US-based scholars in disability studies and the related area of queer theory over the past two decades have grappled with the dilemma of futurity, or the possibility of a desirable queer or crip future, including texts by Alison Kafer, Robert McRuer, José Esteban Muñoz, and Lee Edelman. Such forms of futurity, typically imagined from a late-twentieth- or twenty-first-century standpoint, whether envisioned through creative flourishing or annihilation, tend to work in opposition to familiar heteronormative, ableist, and ultimately eugenic projects of mainstream human reproductive futures in US contexts. In other words, a crip futurity contests and unravels eugenic initiatives, and in fact acquires much of its impact against both contemporary forms of ableist violence and a farther-reaching history of eugenics as an enterprise grounded in the efforts of scientists, physicians, and educators to build a better "race." Eugenic practices in the US, Canada, and parts of Europe included sterilization and immigration bans on those seen as unfit, as well as genocidal projects such as the Nazis' Operation T4, through which over 300,000 disabled people were killed. Crip and queer collective futures survive and flourish today, projecting new spaces, practices, and desires, despite and against long histories of exclusion, annihilation, institutionalization, and the politics of "better breeding." As David Mitchell and Sharon Snyder note, the Berlin T4 memorial includes a quote from a disabled member of the Netzwerk People First Deutshland, who states: "If we had been alive during the war, we wouldn't be here today. Then you would not get to know us anymore" (267). The declaration explicitly posits the affirmative presence of disabled people in the here and now, linking them to those who were murdered during T4 as part of a common group, and reminding the reader that the flourishing of disabled lives in the present and future is possible because of the contestation of eugenic beliefs and practices. In turn, failure to recognize and contest the premises underpinning this violent history puts the lives and well-being of disabled people at risk, now and in the future.[11]

Mexican eugenics and hygiene programs did not include the systematic murder of disabled people, nor is there evidence that sterilizations based on presumed disability or criminal records took place in the Mexican context, as was the case in Germany, the US, and Canada.[12] As noted in the introduction to this book, analysis of Anglo-American, European, and Latin American eugenic discourse and state policies of the early twentieth century reveals marked regional differences, specifically an emphasis on the "soft" eugenics of social medicine in the Mexican context, though often in continuity with elements of "hard" eugenics.[13] As an example of such continuity, in 1942, the Mexican periodical *Eugenesia* refers to "un plan eugenésico . . . contra la ignorancia de las causas de la degeneración, contra el alcoholismo, el sífilis . . . como un símbolo de la higiene de la raza" (Ruiz Escalona 15). [A eugenic plan . . . against ignorance of the causes of degeneration, against alcoholism, syphilis . . . as a symbol of the hygiene of the race.] This combination of practical health programs with the troubling term "hygiene of the race," evoking the German notion of *rassenhygiene*, underscores the particularity of eugenics in Latin American contexts.[14]

As Nancy Leys Stepan writes:

> A central factor in the Lamarckian outlook on preventive eugenics . . . was the idea of "racial poisons," a term eugenists used to refer to such things as alcohol, nicotine, morphine, venereal diseases, and other drugs and infections. These poisons were called "racial" because, though the habits and diseases were often first acquired or experienced in one individual's lifetime, they were believed to lead to permanent, hereditary degenerations that in the long run could affect entire populations or nations. (85)

David Mitchell and Sharon Snyder's notions of "ablenationalism" and of a "eugenic Atlantic" offer a model that emphasizes specific and more clearly demarcated distinctions between individuals accepted into or rejected from a citizen body, particularly in the United States, Great Britain, France, and Germany. Rather than theories of hereditary transmission, the authors focus on sterilization, extermination, exclusion, and institutionalization and mechanisms intended to purify the population. As they write, "the historical development of ablenationalism results in the modern formation of disability as a discrete, sociological minority" ("Ablenationalism" 113).

In contrast, the cultural discourse of eugenics in Mexico, enacted in medical, literary, and popular publications, underscores a temporal fluidity, with reference to the potential future outcomes of eugenic practices. Such narratives of preventive eugenics depend on their reference to the future in relation to practices in the present, yet the relationship often blurs the line between the two or suggests only a potential or hypothetical causality. This is the case in the above-mentioned public messages from the *Weekly Bulletin* of the Ministry of Public Health, in which the texts present their urgent message, and yet insist on the uncertainty and ambiguity of their own temporal logic, obfuscating the differences between the linear and the cyclical, the present and the future.

In the context of this temporally fluid eugenics, disability and racial differences become relatively uncertain markers linking past, present, and future. Unlike in the "ablenationalist" discourse outlined by Mitchell and Snyder, soft eugenics does not easily allow for strict demarcations between rights-bearing citizens and those deemed biologically inferior due to disability or race, primarily because this preventive eugenics suspends differences along a temporal continuum, marked with warnings of danger and exhortations to improvement. The collective quality of this hypothetical reproductive timeline also suggests a more intimate linkage between the notions of disability and race, since all potential markers of biological difference may impact the future of the national body, conceived as a mestizo "race," as evidenced in Stepan's reference to "racial poisons."

The issue increases in complexity, however, when one considers the variety of scientific influences impacting eugenic discourse in Mexico, including emphasis on both biological determinism and social environment, at times contributing to shifting or contradictory notions of heredity, as noted in the introduction. Moreover, scientific theories would be shaped by the transnational aspects of Mexican hygiene and eugenics, as through the figure of the Yucatec Cuban emigré, Eduardo Urzaiz, discussed in chapter 1, and through Mexican participation in numerous international conferences on eugenics, hygiene, and related topics.[15] These points of contact brought Mexican physicians and educators into dialogue with their European, US, and Cuban counterparts, juxtaposing radical or "hard" eugenics, including advocacy of sterilization, with the "soft" eugenics of social medicine.

By accounting for the fluidity of eugenic discourse in Mexico, in which social medicine and hygiene in practice, along with more rigid theories of reproductive control, come to impact a range of public-health and education policies, one allows for clearer recognition of the complex temporality through which disability emerges in this period. This is because eugenics through social medicine projects disability in potential over a broad temporal horizon, while "hard" eugenics identifies disability for eradication at a specific place and time. This duality is related to the contradictory coexistence and blending, noted above, of diverse eugenic theories of social environment and those of biological determinism. As one example, we might consider the work of Dr. Roberto Solís Quiroga, director of the Instituto Nacional de Psicopedagogía, founded in 1937, and founding and long-term active member of the Sociedad Eugénica Mexicana. Dr. Solís Quiroga focused throughout his career on the newly emerging field of special education, or education for "abnormal children," and in 1935 he founded the Instituto Médico Pedagógico, a school located in Mexico's Parque Lira, dedicated to the education of "educable mental weaklings" as well as to research and medical treatment.[16] Solís Quiroga's work in special education fits clearly into a broader paradigm of hygiene, in which social and environmental causes must be identified. As he writes in a 1936 letter: "En el Servicio de Higiene Mental se están estudiando hasta donde es posible los factores etiológicos de las anomalías de conducta" (3). [The Mental Hygiene Service studies to the degree possible etiological factors in abnormal behavior.] (Solís Quiroga, "Carta").

Yet in a 1933 text, within the *Bulletin of the Mexican Eugenics Society*, we find reference to a text by Dr. Solís Quiroga advocating "limitación de la concepción . . . por la existencia de seres indeseables" [limiting conception . . . because of the existence of undesirable beings]. As the reference states, "Hay casos de indicación definida, y casos de indicación menos clara que requieren el conocimiento de la herencia patológica de los cónyuges para neutralización de factores o para desautorizar la union." [There are clearly defined cases, and cases in which the course of action is less clear and requires knowledge of the pathological inheritance of the spouses in order to neutralize factors or to disallow the union.] ("Informe de la última session"). The uncertain shifting between clear and less clearly defined "cases" suggests a combined approach in which the "undesirable" elements are by turns hidden beneath layers of hereditary possibility and exposed as irrevocable fact. Moreover, specific use of the term "*seres indeseables*" [undesirable beings] underscores the notion that eugenics can work to shape a purportedly better future society by literally preventing the existence of certain types of people.

What is undesirable, here and now, emerges paradoxically in this discourse through a framework of hypothetical becoming that is the hallmark of hygienic thinking. In other words, the impetus to violent eradication is ostensibly softened by the context of causality, displaced from the undesirable subject to the factors that may have created or shaped it, or that may do so in the future. Undesirability of course may take on a variety of different forms, displayed through physical or behavioral features, associated at times with notions of race, and at times with disability. The coexistence and dialogue here between the models of "soft" and "hard" eugenics, or if one prefers, hygiene and eugenics, suggest that although social medicine and hygiene rather than hard eugenics were the predominant policies of Mexican post-revolutionary health and education initiatives, such projects nonetheless encapsulate a series of ableist assumptions, grounded in notions of social and biological hierarchy. In other words, the idea of undesirable people, or those without human worth, remains operative here, although overall policy dictates emphasis on attending to hygiene and social environment as causal factors.[17]

Reading these archival documents in relation to disability in the present day, and to notions of crip futurity in current circulation, requires more than a critique of exploitative and discriminatory discourse and practice. After all, such a critique is not difficult to achieve, given the particular and derogatory language of hygiene and eugenics through which disability appears in the archive, as well as in many more recent sources. Rather, at stake here are the processes of temporal displacement through which the texts depict and manage disability, and the ways in which disability becomes integral to a particular temporal and causal arc within Mexican post-revolutionary discourse. From this perspective, imagining a future disability today, with the critical aim of a contestation of past and current ableism, must necessarily account for prior, historically specific modes of futurity in which disability was already deeply inscribed.[18]

Alcoholic Effects

I began this chapter with a reference to the language of an anti-alcoholism campaign of the late 1920s and 1930s, and to the emergence of disability within a temporal trajectory defined by the slogans of the campaign. This temporal arc in turn has allowed me to consider the ambivalent projections and contours of eugenic discourse and its inflections in archival documents, as well as in some present-day representations of disability. In returning now to the context of anti-alcoholism in the post-revolution, I am reminded that for readers today, a link between the notions of alcoholism and disability may not be immediately intuitive, but instead gestures toward potentially fraught conjectures on causality, stereotyping, and "innate predispositions." The language of hygiene in 1920s and '30s Mexico lays out these processes somewhat more clearly; here references to alcoholism point to future risk or serve as lessons about an unfortunate past, yet still leave the reader in the space of conjecture and uncertainty, contemplating possible pasts and futures.

Anti-alcoholism alone does not define the discourse of hygiene and the causal structuring of disability in this period, but it is a prevalent mode through which the dangers of immoral behavior were represented through their impact on reproductive futures. In addition, alcohol operates in many instances as a bridging device between discourses of hygiene and those of racial difference, because of perceived notions of racially or regionally specific drinking practices, particularly related to presumed associations between alcohol abuse and indigeneity, or lower-class status, and efforts to debunk such stereotypes.[19] In this sense, the representation of alcohol abuse emerges as a curious sticking point, through which the denigration of others is framed and displaced by the denigration of a product and its ingestion. Anti-alcohol discourses, it is worth noting, also work through strongly articulated gender divisions, in which men, particularly those who engage in sexual activity when drunk, are seen as the source of reproductive danger, while women are exhorted to play a central role in combating such immoral drinking practices. In my analysis of the 1929 anti-alcohol campaign featured in the journal *El Sembrador*, I pay attention to the role of temporal and reproductive causality as part of the broader discourse of hygiene, but also, as a linked issue, to the dilemma of partial or blurred associations between alcohol and its ingestion, and between those who drink and the presumed outcomes of this practice. In this sense, the question of the degree to which the product and its purported effects seem to adhere to the body and identity of the consumer will occupy center stage.

In 1929, the Ministry of Public Education began publication of the newspaper *El Sembrador*, designed for a rural readership and with the goal of improving literacy rates and promoting state-sponsored projects, particularly those pertaining to hygiene. (Gudiño).[20] The pages of *El Sembrador* became an effective platform for President Portes Gil's anti-alcoholism campaign, and in April of 1929 the newspaper published a portion of the president's speech, outlining a "program of action" for the campaign. In the context of *El Sembrador*, as specifically designed for a campesino population generally depicted as ignorant, the campaign highlights the destructive role of alcohol in broad strokes, quite literally, for the speech excerpt is accompanied by a rough sketch by Diego Rivera, revealing the function of alcohol in destroying the lives of the laboring classes (Rivera and Portes Gil). The image shows a stout man in a three-piece suit and top hat, holding a whip in one hand and a bag marked with a dollar sign in the other. He is seated before what appears to be a maguey plant, with two other money bags at his feet, and he is grinning broadly.

To the right, a human figure lies on the ground, holding a bottle in one hand, his face concealed. Behind him stand other figures, their heads down and their faces hidden by hair or a hat. A woman carries a child on her back and holds an infant in her arms, while a man appears to drink from a jug. The clothing of these figures is simple, rendered in few lines, and the one figure whose feet are visible is barefoot. The infant's body is disproportionate, with thin arms, an elongated torso, and only three visible fingers; the other figures, similarly, have been created with minimal detail and few signs of life, other than the fact of being upright, or of clutching a bottle. At first glance, the image appears primarily to contrast riches with poverty, elegant Western-style clothing with peasant garb, and evil, grinning exploiter with faceless victims. The caption to the image spells out the message more explicitly, at the same time reminding the reader of the efficacy and importance of this communicative process. The caption reads as follows: "El Alcohol es el más eficaz auxiliar de los explotadores del trabajo humano. —La Revolución combate el Alcoholismo, porque ella quiere la libertad, la responsabilidad y la dignificación del trabajador. —El Alcoholismo es el destructor del hogar, y es la mujer quien sufre las consecuencias más tristes y deplorables de este vicio. —Lic. Emilio Portes Gil" [Alcohol is the exploiters' most effective helper. —The Revolution combats alcoholism in favor of liberty, responsibility, and the dignification of the worker. —Alcoholism destroys the home, and women suffer the saddest and most deplorable consequences of this vice]. Below this caption, a brief explanation appears: "Estos tres hondos pensamientos del C. Presidente de la República, interpretados maravillosamente por el fuerte y laureado pincel de Diego Rivera, fueron proporcionados galantemente a "El Sembrador" por la Secretaría de Gobernación, que ha emprendido enérgica y eficaz campaña antialcoholica." [These three profound thoughts from the Citizen President of the Republic, marvelously interpreted by Diego Rivera's acclaimed brush, were gallantly offered by the Ministry of Governance to "El Sembrador," as part of a vigorous and efficient anti-alcohol campaign.]

El Alcohol es el más eficaz auxiliar de los explotadores del rabajo humano.—La Revolución combate el Alcoholismo, porque ella quiere la libertad, la responsabilidad y la dignif cación del trabajador.—El Alcoholismo es el destructor del hogar, y es la mujer quien sufre las consecuencias más tri tes y deplorables de este vicio.—*LIC. EMILIO PORTES GIL.*

Estos tres lucidos pensamientos del C. Presidente de la Repúbl ca, interpretados maravillosamente por el fuerte y laureado pincel de Diego Rivera, fueron proporcionados galantemente a «El Sembrado » por la Secretaría de Gobernación, que ha emprendido enérgica y eficaz campañ antialcohólica.

Fig. 9. A sketch by Diego Rivera depicting a causal relationship between capitalism, alcoholism, and the exploitation of peasants. Published in 1929 in the journal *El Sembrador* as part of an anti-alcohol campaign by the Ministry of Public Education, under the presidency of Emilio Portés Gil. *El Sembrador* #4, 5 de junio de 1929, pp. 8–9. Caja 3553, Ref. 146, exp. 79, folio 164. Archivo General de la Nación.

The message of the campaign, already synthesized in the abridged version of President Portes Gil's speech on the following page, is further broken down in the didactic combination of slogans, illustration, and supplementary gloss, presumably designed to reach an audience with mixed or low levels of literacy. But in fact, the additional explanatory layers provided here complicate an already complex logic through which one evil is said to lead to another. Reading the drawing in tandem with its caption, the notion of alcohol as an auxiliary to exploitation in the context of Mexican revolutionary discourse becomes especially noteworthy. Alcohol itself is side-stepped, at least for a moment, to allow capitalist exploitation to play a central role. In its helper role, alcohol works on behalf of the capitalist, yet the connection is an indirect one, for as the image shows, the man with the money bags sits comfortably, his whip to the ground, while his victims drink or sleep off their drunkenness. Rather than representing alcohol abuse as the specific cause of suffering on its own, the image and text suggest instead that drinking alcohol is a supplementary element within a larger process of economic exploitation. The destructive nature of alcohol here is due not simply to specific debilitating physical effects, but more importantly to its role in the impoverishment of individuals, households, and communities, hence as a means through which labor and needed resources seem to evaporate, as if magically transformed into money and then into drink.

The image of the stout and grinning capitalist may remind viewers of large and detailed murals and other works depicting aspects of the Mexican revolutionary struggle over time. This lesser-known sketch, produced within the context of a more specific didactic purpose, taps into the language of exploitation generated by more iconic works, thus creating a short-hand equivalence between alcoholism and the familiar process of exploitation against which the revolution and the worker must struggle.[21] Although the idea of a link between alcohol and capitalist exploitation is not unique to this setting, the combination of text and image is striking here for effectively illustrating a transformative, cyclical process, linking the alcohol containers to the bags marked with dollar signs, and the fragile, faceless bodies of the peasant-victims to the well-fed figure of their exploiter. It is of course thanks to the capacity of capital to transform both labor and alcohol or other products into abstract and exchangeable commodities that the exploitation cycle may continue. At the same time, the relationship between the peasant, as consumer-producer, and the alcoholic products, is a tangible, viscerally experienced one, defined by the materially transformative processes of ingestion and intoxication.

In addition, the detail of the maguey plant before which the smiling capitalist sits suggests an additional transformative process at work, in which natural resources are fermented and then in some cases distilled into stronger substances, either the traditional fermented pulque or the more potent, distilled mezcal. The image thus suggests two linked causal chains at work simultaneously: one in which human labor and products generate surplus value, and another in which the technologies of fermentation and distillation produce intoxicants from plant sugars. Because Rivera's imagery and its accompanying message underscore addiction to alcohol as an ongoing problem, distillation ultimately produces both alcohol and by extension the promise of further consumption and intoxication. In this way, the physical and chemical changes produced by distillation and intoxication become closely intertwined with the capitalist production of surplus value through labor exploitation. The curious properties of commodities as they enter into relations with one another thus emerge here through intimate dialogue between the magic of Marxist exchange and the similarly mysterious process by which common plant extracts become intoxicating, addictive substances, marked as both valuable and dangerous.

The notion of alcohol abuse as prevalent among indigenous populations is not unique to Mexico. Moreover, it is an association that often reveals the framing devices through which humanity is only partially, rhetorically separated from the differences that are expected to degrade and dehumanize it. Sherene Razack's work on the abuse and death of indigenous people in Canadian police custody serves as a relevant example. As she argues, the attribution of the cause of death to alcoholism effectively produces a notion of the indigenous body as always already dead, and as part of a disappearing race. Here Razack cites from Rod Michalko's influential work, *The Difference that Disability Makes*: "The difference of disability thus becomes the useless-difference borne by anyone victimized (disturbed) by misfortune" (qtd. in Razack 21). Alcoholism, and the disability construed as its effect, is this "useless difference," and becomes both separated from the humanity of the subject to which it is attributed, and ironically, dehumanizing of that subject. As in the context of eugenics and hygiene campaigns, here too, disability and racial difference become mutually constitutive of one another through police documentation of the alcoholic and racialized body. Unlike Razack's depiction of the temporality of death, in which perceptions of alcoholism and its physical effects seal the indigenous body into a closed and predefined history, the texts in my analysis tend to suggest a greater margin of uncertainty and speculation regarding the pasts and futures of the bodies and national population they purport to represent. After all, in the case of Rivera's sketch and the accompanying quotes, the revolution is held out as the hope for a healthier and more just future. Yet in both Razack's analysis and in my discussion of the Mexican archival texts, a partial separation takes place, between the "useless-difference" of alcoholism as disability, and either the potential humanity of the individual, or a promising collective history, extending from past to future.

In contrasting these two models here, I want to emphasize how the perception of temporality and national history becomes integral to the emergence and conceptualization of disability and other differences in early post-revolutionary Mexico. In Razack's argument regarding a contemporary Canadian context, it is the humanity of the individual subject that is at stake in its ambiguous, partial separation from the "useless difference" of disability. In my reading of the Mexican texts it is primarily a collective national history and future that operate in tension with this so-called useless difference. In this case, disability is ironically both outside of conventional time, suspended from history, and disruptive to the logic of past and future, destiny and progress. Whether disability is deferred through projection into the past or future, or obliterated through equation with death, social and political contexts oppressive to disabled individuals and populations remain prevalent. In each context, perceived causes of disability frame and threaten the singular or collective human subject, while at once blurring the bounds that would define humanity and human temporal progression as distinct from the offending differences. This ambivalent blurring between human subjects and the factors that may damage them over time is similarly at work in both the anti-alcoholism campaign featured in *El Sembrador*, and in the previously cited public-health slogans regarding the potential effects of alcohol on the drinkers' offspring.

The "difference" created by alcohol is the dehumanization of the campesino subjects in Rivera's sketch, just as it is the marking of the indigenous body as already dead in Razack's discussion. The sketch also implies the threat of mortality through the figure of the face-down drunken subject, yet at the same time includes the projection of an uncertain future through inclusion of the child and the infant, carried by their mother. The child's face, barely rendered by marks for two eyes and a nose, tells us very little, but the presence of this emergent generation underscores the message that actions of the present unfold in their effects over time, through processes of reproduction and transformation, extending beyond the individual to family and community.

The lines of Rivera's sketch suggest a hastily rendered work, yet this too appears as a self-reflexive quality, as if proclaiming itself as the rough outline of an example of what happens at times, or of what may take place when unfettered capitalism and alcoholism defeat revolutionary principles. The sketch itself is an adjustable hypothesis, and in this sense carries with it ambivalent projections of time and place, reminding us that such a scene may unfold somewhere, may have happened or be still to come. The final version will presumably depend on the actions of the viewers and their ability to assimilate the lesson. The denigration of the drunken subject, like the undesirability of disabled offspring featured in other texts, is only partially displaced by the factors that have caused the damage. A discourse of hygiene persists, in this sense, through the framing of dehumanization, an uncertain separation between the subject and the damage he evokes, embodies, and projects.

The particular message regarding alcoholism and economic exploitation promoted in the 1929 campaign persists in nearly identical form decades later, as the reader may appreciate in the following text from 1986: "Los indios, pues, sólo llegan a conocer las bebidas destiladas de alta concentración al quedar sujetos a la explotación colonial y permanecer en contacto y conversación con los no indios. La sociedad dominante, de entonces a nuestros días, usa el alcohol para extraer surplus de la fuerza de trabajo del indio y para mantenerlo en situación subalterna." [Indians only come into contact with strong, distilled beverages of high alcohol content upon becoming subject to colonial exploitation and ongoing contact with non-Indians. Dominant society, from that time until today, uses alcohol in order to extract surplus value from the Indian's labor and to keep him in a subaltern situation.] (Aguirre Beltrán 142–43). This classic source on medical anthropology exhorts the reader to focus on the economic, structural processes through which the "indio" becomes alcoholic, and through which alcohol simultaneously becomes a tool of exploitation. As in the case of Rivera's sketch in *El Sembrador*, here too the accumulation of capital through the extraction of surplus labor force may be said to suggest a parallel with the distillation and ingestion of alcohol. In both texts, distillation and intoxication as physically transformative processes create an ephemeral excess, one that adheres to the body of the drinker, marking its dehumanization as determined by a cycle of causes and effects. This excess refers to the work of capitalist exploitation, to the recapture of condensed ethanol, and to the measurable effects of concentrated alcohol within the human body. It results in a social and corporeal alcoholization through which bodies acquire their differences.

The dilemma, in reading the question of disability in such depictions of alcohol consumption, is to what extent these forms of excess appear to adhere to the bodies and subjects in question, or to what extent they separate, as contingent qualities, partially or potentially removable frames. As we have seen, the quality of at least partial separation between the alcoholic subject and the causes of his dehumanization is recurrent, and a discourse of temporal contingency generally insists that particular causes, such as poverty and inequality, are to blame. Yet the blurriness of this separation must be considered; in the *Sembrador* text, this blur is conditioned by the notion of excess in capitalism and in alcohol.

In this anti-alcohol text, the individual, intoxicated body suggests a larger pattern of transgenerational addiction, while embodying the physical and social transformations that reveal the production of excess. Images and evocations of the drunken individual, in highlighting physical changes both outside and within the body, thus announce their intertwined complicity with a broader pattern of exploitation and destruction. The image of the drunkard retains its markers of race and class primarily through insistence on the causal structures of colonialist and capitalist exploitation, yet the negatively charged production of economic, physical, and social excess passes through and impacts the body over time, just as the body itself in these texts, in its physical transformation and interaction with alcoholic excess, hosts and extends the repeating blows of dehumanization. It is largely through the structure of a physical interdependence between capitalist production, distillation, and intoxication over time that the texts project the visceral quality of dehumanized excess, a residue that proves difficult to extract from the ongoing generation of racialized and disabled embodiment, and hence from the bodies at stake.

Text and image together in this instance underscore the blurred framing of dehumanization—both external and fused with the subject—as linked to the similarly uncertain temporal structure, in which pasts and futures project beyond but at the same time emerge as one with the moment at hand. A similar process takes place in the public-health slogans on the dangers of alcohol, as cited at the beginning of this chapter. In the first case, the "niños imbéciles" [imbecile children] are postulated as both a warning and as suspected proof of a chain of causality. The actual presence of such children points to their parents, and to the immoral behavior of these parents, even when the parents themselves are nowhere to be seen. The marked child thus potentially embodies a corrupt parental practice, but always through a structure of uncertainty. In a similar sense, the words conjure up an unborn, future child, who may be negatively marked by parental alcoholism, though again the causality is only suggested and not proven. The construction of cause and effect in this case is both compelling and uncertain, or arguably compelling because of the uncertainty on which its logic is based. Fear of a negative future outcome, or suspicion of a past corrupting influence, guides the reader, but never offers a clear explanation of reproductive and moral causality.

Time will not tell, but will only suggest whether morality pays off, and by the same token, the eventual outcome will only appear to prove whether or not the initial action was morally correct. The message of hygiene implies the need to monitor individual and collective practices over time, as part of an ongoing striving toward moral good and reproductive improvement, against the risk of a looming future that threatens to reveal any earlier source of depravity or undesirable difference. Time will not simply produce or fail to produce difference, but will also continually allow for further investigation into the causality of this production. The projected future thus postpones and sustains a discourse of disability as causal and reproductive logic.

The second text, on the vulture who returns to devour the alcoholic's entrails, is anchored in another kind of ambivalent temporality, thanks to its cyclical qualities. Yet closer examination reveals an additional complicating feature. Readers may immediately notice that the text evokes the myth of Prometheus, who was chained to a rock so that an eagle could come each day to devour his liver, which would grow back the following night.[22] By evoking Prometheus through the figure of the alcoholic—who perhaps devours his own liver by drinking—this text references the cyclical quality of the myth, and at the same time insists on a gruesome form of finite, earthly punishment. Prometheus is punished for defying the gods, stealing fire, and thirsting for immortality in the face of mortal consciousness, while the alcoholic experiences the physical and social consequences of drinking, desiring, and continuing to drink.

Each of these two brief texts—slogans of 1930s anti-alcoholism, markedly invested in eugenic discourse—appears to serve as a companion to the other, allowing for complementary notions of temporality in their strongly stated messages. It is fair to note that such complementarity may be a coincidence, because the texts were printed in separate editions of the *Weekly Bulletin*; it is only in the archival folders that they come to appear side by side. Yet taken together, the phrases seem to pinpoint a temporal duality that is not easily resolved, between irrevocable present and ambivalent pasts and futures. This impasse is bound up with the uncertain marking of eugenic dehumanization over time, in which a "hard" notion of biological determinism seeks a foothold alongside or intermingled with a "soft" version, grounded in an emphasis on possible environmental factors.

In tracing out a parent-child causal relationship, these texts exemplify the elision of distance between present and future. The blurring of time in this case, as in Rivera's drawing and accompanying text, also works to foreground the issue of relative contingency, or the extent to which the subjects—and in some cases, communities—are ultimately defined by the apparent ills that threaten or afflict them. As I have suggested, denigrating representations tend to be tempered by the sense that effects can be traced to separate, prior causes, as when the ills of a child are bracketed by the actions of the father who caused them. Still, the fluid intimacy of these boundaries reveals the inextricability of "effects" from "causes," the unresolved yet tenacious capacity of these verbal and visual images to congeal their various pasts and futures.

José Vasconcelos's Temporal Aesthetics

The rhetorical strategy of blurred temporality and its intimate ties to the hovering presence of contingent differences are characteristic of post-revolutionary discourses of hygiene and eugenics, as evidenced in the didactic texts discussed here. As noted at the beginning of this chapter, the problems of temporal causality and contingency also emerge frequently in the broader context of debates on national identity and aesthetics in twentieth-century Mexico, though such debates are not typically framed with emphasis on the role of disability. I now turn to the work of José Vasconcelos, perhaps the best-known Mexican literary eugenicist of the 1920s and '30s. As secretary of public education, 1921–1924, Vasconcelos embarked on major initiatives to promote literacy and national culture, which would transform the post-revolutionary educational landscape. His projects included attention to questions of hygiene and physical education, geared toward practical goals of improved health, but also and far more prominently, to notions of spiritual and aesthetic enhancement of both the individual and the nation.

My reading of Vasconcelos's work here, including his classic *The Cosmic Race* and the more reactionary *Ética*, is intended as a complement to the analysis of the more popular and didactic public-health and education texts of the period. It is offered as a conscious bridging between the discourses of hygiene and aesthetics but also between the practical aims of public officials in a variety of posts, and the loftier philosophical projects that would come to shape Mexican letters throughout the twentieth century.[23] Considered in this broader context, the temporal arc of "soft" and "hard" eugenics also has repercussions for the politics of reading Mexican history. Gareth Williams's discussion of a 1939 text by Alfonso Reyes on the topic of the nineteenth-century liberal intellectual Justo Sierra illustrates this point. Williams's notion of the *homo barbarus* of the Mexican Revolution, or "the displaced, exploited, and expropriated" (109), represents abnormal elements, in contrast with Sierra's "normal history of Mexico" (105). As Williams notes, Reyes celebrates Sierra's vision of history as contained in his *Evolución política del pueblo mexicano*, first published during the Porfiriato (Williams 104). For Reyes, "The Revolution, in other words, was a historical aberration that interrupted normality" (Williams 105). Although Williams does not focus specifically here on questions of race or disability, the structure of historical temporality he describes in Reyes serves to bracket abnormality, much as the texts in my analysis articulate disability and racial difference as ambivalently bound to a history that would ultimately prefer to exclude them. Williams's emphasis on the *homo barbarus* as partially excluded from history, through rigorous analysis of how the combined historical perspectives of Sierra and Reyes articulate this exclusion, thus effectively works to counter "the normal history of Mexico."

In a similar vein, my approach to Vasconcelos in combination with the archival texts discussed here is intended to underscore the specificity of exploited or excluded corporeality, and most crucially, the temporal, contingent conditions through which exclusion or exploitation unfolds. Moreover, expanding the discussion toward philosophies of Mexican identity and national becoming shifts the issue of temporality, expressed in the didactic public-health texts, toward the vaster and more self-reflexive problem of history. Thanks in part to his practical role as education minister, Vasconcelos's work encompasses both the close interrogation of temporal progression and causality pertaining to human reproduction, and broader visions of national, Latin American, and universal historicity. Key moments in *The Cosmic Race* and *Ética* reveal significant focus on eugenics and hygiene, with explicit references to Mendel and Lamarck, in combination with an emphasis on a spiritual vision that continuously pushes toward the transcendence of such mundane concerns yet can never quite abandon them.[24]

Vasconcelos was aware of Mendel's discoveries in the field of genetics, referring to them at several points in *The Cosmic Race*. However, his approach to Mendel reveals his own interest in combining the improvement of genes with the improvement of the soul. He writes, "La ley de Mendel, particularmente cuando confirma 'la intervención de factores vitales en la rueda motriz físico-química', debe formar parte de nuestro nuevo patriotismo. Pues de su texto puede derivarse la conclusión de que las distintas facultades del espíritu toman parte en los procesos del destino" (77). [Mendel's law, particularly when it confirms "the intervention of vital factors in the physico-chemical wheel," must be part of our new patriotism, because from it we can draw the conclusion that the different faculties of the spirit take part in the processes of destiny (36–37).] Race, nation, spirit, and genetic code thus fuse together in this reading of messianic eugenics. The "eugénica misteriosa del gusto estético" (70) ["mysterious eugenics of aesthetic taste" (30)] that Vasconcelos proposes focuses on the broader parameters of race and genetic code, and not only on the existing population. Vasconcelos does not clearly mark the separation between the genes of the future and the bodies of the present, so in this sense a spiritual and aesthetic form of neo-Lamarckian thinking may be said to play a role in *The Cosmic Race*. The constant slippage between spirit and genotype, and between an aesthetics of artistic production and narrative, and one of race, also suggests an ambivalent temporality underpinning the project. In other terms, the text continues to ask the same familiar question: Has the cosmic race arrived yet? Or is it still to come? Similarly, Vasconcelos's proposed narrative and visual aesthetics repeat the same uncertainty, between artistic creation in the present and in the future. His project undoubtedly participates in the eugenic tendencies of nationalist discourse, and in this sense proposes a fluid, progressive future in which the arrival of the cosmic race is continually, ambivalently postponed, just as the eradication of spiritual and racial factors that might interfere with this race's final mission is also postponed.

More specifically, we may note that disability and racial difference occupy an uncertain space in the text of *The Cosmic Race*, and that in part because of this they become crucial to the passage between the material and the spiritual that is the hallmark of much of Vasconcelos's writing. In this sense, the simple exclusion or erasure of differences is inapplicable here. Vasconcelos underscores this point, when he describes the English approach to eugenics and social Darwinism. The English, he writes, "sólo ven el presente del mundo externo . . . la teoría inglesa supone, implícita o francamente, que el negro es una especie de eslabón que está más cerca del mono que el hombre rubio. No queda, por lo mismo, otro recurso que hacerlo desaparecer" (73) [see only the present in the external world. . . . The English theory supposes, implicitly or frankly, that the Black is a sort of link nearer the monkey than the blond man. There is no other recourse, for that reason, but to make him disappear (33).] Such language offers familiar continuity with Vasconcelos's overall pan–Latin American discourse, constructed in provocative tension with a particular vision of Anglo-American and Northern European cultural models.[25] In this case, the opposition compels the Latin American reader or listener to associate utilitarian thinking, described as English, with a specific mode of racism that would be unthinkable in a Latin American context.

Vasconcelos's approach still construes the black "race" in negative terms, however, and suggests that this race will eventually disappear over time, through the process of reproduction ruled by aesthetic taste. Vasconcelos does not propose the absolute exclusion of any racial or genetic element in the present, but instead imagines a process of racial-genetic amalgamation over time. He also famously notes in his predictions that "los muy feos no procrearán" (70) [the very ugly will not procreate (30)], and "en muy pocas generaciones desaparecerán las monstruosidades" (72) [in a very few generations, monstrosities will disappear (32)]. Yet the ambiguity of this process of fusion derives from the degree to which, at various points in the text, the author draws present and future together into a singular time. By the same process, Vasconcelos slides between the material and the spiritual; according to his "law of three states," society moves from the material, to the intellectual, and finally to the spiritual. The text borrows its spirituality from the teachings of theosophy and Christianity; hence the exalted "mystery" of the projected cosmic race parallels the Christian mystery of word made flesh. In this sense, the text upholds the unresolved enigma of a temporality that is simultaneously future and present, and a citizen body that is at once inclusive and diverse, and eugenically purified to reach its cosmic ideal.

Just a few years later, in the text of his *Ética*, published in 1932, Vasconcelos would refer more specifically to Lamarck, this time as part of an explanation of theories of evolution encompassing humans, animals, plants, and minerals. As Vasconcelos explains, Lamarck, unlike Darwin, emphasizes "transformismo." As he writes, "Según Lamarck, las diferentes clases de animales representan grados de organización de lo más incompleto a lo más completo; conforme a este criterio, se pueden organizar series: como el protoplasma como materia común, y en expansión creciente desde la amiba hasta el hombre" (993). [According to Lamarck, the different classes of animals represent levels of organization from the most incomplete to the most complete. According to this criterion, one can organize series: with protoplasm as common matter, in growing expansion from amoeba to man.] According to Vasconcelos's overall reading, relationships between species and individuals must be understood in terms of an overarching system, one that participates in evolutionary linearity, but at the same time, and more importantly, in a universal and divine energy. The theory borrows from the author's reading of other scientific sources as well; as he notes: "Fritz Muller aporta una tesis que parece comprobación de la teoría general transformista: el desarrollo del individuo (ontogenia) es una repetición abreviada, a menudo alterada por circunstancias exteriores, del desarrollo de la estirpe (filogenia)" (992). [Fritz

Muller contributes a thesis that appears to prove the general transformist theory: individual development (ontogeny) is an abbreviated repetition, often altered by external circumstances, of the development of the lineage (phylogeny).]. And he adds that Jung's notion of the subconscious as a kind of summary or microcosm of the history of the species is also derived from this reading of ontogeny. In his own summary of these phenomena, Vasconcelos states, "Lo que late en el subconsciente no es, en consecuencia, el clamor de una falsa línea ancestral, sino el anhelo de las varias potencias de un aparato de vida, semejante en los hombres y en gran número de animales" (1003). [What pulses in the subconscious is not, therefore, the cry of a false ancestral lineage, but rather the longing of the various forces of an organism, similar in men and in a large number of animals.][26]

More than in the text of *The Cosmic Race*, in this portion of *Ética* Vasconcelos insists on simultaneity as the guiding feature of life and of the workings of the universe. He even makes a brief reference within the text of *Ética* to the cosmic race, but collapses the presence of this race into a single instant, as "consumación de una existencia que se sale de la materia como el ovíparo escapa del cascarón" (1015) [consummation of an existence that exits matter like the hatchling that bursts forth from the shell]. This representation remains faithful to the spirit of the earlier text, but with the difference that here the complex racial and cultural history underpinning Vasconcelos's reading of *mestizaje* in the Americas and in the world is more tightly reduced to the singularity of one moment, via the image of a creature bursting forth from its shell. In other words, Vasconcelos here intensifies his emphasis on the moment of "*transmutación*," or the instantaneous transition from matter to spirit.

The temporal structure governing Vasconcelos's texts plays a crucial role in the works' intertwined depictions of disability and racial difference. In both *The Cosmic Race* and *Ética*, particular elements of animal and human life are marked as inferior—the category of *torpeza*, or awkwardness, and the monkey or the rabbit, for example, in *Ética*; the black man, and the ugly or monstrous in *The Cosmic Race*—but the process of marking necessarily rests on the paradox of a deferral that may stretch or shrink the time it requires to occur. Race and disability are contingent on this curious temporal structure, but the degree to which time appears to collapse or expand affects the possibility for a historical reading of the problem of contingency. Specifically, in the case of Vasconcelos's *Ética*, humanity and other life forms are most true to the structure of the cosmos when they abandon the purportedly false linearity of history, and participate in an instantaneous transmutation into divine energy, or in other words, a collapsing of time. On the other hand, when time is stretched over a longer historical trajectory, as is the case in portions of *The Cosmic Race*, human difference expands to fit the timeline, and becomes contingent on specific historical circumstances.

As Beatriz Urías Horcasitas has suggested, the historically specific contingency of difference plays a significant role in mid-twentieth-century Mexican writing on the question of race. For example, in the work of José Gómez Robleda and of other biotypologists of the 1940s to the 1960s, Urías Horcasitas observes, "physiological and mental inferiority" (55) are caused by conditions of poverty and not by intrinsic racial difference.[27] As noted in the introduction to this book and at the beginning of this chapter, insistence on historical contingency also emerges in a trajectory of cultural and philosophical texts on the issue of Mexican national identity, in which Vasconcelos's work undoubtedly participates. While *The Cosmic Race* offers an implied split between what the collective body is and what it might or should become through historical progress, in the text of *Ética*, progress is less contingent on history and more on biological evolutionary processes, which depend in the final instance on instantaneous spiritual transformation. This form of contingency, though nuanced in its negotiation of time and spiritual processes, is ultimately closer to a notion of eugenics than of hygiene as a mode of collective self-fashioning, and in this sense reflects Vasconcelos's increasing turn to conservative politics in his later writings. When read in juxtaposition with *The Cosmic Race* and with the archival texts I have discussed here, however, *Ética* underscores the dilemma of fluidity between "soft" and "hard" eugenics in Mexican scientific and aesthetic discourse, and the complex temporal arcs this eugenics describes.

Throughout the text of *Ética*, Vasconcelos emphasizes both continuity and parallelism between material life forms and the immaterial, or divine. For example, in his explanation of the birth of the soul, he writes of how an integral, eternal soul is produced through individual consciousness and spirit, and exclaims "¡Catálisis de una sustancia hecha ya firmemente espíritu! Es claro que esto deja fuera una infinidad de almas; pero aquí entra otra vez nuestro argumento zoológico-biológico sobre el desperdicio de los ensayos, necesario para que cuajen los tipos" (849). [Catalysis of a substance made spirit! It is clear that this leaves behind an infinite number of souls; but this is where our zoological-biological argument on wasted attempts, necessary so that types may be formed, emerges again.] Just as in nature, countless individuals, groups, and species appear and disappear in a seemingly wasteful process, so in the case of the soul: "muchos son los llamados y pocos los elegidos" (847) [many are called but few are chosen]. In this process of selective exclusion, according to Vasconcelos, souls are not condemned to eternal punishment, but instead simply disappear, as do various forms of biological life. As he writes:

> En la naturaleza, son las causas físicas, climatéricas, y las causas biológicas, enfermedades, muertes, las que determinan la desaparición, la supervivencia de distintos grupos de individuos. En el orden espiritual, y aun dentro, todavía, de la conciencia terrestre, las almas no están sujetas a la contingencia física; ni padecen enfermedades fisiológicas, ni están sujetas a muerte por disolución de los componentes químico-biológicos. Sin embargo, imaginemos el aparecer y el remontarse de las almas, un poco a la manera de las especies zoológicas. (846)

[In nature, physical, climatic and biological causes, illnesses, and deaths, determine the disappearance and the survival of different groups of individuals. In the spiritual order, and even within earthly consciousness, souls are not subject to physical contingencies, nor do they suffer physiological illnesses, nor are they subject to death from the dissolution of chemical-biological components. We nonetheless imagine the appearance and transcendence of souls as somewhat similar to that of zoological species.]

Elsewhere in the same text, we learn of the classification of types of intelligence and their uses, which are judged according to their ability to improve the self, and their convergence with divine energy. In this classification, which the author titles "Valores intelectuales, correspondientes a un orden positivo de existencia" [Intellectual values, corresponding to a positive order of existence], there are two complementary oppositions: "capacidad-torpeza" [ability-awkwardness] and "afirmación-negación" [affirmation-negation]. As in the case of souls that do not achieve eternal glory, and species that disappear from the planet, here too, negative categories tend to disappear: "los términos torpeza-negación corresponden al estado de divergencia en que las energías no aciertan a convivir, menos aún a realizarse en una categoría superior" (880); [the terms awkwardness-negation correspond to the state of divergence in which energies do not succeed in coexisting, much less in rising to a higher state]. Yet here, material life does not simply operate as a metaphor for the spiritual realm, for the continuity or disappearance of the soul as divine energy. Instead in this case, earthly value categories also act as stepping-stones toward a higher plane, so that some elements will actually be discarded before ever reaching the "categoría superior" (880).

However, when he discusses evolution, and in his well-known and repeated attacks on Darwinian theory, Vasconcelos is careful to distance himself from the notion of a hierarchy of life forms. He cites the scientist Edgar Dacque, from a 1931 text, who writes, "'¿No están adaptados todos los seres vivos igualmente y por entero a su mundo, a sus tareas y sus posibilidades vitales? Desde el punto de vista biológico, todos son de igual valor; ¿qué quiere decir entonces superior o inferior?'" (986) [Are not all living beings equally adapted to their world, to their activities and their vital possibilities? From the biological point of view, all are of equal value. Then what does superior or inferior mean?] In the final analysis, what is most important to Vasconcelos is not how evolution does or doesn't take place, but rather his conclusion regarding the spiritual realm: "Lo que mi teoría demuestra es EL RESULTADO OBTENIDO DE LA ACTIVIDAD DE LAS ESPECIES: A SABER: LA TRANSMUTACIÓN DE LA ENERGÍA DESDE LAS FORMAS FÍSICAS A LAS FORMAS INMATERIALES" (988). [What my theory demonstrates is THE RESULT OBTAINED BY THE ACTIVITY OF THE SPECIES, NAMELY: THE TRANSMUTATION OF ENERGY FROM PHYSICAL TO IMMATERIAL FORMS.] Although Vasconcelos does at times postulate the eradication of individuals or categories, at other moments he affirms essential equality between all beings. Ultimately, material features may be denigrated or cast away because they are not the finality or true being of humanity or of other species; instead they give way to the spiritual, or simply disappear before reaching that point.

By concentrating on the moment of the evolutionary leap from matter to spirit as the issue of primary concern, and the movement in which all life forms have a chance to participate, Vasconcelos brackets his own parallel reading of evolution in the more mundane sense. Here, then, the presence and validity of biological differences becomes contingent on adherence to a tightly collapsed temporality, in which the instant of "transmutation of energy" creates a seamless crossover between matter and spirit. As long as this instantaneity persists, differences determined by race, genetics, disability, or other categories may remain perfectly contained in the crystallization of form that encompasses all of life as the force of divine energy. The moment in which the cosmic race is characterized through the metaphor of the "hatchling bursting forth from its shell" and hence as a time of transition from matter to energy, epitomizes the process through which racial difference becomes contingent on the collapsing of time. The survival of difference, and the erasure of value hierarchies of biological life, depends on this idealized instantaneity. Vasconcelos's crystallization of material life goes beyond the ostensibly inclusionary and historically grounded political utopia of the cosmic race and instead operates as a provocative act of temporal suspension, an aestheticization of material difference through spiritual sublimation.

Curiously, Vasconcelos refers elsewhere in the same text of *Ética* to his notion of the cosmic race, but this time in more clearly negative terms, and with a different temporal outlook. He writes:

> Nuestro mestizaje, hasta hoy, no ha hecho sino corromper valores y simular actitudes. Enfermo de apetitos vagos, sin energía para la ambición en grande y atacado de una suerte de epilepsia sentimental, que le ciega ante su propia ignorancia y finge victoria con las más grandes ignominias, no se concibe que, por de pronto, pudiera surgir de allí alguna esperanza para el porvenir de los hombres. En verdad no se ve que las razas de color demuestren aptitud, ya no digo para reemplazar al europeo, ni siquiera para mantenerse a salvo de una regresión a la barbarie ancestral. (914–15)

> [Our racial mixing, thus far, has done nothing but corrupt values and simulate attitudes. Sick with lazy appetites, without energy for higher ambitions and attacked by a sort of sentimental epilepsy that blinds it to its own ignorance and feigns victory in the greatest of disgraces, it is inconceivable that any hope for the future of men could emerge from there. Truly it does not appear that the colored races show aptitude for saving themselves from a regression to ancestral barbarism, much less for replacing the European.]

Here, racial difference characterized negatively as "razas de color" is displayed on a timeline of mankind's progress, with the prognosis of regression to an inferior past that at once defines the racialized present as inferior to imaginary and presumably whiter alternatives. Gone is the instantaneity of divine energy that would be the salvation of all species and individuals, at least in potential. Instead, time is plotted and stretched, marked by the races and civilizations that rise and fall to the rhythm of its singular axis. Hence the flip side of a collapsed temporality that preserves difference in a singular flash is, in this case, an extended sweep of time, saturated from start to finish by a self-defeating race of endless potential regression, and a mode of explicitly "hard" eugenics in which negative characterization predetermines the future of racialized populations.

I read *The Cosmic Race* with *Ética* as a means to underscore how the contingencies of temporality and history impact the potential roles of difference and disability in Vasconcelos's aesthetic vision. I use the term *aesthetic* here because Vasconcelos structures his work as moving toward its culmination in the volume *Estética*, which follows after *Ética*, and because his reading of *transmutismo* as an instantaneous leap from the material to the spiritual, already present in earlier works such as *The Cosmic Race*, is understood as an ascension to the highest of three states, the aesthetic state. The continuous aesthetic drive in Vasconcelos's work, which may be observed over the course of much of his career, from his 1916 experimental play *Prometeo vencedor* to his 1935 *Estética*, is nonetheless grounded by its tension with practical matters of biological theory, racial difference, and seemingly inevitable or avoidable events in history. The relationship between spiritual and material planes offers more than a simple contrasting mechanism, for as we have seen, evolutionary biology provides Vasconcelos with a scaffolding on which to build his process of spiritual ascension. Moreover, spiritual transformation and the sublimation of matter allow the author to justify the disappearance of some biological types and the ascension of others, even while the instantaneous quality of transformation potentially preserves and equalizes all life forms.

The work of *Ética* thus resonates strangely with the projects of more pragmatic public-health texts, such as the previously cited anti-alcoholism slogan with its entrail-devouring vulture, in which alcohol consumption traces a paradoxical path to both eternal suffering and final destruction. By reading the threatening public-health text alongside a key portion of *Ética*, we may appreciate the complexity of Mexican eugenic discourse in its diverse popularized and erudite forms, and its symbiotic fusion of scientific and aesthetic projects. Most importantly, this juxtaposition reveals a fluid combination of "hard" and "soft" eugenics as consistent with a fascist, utopic project of spiritual transformation as a path to the highest state of human perfection.

Promethean Futures

In the concluding section of *Ética*, a transition to the opening of *Estética*, Vasconcelos presents the figure of Prometheus as the personification of the final "ethical revolution," the moment of sacrifice where ethical action transcends its own finality and reaches a higher, aesthetic plane.[28] Prometheus gave fire to humans and helped save them from extreme servitude to the gods; this is why Zeus punished him, hence the classic image of Prometheus chained to a rock, victim of the liver-eating eagle and its daily visitations. In Vasconcelos's reading, Prometheus transcends his punishment by recognizing the injustice of the law he has ostensibly broken: "En su pecho arde llama nueva. Interiormente se sabe apartado de la necesidad inflexible; a salvo de venganzas semidivinas. La norma ha dejado de serlo, puesto que él la violó provechosamente, no caprichosamente" (1108–9). [A new flame burns in his chest. Internally, he recognizes that he is not subject to inflexible need; spared from semi-divine revenge. The standard is no longer, because he violated it beneficially, not capriciously.] Prometheus comes to represent the cycle of Vasconcelos's work, emblematic of the transition from human, directed action, to mystical vision. Yet because the tripartite structure of Vasconcelos's overarching plan (material, intellectual, spiritual) depends on perfect continuity between the three stages, the moment of transcendence to the aesthetic (or spiritual) plane always reverts back to the earlier stages. The aesthetic moment of Prometheus is part of a fluid movement that gives meaning to ethical action (*lo ético*), according to the author, and as he explains further, "De igual suerte, la ética revierte hacia la fisiología y hacia el átomo, determinando las cuantas moleculares que son indispensables a la construcción del metal, el cristal" (1109). [In the same way, ethics reverts toward physiology and toward the atom, determining the molecular quanta which are indispensable in the construction of metal and crystal.][29] The transition from *Ética* to *Estética* here occurs as both a transcendent leap, or line of flight from the earthly to the spiritual, and the repetition of a cyclical movement, doubling back to an earlier stage. In fact, the author notes in the final paragraph of *Ética*, "no se trata de cerrar un ciclo, sino nada más del eslabón de una cadena que se continúa en la 'Estética'" (1109) [the idea is not to end a cycle, but only one link in a chain that continues in *Aesthetics*]. This statement suggests both the linearity of an argument that will proceed from here to the next stage, and the circularity of a chain, defined by each of its intersecting links.

Unlike Vasconcelos's writing, the aphoristic texts of the *Weekly Bulletin* of the Department of Public Health, as cited at the beginning of this chapter, tend to be short and eye-catching, designed to convey a strong message quickly and graphically, and to serve as powerful examples of hygienic propaganda that might be further promoted by healthcare workers to their patients and communities. Yet the broader goal or "ethics" of the campaign of which these texts formed a part was the improvement of nation and race, through the eradication of illness and moral vice. In this sense, they operate as a mode of action akin to the second or ethical stage of Vasconcelos's overall system, and their message dovetails with much of the practical, programmatic argument of *The Cosmic Race*.

As cited earlier, one of the texts reads: "El alcohol es un buitre que arrancará lentamente las entrañas del bebedor. El bebedor está siempre atado en la roca del infortunio." [Alcohol is a vulture that slowly rips out the entrails of the drinker. The drinker is always tied to the rock of misfortune.] The figure of the alcoholic suggests both the cyclical quality of the Prometheus myth, since he is permanently bound to the rock, and the linear narrative of gradual, painful death and destruction, since eventually he will lose his entrails and die. In a complementary sense, Prometheus, in Vasconcelos's reading, occupies the site of endless, cyclical, corporeal pain and punishment, thanks to the regrowth of his liver and the daily return of the eagle, and at the same time, a linear escape from this circularity, as his just opposition to the cruelty of the gods elevates him to the aesthetic, spiritual plane where man transcends materiality. Both texts thus present the paradox of a combined cyclical and linear temporal model, yet in Vasconcelos, linear chronology occurs as spiritual transcendence, while in the *Bulletin* it works in the opposing sense, signaling toward decline and death. Once self-destruction is complete, the alcoholic is severed from his metaphorical rock, and rejoins the materiality of his own body in death.

As we have seen, in the context of Mexico's public-health and hygiene campaigns of the 1920s and '30s, alcoholism signifies disorder, depravity, and corruption, potentially impacting future generations by contaminating and disabling hypothetical offspring. As an ambivalent marker of cause and effect in human reproduction, it also intersects with representations of racial difference in reproduction, and with cultural anxiety about such representations. The figure of Prometheus celebrated by Vasconcelos, in juxtaposition with the "Promethean" alcoholic from the *Weekly Bulletin*, published just one year earlier, offers an approach to this dilemma of temporal contingency, by mutually overlaying aesthetic transcendence with the chronology of bodily mortality. We may read the representation of the alcoholic, chained to his rock, as a caricature of the Prometheus myth, a crude rendering of a warning to the masses, unlike Vasconcelos's more refined vision of the spiritual sublimation of the evolutionary cycle. In Vasconcelos's reading, physical differences are collapsed into the instant of spiritual sublimation and re-released into circulation in an all-encompassing cycle of three states: material, ethical, and aesthetic. Material differences remain parenthetical and hypothetical, tightly contained by the instantaneity of transformation from body to spirit. Vasconcelos's reading of this transcendental leap exemplifies the fascist tendencies apparent in his work of this period, since it is here that the ethical and political become aesthetic at the moment of transformation to the spiritual realm.[30] The appearance of the text of the *Weekly Bulletin* in this equation, on the other hand, ultimately insists that corporeal difference will persist in the here and now. Disability will not disappear, and the body of the alcoholic continues to depict its own suffering; it signals imminent death even as it serves as a repeating warning to others.

Combining Vasconcelos's transcendent vision of overarching aesthetics with the public-health bulletin's more direct and practical approach to the temporal and reproductive trajectory of corporeal difference suggests certain points of contact between the two. As noted, both texts contain the paradox of cyclical and linear temporal structures, through which mythic perpetuity reverts to a linear pathway, and spirit is grounded in a material substrate. Moreover, beyond their common use of popularized mythology in distinct cultural registers, these texts together reveal the difficulty of separating "hard" from "soft" eugenics, or determinism from temporal contingencies. Even within the context of public-hygiene campaigns that insist on the horizon of future reproductive health as contingent on individual and collective behavior, negative consequences are dramatic and deadly, operating through a rhetoric of mythic eternity and divine condemnation from which few if any could hope to escape. In the case of *Ética*, the creative leap of spiritual transcendence defines superior future life by distilling it from abandoned biological categories, yet seems to potentially retain all life forms through the instantaneous process of transformation from the material to the spiritual. This somewhat unlikely juxtaposition of readings ultimately reveals disability and its temporal contingencies—"useless" differences that hover on a timeline, or saturate the here and now—as central to the philosophical negotiation of post-revolutionary national identity.

My encounter with these literary and archival documents, as I noted at the beginning of this chapter, is conceived as a present-day, embodied practice, attuned to the question of how the disability of here and now, and the disability to come, might resonate in relation to the complex temporality of hygiene and eugenics in post-revolutionary Mexico. In Robert McRuer's terms, crip futurity entails in part a desire for the disability of the future, or a world in which disability would not be deployed as "the raw material against which the imagined future world is formed" (*Crip Theory* 72). In a similar sense, Alison Kafer writes of her longing for a future that would embrace disabled people, stemming in part from the recognition that currently "disability too often serves as the agreed-upon limit of our collective future" (27). In his analysis of corporeal cartography and precarity, the Mexican anthropologist and disability studies scholar Jhonatthan Maldonado Ramírez proposes a "crip fantasy" (*fantasia tullida*): "Hay que reinventar nuevos horizontes que posicionen de otra manera el cuerpo considerado "humano" y para eso la fantasía también es fundamental" (60). [We must reinvent new horizons that position in other ways the body considered "human," and for that, fantasy is also crucial.]

In the texts of the Mexican post-revolution discussed here, disability already occupies an extended temporal horizon, with material and discursive effects inseparable from hypothetical pasts, imaginary futures, and the dilemmas of collective identity in history.[31] Our task is therefore not only to seek a hopeful disability to come, or as Puar writes, "multiple futures where bodily capacities and debilities are embraced rather than weaponized" (xxiv). It is also to recognize the persistent temporal contours of human differences and the potential violence contained in both deterministic biological categorization and the hovering contingencies of cause and effect; then, now, and later. Despite these risks, welcoming a disability to come need not—and indeed cannot—entail abandoning notions of chronology or insisting that disability should be somehow independent of stories and processes of becoming. Instead, disability future might include an insistence on the experiences of temporality and human differences as only partially co-constitutive. Hopefully, such a future would remain crucially generative of unpredictable asymmetries and uncertainties in the production of chronology and embodiment. Turning our focus to what is not clearly known, defined, or predictable allows us to wonder, as Tanya Titchkosky suggests, how disability has come to occupy a perceived horizon of certainty, and how we might perceive otherwise (132–33). This refocusing may allow for an alternative horizon as well, for the "crip fantasy" to which Maldonado Ramírez refers. Our future disability might then, sometimes, refuse or reimagine the pasts and futures so often expected of it.

Three

Psychopedagogy and the Cityscape

Bodies and Buildings

Schools in Mexico City of the 1920s and '30s received regular visits from a *médico escolar*, or school physician, tasked not only with examining students and documenting their health conditions, but with assessing the hygienic conditions of school buildings, their location, construction, materials, and maintenance. The notion of hygiene as a quality pertaining to buildings is not unique to Mexico, nor was it new in this period. Yet it is nonetheless worth pausing to consider the particular role of school physicians, who were employed by the Department of Psychopedagogy and Hygiene (DPH) within the Ministry of Public Education. The *médico escolar* was trained and recognized as a medical doctor, yet was expected to conduct extensive and detailed measurements of school buildings, and to make professional recommendations on the construction of new schools as well as the rehabilitation or restoration of houses for pedagogical purposes. The repeating appearance of the figure of the school physician in archival documents might cause us to wonder how the same person would go about diagnosing children's illnesses and IQ scores, measuring windows, and registering the proper or improper installation of plumbing fixtures. We might wonder as well how such a figure would have appeared to teachers, schoolchildren, and construction and maintenance personnel, and how these actors would have perceived their own bodies and material surroundings.

Equipped with both medical authority and the practical trappings of on-site engineers, school physicians documented the ailments of sick children and sick buildings, determining who should be kept at home until contagion passed, and who should be sent to a central clinic, which schools should be shuttered, and which ones required urgent repairs, particularly pertaining to water access and sanitation facilities. They were also at the forefront of the compilation of anthropometric and psychometric data, measuring children's bodies and assessing their respiratory function, hearing, vision, physical strength, and intelligence, with the goals of identifying common and abnormal characteristics and establishing homogeneous student groups. In lingering over the figure of the *médico escolar*, and the question of hygiene as a conduit between the human body and its material surroundings, I wish to consider how disability circulates within the state-sponsored pedagogical landscape of post-revolutionary Mexico City. I also want to pay particular attention to the surprising incarnation of the medical doctor as building inspector, because of the way this role brings urban infrastructure to life, while at the same time instrumentalizing the bodies of young students as both quantifiable resource and burden to an overtaxed system. The incongruous figure of the school physician, who we might imagine today with hard hat, stethoscope, and measuring tape, may serve to remind the reader of the porous limits of the human body in this pedagogical setting, and of how notions of construction and rehabilitation, disability and dilapidation, move almost imperceptibly between flesh and concrete.[1]

From the previous chapter's emphasis on the temporally determined causality of disability, as when alcoholism serves as a predictor for "idiocy" and other ills in future generations, I shift here toward the more immediate and material, spatially rendered determinants of urban infrastructure, as schoolchildren interact with their built environments. School buildings, however, do not simply serve as blueprints, whether literally or metaphorically, for the relative health and normalcy of the children who frequent them. Instead, the dilemma of hygiene occupies a broad and multicontoured space, flowing between the bodies of living beings, their behavior or habits, and the buildings in which they spend much of their days. If disability, as discussed in chapter 2, is bracketed by the contingencies that may potentially cause it, or by the time over which human differences unfold, in the present chapter the contingency of disability emerges through spatial as well as temporal coordinates. Within the discourse of the Department of Psychopedagogy and Hygiene, built structures shape the bodies and behaviors of schoolchildren, yet it is also true that the children and the qualities and categories ascribed to them in turn shape building inspection reports, architectural debates, and the buildings themselves. Moreover, tangible elements such as textbooks, school supplies, and furniture, along with more nebulous factors including lighting, ventilation, and neighborhood noise levels, also enter the hygienic landscape. In this context, disability as intimately linked to the fraught pursuit of hygiene, defines and constructs the evolving conditions and spaces of pedagogy.

The first part of this chapter focuses on the work of the DPH, later the National Institute of Psychopedagogy, and in particular on the assessment of the hygienic conditions of a diverse ecosystem encompassing school buildings and infrastructure, students, their families, and pedagogical methods. The dynamic hygiene network linking students to their material surroundings also extends in this reading to include the complex rhetoric of hygiene through which institutional and individual actors negotiate impasses between problems and proposed solutions pertaining to pedagogy, health, and the built environment. I offer a brief overview of the history of the testing and classification of schoolchildren in Mexico, and of school-building inspections, with emphasis on the role of the DPH, founded in 1925. I pay attention in this context to the work of school physicians and their documentation of hygiene problems encountered in buildings and among the students. My analysis then proceeds to the founding of the National Institute of Psychopedagogy in 1937, and to the evolution of psychopedagogy as a state-sponsored research paradigm.

In the second part of the chapter, I turn to the figure of the architect and artist Juan O'Gorman, who, working with the Ministry of Public Education, designed a number of Mexico City primary schools in the early 1930s, according to the functionalist precept of maximum efficiency for minimum cost. In many ways O'Gorman's own rhetoric of hygiene dovetails with that of the *médicos escolares* and other actors, as he advocates for precise accountability and high standards in efficient building design and construction, presenting these efforts as integral to the health and well-being of children. At the same time, O'Gorman's increasing anger and frustration at disjunctures between his technical principles and the evolving roles of the market and of state ideology in the built environment suggest the uneasy and troubled qualities of hygiene and of the institutions eager to define and implement it.

My juxtaposition of archival texts of school physicians and psychopedagogues with the work of internationally renowned architect and muralist O'Gorman echoes a similar gesture in chapter 2, in which the practical measures of anti-alcohol campaigns find a link to José Vasconcelos's philosophical discourse on national identity. In both cases, connections between the practical implementation of hygienic measures and the construction of nationalist rhetoric suggest that the dilemmas of corporeal difference and technical infrastructure ultimately play a role in broader, speculative questions on Mexican identity, history, and future. In the case of Juan O'Gorman's work, the relationship between materially specific, technical problems and overarching philosophy becomes central to the impasse and impending failure of Mexico's hygiene project. The troubled and paradoxical representation of hygiene evident in Juan O'Gorman's writing also begins to emerge in the rhetoric and the organizational charting of the National Institute of Psychopedagogy. These texts underscore the problem of the pursuit of hygiene and its continuous, unresolved circulation in material and social spaces. In so doing, they reveal a progression of conflicts extending from practical dilemmas regarding the classification of "abnormal" students, to more abstract questions on the nature of national identity in relation to history, economic development, and the built environment. Emphasis on the continuity between pedagogy and architecture, and on the glaring problem of hygiene as an unresolved conduit between humans and their environments, allows us to recognize the active role of disability in shaping both Mexican urban landscapes and debates on national identity and future.

The turn to the built environment in this chapter might appear to point toward a familiar juncture in the history of disability studies scholarship. The rise of the social model since the early 1980s led to ongoing efforts by activists and scholars to educate a mainstream public on the notion that disability cannot simply be located and defined within an individual human body, but rather occurs as the result of socially and materially constructed environmental barriers.[2] Despite an obvious emphasis on the *social* nature of the environment in the term "social model," didactic materials to illustrate its function have often privileged images of physical barriers in the environment. Hence the classic illustration of the wheelchair user before a staircase and no elevator or ramp at hand, as a way to show that the solution to the "problem" of disability lies not in the human body but rather in changes to building codes. As revisions of the earlier social model and new materialist approaches to disability studies show, however, the notion of physical and social environments as discrete factors to be localized in relation to one another and to human subjects bears revisiting; disability circulates in forms that are simultaneously embodied, social, and material, as well as human, animal, and inorganic; indeed, the radical inextricability of these qualities comes to define what, or who, we are.[3] In this sense, the history of hygiene as discourse and practice in early post-revolutionary Mexico also has much to tell us about disability and about the fluidity of human and nonhuman embodiment in its material and social facets. Similarly, revisiting the complex history of hygiene in Mexican school buildings and related infrastructure from the perspective of twenty-first-century disability studies may remind us that the notion of disability need not always begin and end with human subjects. Instead, disability comes to occupy and inflect a broader field, as key to human experience, but also permeating material and metaphorical landscapes.[4]

School hygiene practice and discourse in post-revolutionary Mexico make evident the complex interplay of bodies, building features, and social environment, and at times the difficulty of defining these elements as separate from one another. In their continued emphasis on the urgency of constructing or repairing hygienic school facilities, the *médicos escolares* participate in the circulation of disability as irrevocably material, social, and in need of radical intervention. Reading the complex role of the *médico escolar* in continuous movement between attention to bodies and buildings serves to underscore that this iteration of a medical model of disability is complicated by its interpenetration with social and environmental as well as technical architectural concerns.

Inspecting Abnormality

The DPH, part of the Ministry of Public Education was founded in 1925, under the directorship of Dr. Rafael Santamarina. The DPH included five sections: psychopedagogy, with the subsections of anthropometrics, psychognosis, and pedagogy; school hygiene; social prevention, with the subsection of professional orientation; special schools; and statistics (Bravo Gómez, "Higiene escolar"). Dr. Santamarina, already well known for his prior work and active role in the 1921 Child Congress, was to play a key role in advocating for and administering the testing of schoolchildren, to establish the average characteristics of the Mexican child and to differentiate between various forms and degrees of so-called mental abnormality.[5] As Santamarina himself recounted in 1928, the Binet-Simon IQ test was first adapted to the Mexican context in 1922, and in 1924 US Army IQ tests were applied to 300 Mexican soldiers. He noted that in the year of its establishment, the department began to administer collective, group tests. In the same year 8,000 schoolchildren received the Fay test, and 1,500 the Descoeudres test, while additional tests would be incorporated later (3 de febrero 1928). The 1920s did not mark the beginning of measuring of Mexican schoolchildren and school buildings, however; institutional concerns about school hygiene, student intelligence, and the identification of normal and abnormal characteristics in children can be traced to the Porfiriato, as the late-nineteenth- to early-twentieth-century dictatorship of Porfirio Díaz is generally known. The 1882 Medical Pedagogical Congress held in Mexico City was particularly significant for establishing specific norms governing the construction of school buildings, standards for school furniture and materials, pedagogical methods, and the avoidance of the spread of contagious illnesses (Carrillo). Many of these standards would be reiterated in the writings of the school physicians of the 1920s and '30s, and it is likely that the ongoing emphasis on precise measurements and documentation stems in large part from the 1882 Conference Proceedings. A contextual difference, however, between the hygiene policies of the late nineteenth century and those of the post-revolutionary period, was the shift from local and state to federal authority regarding the mandated implementation of hygiene campaigns. In this sense, the classic 1917 speech by the physician and military general, José María Rodríguez, in which he advocated for the necessity of a "sanitary dictatorship" with a national public-health department under the executive power of the state, marks a key transition (Aréchiga Córdoba 60–61). School hygiene of the post-revolutionary period would thus re-emerge with increased vigor through the centralized backing of the state, setting the stage for the growth of psychopedagogy and its detailed attention to abnormality in schoolchildren and educational infrastructure.

School medical inspections first took place in Mexico in 1896, the same year in which Dr. Luis C. Ruiz established the School Hygiene Service ("Higiene Escolar"), and by 1906, medical inspectors working within the General Directorate of Primary Instruction of the Federal District initiated the systematic study of the health and anthropometrics of schoolchildren (Castillo Troncoso 89). The year 1908 would see an increase in the number of school physicians, and newly implemented rules on school hygiene; a Department of Anthropometrics was created in 1909 (Jiménez). Although the earlier tests and measurements of schoolchildren and buildings included attention to determining normal and abnormal characteristics, the work of the DPH beginning in 1925 stands out for its expansion and systematization of testing, incorporation of a battery of imported IQ tests, and emphasis on statistics and data compilation (Stern, "Responsible," 384–85). The DPH records also reveal a particular interest in defining, identifying, and explaining various forms of mental abnormality and delays, or *retraso*, in schoolchildren, leading to the segregation and institutionalization of "the feebleminded" and others deemed unfit for regular schooling.[6] As Dr. Santamarina himself would later note, it was only in 1925 that research began to establish the parameters of normal development in schoolchildren, to adapt mental tests, and to identify "mental deficients" ("Bases" 227). Along with the anthropometric and psychometric testing of children, the DPH continued its work in regular school inspections, with reports that frequently highlighted a causal relationship between improper environment and maladapted students, as well as between physical and mental abnormalities.

School physicians were required to fill out a three-page standardized form documenting the details of each visit to a school. This form, created by the DPH of the Ministry of Public Education, included details on the location of the school, date of the visit, name of physician, and accompanying nurse in some cases, and extensive sections to document the condition of the building, number and measurements of classrooms, windows, and bathroom facilities, among other features. On January 23, 1935, the school physician Dr. Miguel Cabrera visited primary school 13-9, located in Mexico City's Colonia Obrera, which the doctor described as a "mala urbanización" [bad neighborhood]. He noted that the building was a house, privately owned by a Dr. R. Sánchez, but used as a school. It was comprised of nine classrooms, measuring a total of 251.71 square meters. The form included a space for the number of students enrolled, in this case, 460, and another space for the number who should be enrolled, here 250. This feature on the form appears to anticipate the fact that many public primary schools in Mexico City were vastly overenrolled, and indeed most available forms indicate massive discrepancies between "number of students" and the "number there should be." Dr. Cabrera described the facade of the building as "triste, destartalada" [sad, dilapidated] and the overall condition of the building as poor.

The second page of the form included a chart for data on each of the classrooms, including shape, size, number of windows and doors, and their corresponding measurements, ventilation, angle of lighting, and overall cleanliness. In this case, we may note that of the nine classrooms, only two included windows, and that the physician found lighting to be irregular and ventilation poor. In the section on sanitary facilities, he noted the presence of four toilets for the students, one for the teacher, and one communal urinal, in each case poorly installed. On furniture, the size and number of student desks were included, with a total of 350 individual desks for the 460 students. In the concluding "results" section on the third page of the form, Dr. Cabrera wrote that although improvements could be made by adding toilets, sinks, drinking fountains, and bathing facilities, nothing could be done to change the fundamental issue of the building itself, which "cannot be accepted as a school." Although the form included an additional portion for listing repairs to be undertaken, and a space for the head of the school hygiene section to sign indicating that the school could remain open, these were left blank ("Informe sobre las condiciones higiénicas").

In studying Dr. Cabrera's form and others similar to it from the mid 1920s

INFORME sobre las condiciones higiénicas de la Escuela. 13 - 9

de propiedad del Sr. R. Sánchez dedicada a escuela primaria

visitada el día 23 enero por el Médico Escolar Miguel Cabrera

acompañado por

I.- DATOS GENERALES.

Situación al sur de la ciudad, en la Colonia Obrera (nada urbanización)

Ubicación Calles Juan de Dios Peza #157 y Fernando Ramírez 154.

Orientación O.N. a S.

Elevación 2 piso

Fachada triste distributiva

Distribución en una sola ala

Núm.de salones 9 Superficie total de ellos 251.71 m²

Núm.de alumnos inscritos 400 Núm. de ellos que debe haber 250

Núm.de grupos escolares 9 Núm.que debe haber 5

Condiciones sanitarias generales malas.

RESUMEN: por los datos anteriores este edificio no está adaptado.

II.- DEPARTAMENTO MEDICO.

Datos generales y detalles no tiene

III.- DEPENDENCIAS.

Entrada y vestíbulos La entrada deberá ser por la calle de Fernando
Ramírez # 154; pero actualmente se encuentra cerrada. Se hace por Juan
de Dios Peza 157 carece de vestíbulo.
Corredores no tiene.

Patios de juego 2. El 1° de 7.5 × 5, 37.5 m² y el 2° de 10×4, 40 m²
Con pavimento de cemento

Gimnasio no tiene

Fig. 10. Detail from an inspection report on the hygienic conditions of a primary school. The report was completed by Dr. Miguel Cabrera on January 23, 1935, and documents the poor sanitary conditions of the school, as well as its "sad, dilapidated" appearance. Caja 35540, 17-13-5-94. "Informe sobre las condiciones higienicas de la escuela 13–9 III-421.1 (II-21-13-9)-1. Escuela Primaria #13–9 Pino Suárez #44 cd. Archivo General de la Nación.

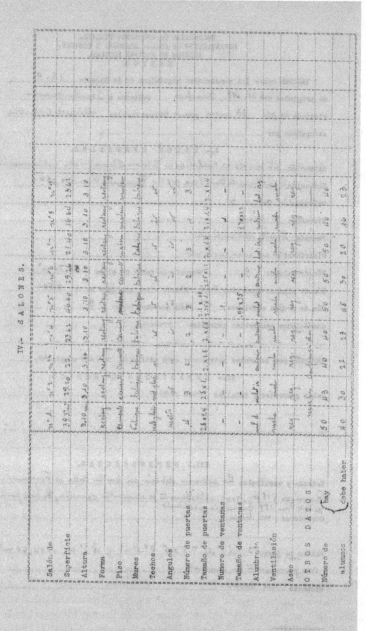

Fig. 11. Detail from the second page of Dr. Cabrera's report. The chart includes measurements of various rooms, quality of ventilation and lighting, actual number of children in each room, and number there should be. Caja 35540, 17-13-5-94. "Informe sobre las condiciones higienicas de la escuela 13-9. III-421.1 (II-21-13-9)-1. Escuela Primaria #13-9 Pino Suárez #44 cd. Archivo General de la Nación.

to the mid 1930s, it is easy to be struck by the deplorable conditions in which large numbers of Mexico City schoolchildren spent their days. Despite the construction of a number of new schools and the installation of improved sanitation facilities, it would seem that in many cases, little had changed since 1908, when government medical inspectors initiated the systematic assessment of school hygiene conditions (Chaoul Pereyra 121–22). From the exterior impression of a sad and dilapidated building, to the poorly ventilated and overcrowded classrooms within, Dr. Cabrera was unimpressed, to the degree that he concluded that nothing could be done to remedy the unacceptable state of the school. Yet in addition to the troubling or even insurmountable task faced by the *médico escolar*, this form reveals a particular institutionalized emphasis on accurate, quantified, graphically rendered and systematized data collection. Use of the data table with its carefully plotted grid lines to record and visualize classroom measurements suggests the expectation of uniformity in information processing, corresponding to similarly standardized regulations regarding the hygienic qualities of school infrastructure, pedagogical methods, and student anthropometrics. Boxes on the table are to be filled with numbers corresponding to measurements, or in some cases with words, brief, recognizable, and often abbreviated to fit the spaces: irreg., ant. (for anterior), *madera, tabique, concreto* [wood, brick, concrete].

A similar form was used to record the health conditions of students, and documentation of the inspection of buildings and of children often appears together in the archived folders. This second form was apparently designed to offer an overall view of health issues, and contagious conditions in particular, that were present at a given school, for rather than including student names, the data chart allows space for listing health conditions, and boxes for numbers of students found with each condition. Anemia appears as a common diagnosis, as do cavities. In the forms I observed, physicians generally wrote out the names of health conditions by hand on their data charts. Yet perhaps with the aim of greater systematization and efficiency, a 1934 chart by Dr. Ignacio Millán, head of the DPH, provides numerical codes for a list of 156 illnesses and conditions. These include myopia, cavities, epilepsy, warts, ringworm, and both acquired and congenital deformities, to name just a few.

In addition to the basic health inspection form for the student population of each school, other standard charts included a Physical and Physiological Exam for each individual student. This was a more detailed document, divided into various quadrants with spaces to record the results of six different exams, pertaining to each of the six years of required primary school. Information to be recorded included pathological antecedents and vaccination history,

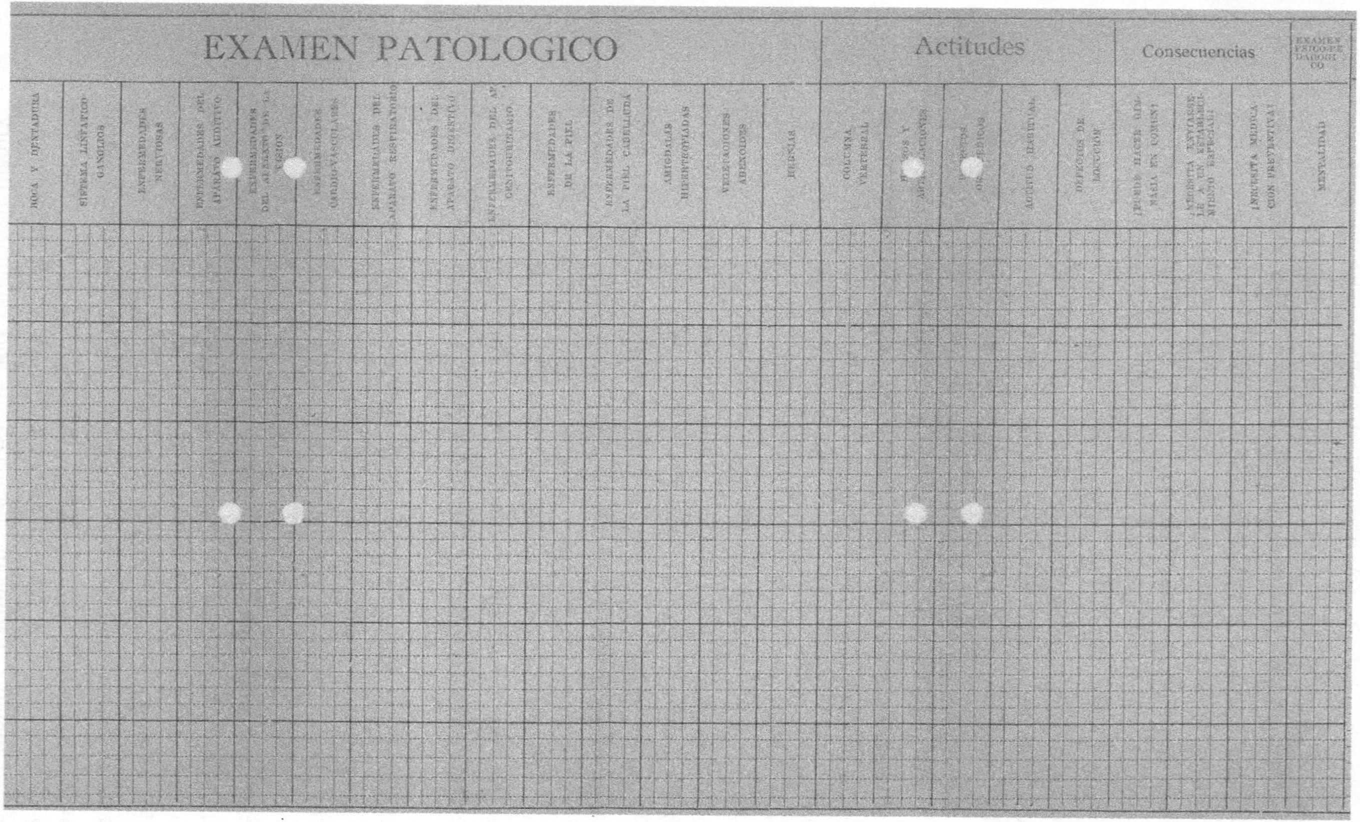

Fig. 12. Detail from a physical and physiological exam for primary school students. The list of "attitudes" includes "hernias," "vertebral column," "bones and joints," "orthopedic defects," "habitual attitude," and "speech defects." Questions to be answered under "consequences" include "Can the student participate in group sports?" "Does he/she need to be sent to a special institution?" "Does he/she need preventive medication?" and "mentality." Caja 35479, ref. 134, exp. 21, 1923. "[R]egistro escolar del alumno" Jesús A. Rojas. Folio 15. Archivo General de la Nación.

muscle strength, vision and auditory capacity, height, weight, and biacromial diameter. Another section covered the categories of "attitudes" and "consequences." Among the attitudes we find reference to the vertebral column, to "orthopedic defects," and to "speech impediments," while the consequences are mainly articulated as a series of questions: Can the student participate in group physical education? Does he/she need to be sent to a special school? Does he/she require preventive medication? (Rojas).

The compilation of these forms, folded and produced with their characteristic grids of solid and dotted lines for systematized data entry, suggest an insistence on the accumulation of knowledge regarding the young students and their physical environments, as well as a spatialized approach to the representation of that knowledge. The Physical and Physiological exam, compiled with data charts for height, weight, various health conditions, and other observations, unfolds and extends like a delicate blueprint, its layout evoking the sketch of a building. The building inspection report, for its part, takes the visitor from facade to interior, laying out the classroom dimensions in ordered quadrants, revealing bathrooms and windows in need of repair, and counting ideal and actual numbers of students, room by room. The reports together evoke the space and dynamics of interaction between schoolchildren and school buildings, plotted in relation to hygienic institutional expectations.

The same Dr. Miguel Cabrera, writing in a separate 1935 report, offered a more general account of the work of the DPH. As he noted, "Las actividades llevadas al cabo por el Departamento han tenido siempre como finalidad, el mejoramiento del niño en todos sus aspectos." [Activities carried out by the Department have always had as their goal the improvement of the child in all aspects.] Yet he also expressed his concern over the amount of work expected of the school physician, having 6,000 or more students to assess. Each had to receive visual, auditory, and medical exams, to be weighed, measured, and classified according to physical state; documents had to be created to incorporate the data and create health cards (*tarjetas sanitarias*); conferences on hygiene-related topics had to be given, and school buildings inspected regularly. Given these multiple tasks and the large number of students, Dr. Cabrera expressed the need for more medical personnel, improvements to buildings, fewer students per doctor, and better coordination among the departments of the Education Ministry ("Informe del médico escolar").

This report makes clear that the same physicians involved in school building inspections were also directly responsible for attending to the health of the student population, and for the compilation, organization, and transmission of data accounting for the hygiene of schools and students. Moreover, these tasks together contributed to an overarching logic of hygiene in which each element would ideally function within a cohesive whole, despite the school physician's familiar laments of excessive workload and inadequate institutional coordination. In addition, rather than simply conducting medical exams and measuring classrooms, school physicians also reflected and wrote on their roles, and on the importance of improvements in hygiene and in the study and compilation of appropriate data. In a sense, the active pursuit of research and knowledge in this area—or what we might term meta-hygiene—turns out to be inseparable from the pursuit of hygiene itself. Writing in 1926 in his thesis for the degree of *médico escolar*, Dr. Jesús Sola proclaimed that "si no se conoce de una manera real el TIPO del niño será imposible dictar medidas tendientes a conservarlo o a mejorarlo en su caso." [If the TYPE of child is not known in a real sense it will be impossible to dictate the means to conserve or improve him.] (148). Knowing the "type" of child in this case refers to a racial category, but also to other contextual features: "Considerando el punto de vista individual, la talla de un niño no puede compararse más que con el promedio de su raza, de su medio climatólogico y de su ambiente social." [Considering the individual point of view, a child's height can only be compared with the average of his race, of his climatological and social environments.] (152). For Dr. Sola, who also completed his own share of archived school-building inspection reports, measurements had to be contextualized and studied in terms of the indices they generated, and not read as isolated cases (159).[7] The work of hygiene moves beyond the body of the specific child and into the realm of comparative data. Improvements can only be made, the physician argues, if the child is approached not as an individual, but as a type. Hygiene as research thus moves continuously between particular bodies and the more abstract indices of data they generate. For the *médico escolar*, it is the ability to establish coherent links between information sets, to situate a given measurement within a system of coordinates, and to understand the relationship between environments, types, and data, that defines effective hygiene. The emphasis on the relativity of measurements also extends to the movement between buildings and bodies, as we have seen. In addition, the shift from a particular case toward abstract data offers a form of ordered cleansing, converting material embodiment to numerical sets, and illegible individuality to clarified group systematization.

In many cases, proximity between the hygiene of the body and that of its physical, social, and rhetorical environments emerges through the use of explicitly metaphorical language. This is the case in a 1925 text, "Ideas generales sobre la higiene escolar," by Dr. Alberto Lozano Garza, a school physician whose work often focused on questions of abnormality in students, and who would later become director of the DPH. As Lozano writes, "Después de hurgar con la punta de nuestros escalpelos hasta el más oculto rincón de los misteriosos órganos que integran nuestro sistema, nos hemos abocado al estudio de las leyes que rigen todo ese movimiento que se llama 'vida normal' para pasar después al conocimiento de los fenómenos que ocurren en estado anormal, en estado de enfermedad" (1). [After probing with the tip of our scalpels to the most hidden corner of the mysterious organs that make up our system, we have approached the study of the laws that rule all that movement known as "normal life" to turn afterwards to the knowledge of those phenomena that occur in an abnormal state, a state of illness.] Although Lozano does in one sense refer literally to a scalpel that actually probes human "mysterious organs," here instrument, organs, and the overall system also take on metaphorical connotations, as the probing gives way to more subtle revelations regarding the laws of "normal" and "abnormal" life. As he explains further, understanding the causes of abnormality and ways to avoid it—through research with a "scalpel"—constitutes the ideal of hygiene. Dr. Lozano's text includes extensive reference to the question of school building and furniture; as he notes, improperly sized or situated furniture "será causante de antiestéticas y desgraciadas deformaciones de los tiernos cuerpecitos de los niños" (3) [will be the cause of anti-aesthetic and unfortunate deformations of the tender little bodies of the children]. He dedicates additional attention to "abnormal" children, particularly regarding intelligence, and to the importance of creating homogeneous groups through the classification of students. Proper adherence to the laws of hygiene meant, first and foremost, separating children according to classified differences.[8] It also meant avoiding factors that would cause further abnormality, along with the careful study of a system in which bodies, organs, medical instruments, pedagogical classification, and school infrastructure all operated in accordance with a singular hygienic logic.

Elsewhere, the language of illness and abnormality emerges in discussions of school buildings and facilities. In one case, a letter from the school physician Dr. Pedro Bravo Gómez, reporting to the director of school hygiene and describing the conditions of Centro Educativo 13-11 after his visit, underscores the problematic qualities of the construction in question: "Estos salones aquí descritos dan salida a multitud de alumnos que tienen que pasar por un raquítico pasillo como de sesenta centímetros de ancho" (2). [The rooms described here provide outlets to a multitude of pupils who have to pass through a rickety hallway of about 60 centimeters in width.] Use of the term *raquítico*, or "rickety," was common in discussions of the health conditions of schoolchildren of the period, whether as a literal reference to rickets as an illness, or as a vaguer and more general way of denoting the appearance of poor health, particularly as caused by malnourishment. In this case, however, the effects of malnourishment and the illness it may cause are transposed to become part of the description of a hallway. The physician suggests further that potential outcomes of use of this *raquítico pasillo* are accidents that might occur as many children try to pass through a narrow space at once. In this way, a quality commonly ascribed to the bodies of impoverished schoolchildren turns out to characterize part of the built environment they inhabit, one that in turn is likely to produce further injury or abnormality. Poor hygiene here thus takes on a cyclical aspect, shifting between cause and effect, as well as built structure and human body. In these cases, it is the intervening substance of metaphorical language that links bodies to infrastructure, making explicit the continuity of hygienic discourse and of the ills that are said to plague bodies and buildings. In common usage today, "rickety" (or *raquítico*) is more likely to refer to buildings or furniture in poor condition than a person with rickets, perhaps because, thanks to medical advances, rickets is relatively uncommon today in the industrialized world. Yet in the context of 1920s and '30s Mexico, rickets was common in schoolchildren, as were references to its risk factors, prevention, and cure, and use of the term *raquítico* could be equally applied to human beings or to inanimate objects. Reading Bravo Gómez's description today re-enlivens the objects he refers to, and that we might still call "rickety," infusing built structures with the living qualities of organisms marked by disease. The language of the school physician thus shows us how disability becomes a transhistorical and dynamic property of buildings and furniture.

Part of the problem that Dr. Bravo Gómez notes in his inspection stems from the initial construction of the school, since, as he states, no doctor or pedagogue was consulted in this process. Similarly, as the *médico escolar* Dr. Carlos Jiménez would note in his 1926 thesis, "El médico escolar debería intervenir en la construcción de todo edificio escolar para vigilar la buena elección del terreno, la orientación, ventilación, iluminación, patios, dotación de agua, drenaje, bebederos, excusados, mingitorios, lavabos, baños . . ." (9) [The school physician should intervene in the construction of all school buildings so as to oversee the proper selection of the terrain, the orientation, ventilation, lighting, patios, water sources, drainage, drinking fountains, toilets, urinals, sinks, baths . . . .] Curiously, the same physician also uses the term *raquítico* in his text, this time to describe a moment in the history of the

School Hygiene Service, in which this office was less effective: "A pesar de las épocas de duras pruebas, de las oposiciones sistemáticas, de los prejuicios, de la ignorancia de las autoridades o de la falta de preparación del personal docente, hay que convenir en que la Institución no llegó a desaparecer y se mantuvo, raquítica y bastante deficiente, en espera de una nueva época (6)." [Despite the periods of hard trials, of systematic opposition, of prejudices, of the ignorance of the authorities or of the lack of preparation on the part of personnel, one has to agree that the Institution did not disappear, but remained, rickety and fairly deficient, awaiting a new phase.] The physician's language in this case takes on an optimistic and hopeful tone, for despite a "rickety" past, school hygiene continued to wait for a time of better direction in which it might fulfill its goals (6). Institutionalized hygiene itself, like the bodies and buildings to which it refers, is subject here to the perils of ill health that may weaken it, but against which it ultimately prevails as the master discourse of a stronger and better future.

Institutional Structures

The DPH would in fact enjoy further support and success; in 1936 under the government of President Lázaro Cárdenas and the directorship of Dr. Lauro Ortega Martínez, the National Institute of Psychopedagogy (INP) was inaugurated to replace the former DPH. The new institute represented an expansion of the reach and mandate of its predecessor and was comprised of seven "services": psychophysiology, psychometrics, pedagogy (*paidotecnia*), statistics (*paidografía*), special education, professional orientation, and mental hygiene and the behavioral clinic (Instituto Nacional de Psicopedagogía). Comparison between the structure of the DPH and that of the INP reveals several key differences; terms used for the names of sections and subsections such as *Estadística* or *Pedagogía* were replaced with more technical and modern-sounding ones such as *Paidografía* and *Paidotecnia*. The Service of Mental Hygiene and the Behavioral Clinic represented a new focus for the INP, with emphasis on so-called problem children; prevention and cure focused on family and school context and social environment. This service was also responsible for the creation and distribution of information designed to improve students' mental health conditions, and for the statistical study of various common neuroses (Ríos Molina, *Cómo prevenir*, 112–13). In addition, the large and historically significant DPH section on School Hygiene no longer appears as a discrete entity within the INP. School-building inspection reports nonetheless continued in this period; moreover, the legacy of school hygiene history, with its unwavering emphasis on the built environment, still prevailed in the rhetoric of the new institute. The inaugural publication of the INP featured descriptions of the roles of each of the services, along with detailed graphics to illustrate the structure of the organization. In the case of the psychometrics service, responsible for testing and grouping schoolchildren according to their mental capacity, the description offers explicit reference to the issue of material infrastructure:

> Para que el Maestro realice con el mayor éxito posible la importante tarea educativa que le está encomendada y con objeto de que su labor sea científica y útil, necesita conocer minuciosamente el material humano que se le confía, así como al ingeniero que trata de levantar un edificio se sirve del conocimiento de la resistencia de los materiales para proporcionar a la obra la solidez indispensable, o como el técnico que pone en trabajo una fábrica o indaga las características de la maquinaria para fijar un rendimiento determinado y calcular la velocidad de trabajo. (Instituto Nacional de Psicopedagogía, 49)

> [In order that the teacher may carry out the important educational role to which he is charged with the maximum success, and so that his work may be scientific and useful, he needs to have precise knowledge of the human material entrusted to him, just as the engineer who bases his construction of a building on his knowledge of the materials' resistance in order to give the work the necessary solidity, or the technician who puts a factory in operation or investigates the qualities of the machinery so as to establish a given level of productivity and calculate work speed.]

The curious use of technical, structural metaphors here to describe the schoolteacher's required knowledge of his students' mental capacity purports to portray psychometrics as an industrial science, and cognitive measurements as building materials with tangible, physical properties. Although the document does not refer to school buildings in a literal or direct sense, it manages to retain the language of construction, transposing the dilemmas of materials and design to the more abstract realm of student ability and pedagogy. Within this metaphorical depiction of the science of education, students and teacher become components in a cycle of labor and production, one that requires proper technical supervision to operate at maximum efficiency. For the medical staff charged with administering cognitive tests to students, the goal was thorough knowledge of the "human material" with which the future would be built. Their work also offered a more practical outcome; mental tests facilitated the creation of homogenous student groups, and the identification and removal of "mental defectives," who would otherwise be a burden (*lastre*) (49).

The descriptive publication of the new Institute insisted on its characteristics of precise, efficient organization and professional expertise in the research and dissemination of specialized knowledge. A noteworthy attribute here is the emphasis on the institute's role in research; the explicitly stated goals are not simply to improve education or children's health, but instead focus on the centralized acquisition of knowledge. As Dr. Lauro Ortega writes:

> El conocimiento exacto de las características del niño mexicano, su clasificación, la educación especial que requieren los debiles mentales, la recuperación física de los escolares desnutridos, la educación de los lisiados, la orientación profesional, la integridad mental de los escolares, la organización, métodos, programas, horarios, etc., sobre bases científicas, constituyen el objeto de los distintos servicios de este Instituto. (9)

> [The exact knowledge and classification of the characteristics of the Mexican child, the special education required by the feebleminded, the physical recuperation of malnourished schoolchildren, the education of the crippled, professional orientation, students' mental integrity, the organization, methods, programs, schedules, etc., supported by scientific bases, constitute the objectives of the various services of this Institute.]

Emphasis on research and the acquisition of precise knowledge of the Mexican child represented continuity with the earlier mission of the DPH, yet the founding of the INP further emphasized the codification and formalization of this initiative, within a framework determined by the demand for a new, revolutionary, socialist education, properly based on scientific principles. As the text describing the INP further states, the essential function of the institute "Consiste en llevar a cabo las investigaciones científicas necesarias para construir la base sobre la cual habrá de edificarse la técnica de la EDUCACIÓN SOCIALISTA" (15) [Consists of carrying out the scientific research necessary to construct the base upon which the technique of SOCIALIST EDUCATION will be built]. In this context, research itself takes center stage, sustaining yet another structural metaphor through which the reader might visualize the state's pedagogical project, as a building under construction from the ground up.

The inaugural, descriptive text on the newly founded National Institute of Psychopedagogy is striking for the way in which it fuses insistence on the research enterprise with a tangible, spatial ordering of the Institute's own organizational structure. Hygiene, in this sense, emerges as both abstract technique and as materially rendered, visible presence. The organizational charts (*organigramas*) included throughout the text illustrate the division of labor and the relationships between the various services and departments comprising the institute. They also work to make explicit the movement between modern and technical systems for the acquisition of knowledge and the ordered occupation of physical space, depicted through symmetrical line drawings with minimal art deco flourishes. Building for the future in this sense means sustaining a discourse of hygiene as both the abstraction and the embodiment of knowledge.

Organizational charts with some similarities to those of the 1930s are familiar today and can be found on the websites of many companies and government entities, offering a spatial and visual means to depict hierarchies and communication channels, and to reflect labor structures that might otherwise be difficult to conceptualize. In the text of the INP, however, the charts truly dominate, proliferating in each section, with the largest, master chart encompassing all the services of the institute, and separate charts showing the more detailed relationships within each individual service. The descriptive text includes an impressive total of eight organizational charts. Charts for each of the seven services include a list of their functions, linked to boxes showing the "medios" or spaces in which these functions are to be carried out. In the case of the Psychophysiology Service, for example, functions include "Investigación de las características mentales" [research in mental characteristics] and "Estudio de la herencia" [study of heredity], and "medios" include a series of laboratories for experimentation and measurement (23). The textual and structural detail of the full collection of charts is too vast to be captured on a single page, for the work insists on a tangible rendering that captures both the organizational and spatial divisions of the institute and a textual description of each unit. Taken together, these charts thus offer a hygienic universe that seamlessly fuses a material, spatial order with the abstract functioning of each of its parts. We might imagine the overall rendering as a map, one that is either too vast to be taken in by the human gaze, or so elaborate that its details could only be captured through a microscope.

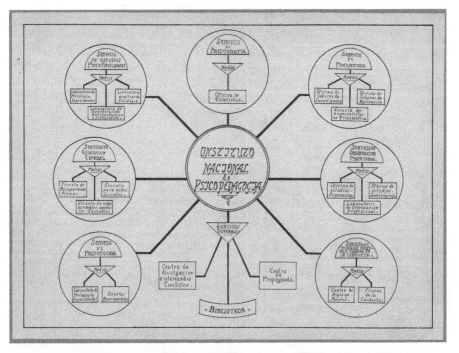

Fig. 13. Organizational chart from the Instituto Nacional de Psicopedagogía [National Institute of Psychopedagogy], founded in 1936. Caja 35520, Ref III/161 (III-5)-2. Instituto Nacional de Psicopedagogía, 17-13-9-276 (1936), Folio 91. Archivo General de la Nación.

The problem of hygiene emerges here as an exquisitely rendered paradox, in which the organizational chart, like the school building and infrastructure it evokes, simultaneously delineates physical spaces and expresses the functions of psychopedagogy. These functions, including research as well as its practical application in educational methods, suture infrastructure to outcomes, spaces to actions, and the identification of problems to the affirmation of solutions. If the potential presence of mentally "abnormal" students is a problem, for example, it is solved by identifying and separating those students into special groups to maintain homogenous classrooms. In this way, classification works to both define and solve a pedagogical problem, represented in terms of bodies in enclosed spaces. The charts' outlined shapes designate different laboratories and classrooms, evoking both the physical spaces of buildings and rooms and the functions to be carried out within them. As in the case of the physicians' reports on students and school buildings dis-

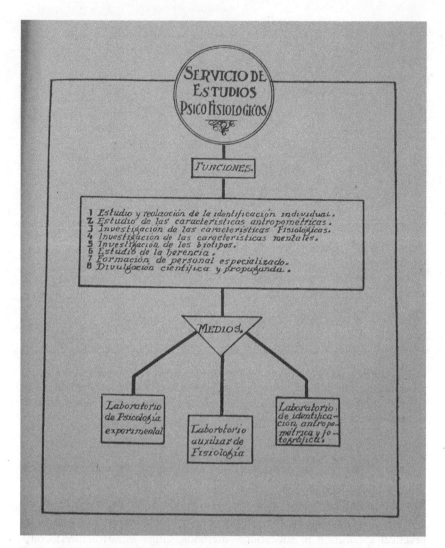

Fig. 14. Organizational chart from the Psychophysiology Service, within the
National Institute of Psychopedagogy. *Instituto Nacional de Psicopedagogía*. Secretaría
de Educación Pública, Departamento de Psicopedagogía y Médico Escolar. Talleres
gráficos de la nación, 1936, p. 23.

cussed previously, here too disability circulates as central to the research and educational enterprise, as the material expression of hygiene in action. The paradox of hygiene suggested in the organizational charts is also akin to the frustration expressed by architect Juan O'Gorman, to be addressed in the next section of this chapter. For O'Gorman, as I will discuss further, the paradoxical problem and virtue of architectural functionalism turns out to be the inseparability of form and function, problem and solution. The organizational charts of the INP in many ways also reflect this functionalist paradigm, and the expressions of disability and hygiene within it.

The explicitly central role of disability in the INP emerges in the details of each service's functions, and also in the overall mission of the organization. Dr. Lauro Ortega's introductory text focuses first on "knowledge and classification of the characteristics of the Mexican child," which had long been a goal among school hygiene professionals.[9] Yet immediately following this evocation of a national type, the director enumerates more specific focal areas of the institute, including special education, attention to malnourished schoolchildren, and the education of the "crippled." The fact that these three areas appear in the formal opening passages of the book and as key to the institute's project of developing a scientifically grounded pedagogy centered on knowledge of "the Mexican child" reminds us, of course, that prototype and differences are tightly and recognizably enmeshed within the research enterprise.[10] While the study of abnormality and the use of statistical data as a means to study and plot a normal curve are unsurprising, this formal, graphic unveiling of the new institute is unique for the way it makes visible the causes and forms of disability. In this depiction, disability appears in close proximity to "the Mexican child," and plays a crucial role in the scientific development of socialist education.

The making visible of disability in this text, and the tangible rendering of institutional structures through illustrations and charts, coincides with shifts in the overall visualization of children and childhood in this period, particularly corresponding to images of the proletarian child.[11] In addition to the carefully sketched, symmetrical organigrams depicting the organizational structure of the Institute, this text includes a number of drawings of children, individually or in groups, many of them wearing the traditional overalls associated with workers and peasants. These illustrations are startling for their attention to detail, minute depiction of children's bodies and faces, and their artistic incorporation of the tools of statistics and scientific measurement (Vargas Parra 54).

The illustration accompanying the section on special education is somewhat distinct from the others. Rather than featuring children's faces and bodies superimposed on bar graphs or vital-signs charts, as in other drawings, here the nebulous silhouette of an upright, maternal figure shelters three children. One leans on a crutch, another presses his head into the woman's leg, and a third gazes downward with a sad expression. The hazy shading of the woman's outline, and the spreading base of her dress, akin to tree roots, combine to suggest a symbolic notion of protective motherhood, the emblem of a nation watching over her children rather than their actual mother. The children, for their part, straddle a line between stereotypes of abnormality and individual particularity, each with a detailed and directed gaze. The caption to the image reads as follows: "El Servicio de Educación Especial realiza la labor que reclama la educación de los niños anormales mentales, débiles físicos y lisiados" (77). [The Special Education Service carries out the labor required for the education of mentally abnormal children, weaklings, and cripples.]

Within the transparently organized and research-based structure of the National Institute of Psychopedagogy, disability itself must be explicitly shown and located in relation to an overarching project of "knowledge and classification of the Mexican child." Curiously, although children considered abnormal were to be removed from regular classrooms to facilitate the creation of "homogenous groups," the supposedly abnormal students nonetheless acquire a presence and a specificity in the institutional text, as a key and distinct complement to their "normal" peers. The text of the INP, as we have seen, does not refer to school buildings or other material infrastructure, but instead shifts toward an insistence on metaphors of construction and on the tangible spatialization of its own organizing principles. Within these structures, disability appears in a literal and graphic fashion through artistic illustration and the naming of conditions, and also through a rhetoric of hygiene, in which problem and solution, structure and function, are fused in the depiction of a paradoxically cohesive universe. In the work of Juan O'Gorman, to be discussed in the next section, the role of hygiene in school buildings is similarly of key importance, since proper and efficient building is explicitly linked to the prevention of childhood illness. In addition, hygiene becomes an increasingly complex and problematic notion for O'Gorman in his writing and artistic production, as technical, material detail in building design often fails to cohere with the broader, state-sponsored principles of building for the future. The troubled quality of hygiene in architecture, presented at times through metaphors of the functioning of human bodies and populations, thus reveals the spatially—as well as temporally—rendered, dynamic role of disability, key to the modern Mexican cityscape and its pedagogical mission.

El Servicio de Educación Especial realiza la labor
que reclama la educación de los niños anormales mentales, débiles físicos y lisiados.

Fig. 15. Drawing illustrating the Special Education Service within the National
Institute of Psychopedagogy, 1936. The drawing shows a woman standing
protectively over three children, one with a crutch, and all with mournful
expressions. *Instituto Nacional de Psicopedagogía*. Secretaría de Educación Pública,
Departamento de Psicopedagogía y Médico Escolar. Talleres gráficos de la nación,
1936, p. 77.

Technical Hygiene

Writing in the early 1930s, functionalist architect Juan O'Gorman effectively summarized the dilemma of urban planning, and specifically the construction of schools in a Mexico City faced with a severe housing and sanitation crisis: "Respecto al problema de la escuela primaria en México, en el que sabemos existe un 50% de escuelas-tugurios, inmundos sitios donde se tuberculizan un buen porcentaje de estos niños, ¿qué hace el arquitecto frente a esta situación? ¿Obras de arte o ingeniería de edificios?" ("Arquitectura funcional" 123). [Regarding the problem of primary schools in Mexico, in which we know that 50% are hovels, unworldly places where a high percentage of children contract tuberculosis, how does the architect respond to this situation? With works of art, or with the engineering of buildings?] O'Gorman here follows his often-repeated functionalist mandate of "maximum efficiency for minimum effort"—in which "effort" primarily designates cost—and at the same time suggests moral indignation through his rhetorical questions, at the thought that some might attempt to create works of art as a response to the needs of poor, sick children.[12]

O'Gorman's words here reflect an important link that would also appear elsewhere in his writings, particularly of this period, between the question of hygiene, the built environment of the city, and the moral imperative that ostensibly ties the two together. The construction of a hygienic cityscape becomes a crucial means of fulfilling the promise of the revolution, and hygiene itself operates as the paradigm of correct action for the good of the people; in O'Gorman's case, hygiene defines successful architecture. I consider O'Gorman's rhetoric of hygiene as central to his increasingly conflictive view of urbanization in Mexico, and his perception of the failures of the revolution. This rhetoric of hygiene goes to work on the problems of social inequality, health conditions, corruption, and mismanagement, but at the same time defines the processes of circulation and exchange between human bodies, the spaces they inhabit, and the political and economic forces through which they emerge.[13] In other words, O'Gorman's distinctive insistence on the notion of hygiene expresses both the problems of inequality and asymmetry in urban spaces, and the proposed solutions to these problems. By articulating a rhetoric of hygiene in which the description of the problem becomes increasingly entangled with the action of solving it, O'Gorman's work conveys a self-reflexive disillusion with the urban built environment as national project. Yet by the same token, the author at once participates in a post-revolutionary national aesthetics—inseparable from the state-sponsored project of hygiene and eugenics—typified by the elision of distance between present and future. In the early stages of his career O'Gorman was adamant in his verbal rejection of what he termed "aesthetics." In this sense I read his participation in a national aesthetic project during the early 1930s as unwitting and paradoxical, and often running counter to the intentions he articulates.

As O'Gorman would write, in reference to the initiative of building cost-efficient, rationally planned schools, "si se lograra sacarlo avante sería, a mi juicio, ser buen mexicano y resolver problemas mexicanos" ("Conferencia en la sociedad de arquitectos mexicanos," 112); [if one were able to carry this out it would mean, in my opinion, being a good Mexican and solving Mexican problems]. In O'Gorman's writing, hygiene thus functions as a primary site for the expression of the author's partial and conflicted participation in a broader nationalist, eugenic aesthetics. The ambivalent location and expression of hygiene is significant here because it reveals the fraught complexity of O'Gorman's relationship—as architect and writer—to the state-sponsored discourse in which he participated. But perhaps more importantly, the role of hygiene in these texts demonstrates the splintered and shifting quality of what might otherwise be read as a monolithic post-revolutionary nationalist project.[14] Within this context, hygiene itself thus turns out to be a troubled and messy endeavor.

Part of the uncertainty of O'Gorman's relationship to nationalist aesthetics, and to the role of hygiene in the revolutionary aesthetic project, lies in the architect's emphasis on strict principles of the technical. In his book *Mexican Modernity: The Avant-Garde and the Technological Revolution*, Rubén Gallo discusses how post-revolutionary Mexican artists and practitioners in diverse media, such as photography, typewriting, radio, cement, and stadiums, aimed to aestheticize the technical, creating new modes of artistic and cultural production through a celebratory use of these technologies. O'Gorman's discourse of the 1930s, in contrast, reveals a near-obsessive concern with the technical as such, and with the frustrated goal of uncoupling "parasitic" art from his own version of technical, hygienic fluidity. Emphasis on the technical, rather than on aesthetic principles, shifts the contours of revolutionary politics, and the role of hygiene in this politics.

In this sense, the architect's technical hygiene differs from the concept of aesthetic, eugenic hygiene, as promoted by José Vasconcelos, for example, in his classic work, *La raza cósmica* as well as later texts such as *Ética*, both discussed in chapter 2. In those texts, eugenics is presented as continuous with a vast sweep of history, and with the spiritual and aesthetic improvement of individuals and species; it is also congruent with a more programmatic discourse of racial hygiene. For Vasconcelos, the necessary apex of national and universal history is racial and spiritual transformation, which continually collapses matter into spirit, and present into future. Vasconcelos's brief discussion of "modern architecture" in *Estética* offers an additional point of contrast to O'Gorman's views. His overall impression of this architecture is primarily negative due to its lack of aesthetic appeal and adornment. He notes for example the "stinginess" (*mezquindad*) of the staircases and blames the "greedy hearts of the industrial era" (1611).

In contrast to the mode of aesthetics observed briefly here in Vasconcelos's work, O'Gorman's technical hygiene purports to solve national, technical problems, and resists the sweep of an aestheticized, racialized, teleological history. The architect's technical version of hygiene attempts to remain separate from aesthetic intentions that he regarded as superfluous, but cannot fully avoid participating in a nationalist agenda, within which the concepts of hygiene and eugenics—broadly articulated—operate as conduits toward a Mexican future.[15] In particular the dilemma of uncertain transition between present and future, as mentioned above, surfaces in the architect's writings, as both a problem of hygiene and a link to nationalist aesthetics.

The more general idea of hygiene corresponds to the particular context of Mexican public-health and education policies from the 1920s to the 1940s, as expressed in anti-alcohol campaigns, studies in biotypology, school inspection reports, and the functions of the DPH and later the National Institute of Psychopedogogy, among other areas discussed in this book. The linkage between hygiene and ("soft") eugenics, which I wish to underscore here once more, rests on their mutual insistence on the biological improvement of the future through action undertaken in the present.[16] This occurs, for example, in anti-alcohol campaigns, through arguments that the avoidance of alcohol will prevent epilepsy or idiocy in future generations, as discussed in the previous chapter. In this sense, as we have seen, health policies designed to improve the well-being of the current population translate to the future improvement of the nation and race. Eugenics and hygiene, at times blurred into a singular concept, operate in this context as part of a biopolitical mode of aesthetics defined by both the projection of an ideal into the nation's future, and the points of conflict between the idealized projection and the (human, material) disruptions to its fluidity. Whether or not O'Gorman's notion of the technical as hygienic operates as a mode of such disruption remains a key indeterminacy here, one that reveals the uncertain and problematic role of hygiene in the revolution.

In a slightly different sense, disability also suggests the presence of human disruption, due to its departure from an ideal or standard, and because it is frequently depicted through material, embodied forms. This is the case, for example, in school hygiene documentation of "abnormality" or illness among students, and of inadequate facilities, as we have seen. Such instances conflict with the goals of homogenous classroom groups and scientifically ordered pedagogical infrastructure and methods, yet are paradoxically key to the research agendas of psychopedagogy and hygiene. O'Gorman's technical hygiene appears to negotiate a related form of disruption, focusing on a specific, material issue to be resolved, positing symmetry between form and function, problem and solution, but wary of the broader aesthetic project that would subsume this symmetry into its overarching mission.

As Luis Carranza notes, studies of the trajectory of O'Gorman's work have paid attention to the significant shift between his earlier emphasis on functionalism, from approximately 1929 to 1936, and his eventual abandonment of architecture and turn to realist painting (158). In Carranza's fascinating reading of O'Gorman's functionalism, partially based on Adorno's essay "Functionalism Today," the architect's goal of serving the masses through functionalist building is shown to have been ultimately co-opted by bourgeois interests, for the advancement of capitalism and the maximization of profits (Carranza 161).[17] Though such co-optation was already present in the early 1930s period of functionalist architecture in Mexico, O'Gorman would only abandon functionalism on becoming increasingly aware of its pitfalls and contradictions. Although this shift and O'Gorman's eventual rejection of functionalist principles are undeniable, here I am particularly interested in considering how the work and discourse of hygiene continually permeate O'Gorman's approach to functionalism from the early 1930s to midcentury and beyond. The role of hygiene in this work, inextricably tied to the economics and contradictions of functionalism in the context of post-revolutionary urban Mexico, reveals O'Gorman's conflicts and points of contact with state ideology, as well as the fluid temporality underpinning the nationalist politics and aesthetics of the period.

Hygiene, for O'Gorman, certainly refers to urgent questions of health and sanitation, as is most obviously the case in the early 1930s when he designed a series of primary schools for Mexico City's working-class population, under the mandate of the Secretaría de Educación Pública. Yet beyond that specific case, the concept of hygiene becomes relevant in O'Gorman's work as a rhetorical device, one that underpins his overall critique of urbanization in Mexico. In O'Gorman's increasingly negative views of architectural trends and his pessimism with respect to the future of the city and its

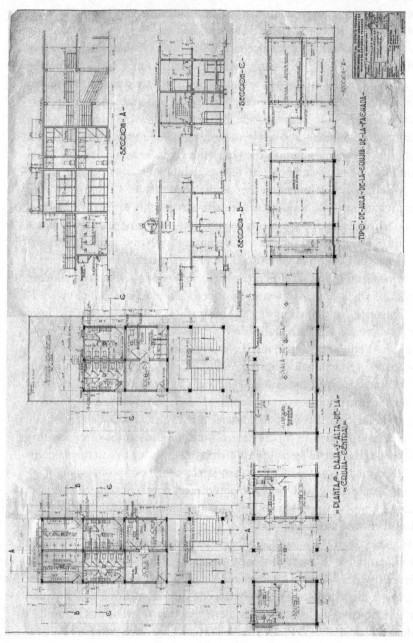

Fig. 16. Architectural blueprint for a school designed by Juan O'Gorman to be built in the Colonia Industrial in 1932. Archivo Histórico de la Ciudad de México, Planoteca, Módulo 4, planero 2, fajilla 4. Clave 415.6 (073)/93.

people, hygiene, as concept and structure, circulates as part of the fluidity of relations between the state, its citizens, and the market. I underscore the ideas of fluidity and circulation here to illustrate a dilemma that repeatedly emerges in O'Gorman's work, one that is crucial to the discourses of eugenics and aesthetics of the period. The issue relates to the spatialized depiction of school hygiene as described in the earlier part of this chapter, in which school buildings, infrastructure, and children's bodies operate as materially and causally linked entities, and where diagnosis, cure, inspection, and reconstruction share a common language, thanks to the work of the school physicians. The fluidity of hygiene in O'Gorman's work also occurs in a temporal sense, and might be summarized as a concern for how action undertaken in the present—by the state, or by an architect, for example—impacts the future of the urban population, and to what degree this human population becomes inseparable from the circuits of state and market causes and effects. Michel Foucault addresses this problem in his discussion of human capital, where he describes the worker as an "active economic subject" (*The Birth of Biopolitics*, 223) or "*homo œconomicus*" (225). In Foucault's reading, this subject, as entrepreneur, accumulates human capital, which may also be acquired for future generations through genetic selectivity in reproduction, and through education. And although he does not literally conflate genetics with hygiene, Foucault does state, "Thus, all the problems of health care and public hygiene must, or at any rate, can be rethought as elements which may or may not improve human capital" (230). This analysis emphasizes the active role of the worker as subject, whose behavior constitutes part of a process of investment and exchange, hence part of the fluid circulation of the market.[18] In addition, by helping to determine his human capital, the worker participates in the determination of his own health, and that of the present and future population. In this sense, the inseparability of the *homo œconomicus*, as active agent of his own value, from the market as a whole parallels the continuity between value in the present and in the future.

The primary schools designed by O'Gorman in 1932 would be constructed under the mandate of the Secretaría de Educación Pública, headed by Narciso Bassols, who appointed O'Gorman to lead the building department of the SEP. Bassols would remain in his position for only two years, thanks to a group of parents who protested his promotion of coeducation and "sexual education" (Olsen 85), yet his commitment to mass, socialist education had an ongoing impact, most visibly through O'Gorman's functionalist school buildings, which sought to put the ideals of the revolution into practice. As the authors of *Utopía-no utopia*, an illuminating study of O'Gorman's school-building project, argue, this project was designed and constructed within the context of the state's hygenicist ideology, which meant a focus on the necessity of regulating "el flujo de la luz por las ventanas, la circulación de los fluidos del cuerpo ocultos en las tuberías, el bienestar infantil" (15) [the streaming of light through the windows, the hidden circulation of bodily fluids in the pipes, the children's well-being].[19]

The project may be said to operate within a eugenicist paradigm, broadly defined, in which emphasis on hygiene in building for the present population inevitably pointed toward the broader goal of massive social improvement for the future. In addition, a closer examination of O'Gorman's use of language with respect to the question of hygiene and functionalist architecture reveals how hygiene itself also begins to determine the logic of the architect's verbal expression. Conflicts arise as a result of this expression, in part because O'Gorman's version of technical hygiene differs somewhat from hygiene as more broadly conceived in the national eugenic project. In his essay "Arquitectura funcional," cited above, O'Gorman presents the dilemma of those who would like to see architecture resolve both basic housing necessities at minimum cost, and "aesthetic necessities" (122). Ultimately, O'Gorman will insist that the two are entirely incompatible, and he is quick to anticipate objections to his idea. With respect to the dilemma of the architect who must design schools for a population in which half the children currently attend "hovels" [escuelas-tugurios] with a high incidence of tuberculosis (as cited above), O'Gorman writes, "Indiscutiblemente que el deber primordial del arquitecto frente a esta situación es el de no gastar ni un céntimo que no sea indispensable y útil. No se trata en este caso de un problema de arte ni nada que se le parezca. Se trata de un problema técnico, de funcionalismo estricto, de funcionalismo mecánico, de un problema de emergencia, de un problema de economía y a fin de cuentas de un problema de ingeniería de edificios y no de expresiones de la imaginación humana" (123). [Undeniably the primary responsibility of the architect faced with this situation is to not spend even a cent that is not indispensible and useful. In this case it is not about a problem of art or anything resembling it. It's a technical problem, of strict functionalism, mechanical functionalism, an emergency, an economic problem, and finally, a problem of the engineering of buildings and not of expressions of human imagination.]

O'Gorman's strict, technical concept of functionalism here differs from the functionalist architecture—and what came to be known as International Style modernism[20]—that became widespread in Europe and the United

States, thanks in large part to the influence of Le Corbusier.[21] The radical frugality and rigid definition of O'Gorman's functionalism are also what define it specifically as Mexican functionalism, appropriate to local context. As Alberto Pérez-Gómez states, in an interview with Edward Burian, "what Mexican architects understand as functional architecture, is simply the idea that somehow all that matters is the resolution of the programmatic questions as economically and efficiently as possible so that form might 'follow,' excluding the architect's potential to indulge his imagination" (34).[22] Here O'Gorman makes clear that the architect is operating within the confines of a limited budget, and that both the problem and the solution are defined in strictly economic terms. The value of the architectural intervention in the problem of public health stems in part from the specificity with which it may be measured; since every last cent must be accounted for, the value of each cent will therefore translate into a precise and necessary unit of use. Obedience to a functionalist ethics in this case also means obedience to a perfectly measured frugality. In other words, the overall value of functionalism stems from its close attention to value as such, and to its perfected conversion from cost to use value. As O'Gorman writes, "It's a technical problem," and then continues the sentence with a crescendoing series of terms, each of which describes the "problem" faced by the architect, while at once implying the type of solution that will be appropriate to it. Finally, as O'Gorman concludes here, the problem is adamantly not one of the "expression of human imagination," as this term opposes all of those that precede it in the same sentence. The task of the functionalist architect as writer is to separate terms such as "human imagination" and "aesthetics" from references to technical problems. The strict efficiency of the solution to the problem appears to leave no margin for a blurring of categories, no space for the expression of art.[23] The explanation here might be considered hygienic in the sense of the clarity and marked quality, or "cleanliness," of its divisions, and economic, of course, in its insistence on the value of each cent, indispensable to the project at hand. Yet by the same token, the description cuts short the possibility of fluidity between the problem and the expression of human imagination, by insisting on a radical separation between the two. The conflictive and cutting spirit of these lines will be echoed elsewhere in O'Gorman's writing, where more explicit contradictions between fluidity and separation emerge. And significantly, this passage does suggest an intimate link between hygiene and economics, not only because in O'Gorman's broader argument, saving more money on the construction of schools means saving more children from tuberculosis and related conditions, but also because the fastidious precision with which the architect separates the artistic from the technical mirrors his accounting for every last indispensable cent—and vice versa.

In O'Gorman's essay cited here, "Arquitectura funcional," as is often the case elsewhere, the author adopts a somewhat aggressive tone, immediately anticipating the objections of his listeners, responding by defending his points, and critiquing the foolishness of their imagined responses. For example, he imagines a reader who might propose a combination of aesthetics and functionality in architecture, and states: "Se me dirá que una tesis no excluye a la otra y que en lo funcional está contenido lo expresivo, lo que podemos llamar la producción de arte. Esto no es exacto e implica una falsificación, pues una tesis sí excluye a la otra. La arquitectura como obra de arte no puede ser la conclusión de la función mecánica y de la arquitectura mecánica funcional. La ingeniería de edificios no puede ser nada que no sea la expresión de la función mecánica y ésta, la expresión mecánica, no es expresión de arte" (123–24). [I will be told that one thesis does not exclude the other, and that the expressive, what we might call the production of art, is contained in the functional. This is inexact and implies a falsification, for one thesis does exclude the other. Architecture as art cannot be the outcome of mechanical function and of mechanical functional architecture. The engineering of buildings cannot be anything but the expression of mechanical function, and this, mechanical expression, is not artistic expression.]

Here again, the author insists on a strict separation between the "functional" and the "expressive," yet the situation is complicated by the notion of expression, a term repeated several times in the passage. Initially, the expressive appears to denote artistic expression, yet further in the passage it turns out that the mechanical offers its own form of expression, "the expression of mechanical function," or "mechanical expression." In this sense, the division between function and expression can be understood as one of cause and effect; function is the primary term, while expression is its conclusion, outcome, or outward manifestation. "The engineering of buildings cannot be anything but the expression of mechanical function" equates engineering with expression, and underscores the idea that expression and function are, or should be, two sides of the same coin. The mandate that expression should express only function suggests that an engineering solution to a mechanical problem must remain mechanical, and not deviate into the realm of art. Likewise, expression should be true to the function it expresses, so that what is in fact purely an aesthetic design choice should not masquerade as an engineering solution. O'Gorman's increasing levels of apparent anger and frustration in attempting to separate art from function, while at once maintaining continuity between the primary function of a given object and its outward appearance, or "expression," imply a necessary duality between form and function that is always in danger of deviating from its ostensibly practical, symmetrical structure. The fact that the type of building O'Gorman privileges here comes into being as an "*expression* of mechanical function," (my emphasis) highlights the idea that even the material existence of the building might already jeopardize its obedience to the principle of pure, technical functionality. Moreover, perhaps it is obvious that the more closely a given building or construction displays coherence between form (expression) and function, the more likely it is that viewers or critics might interpret the aesthetics of this building (as work of art) as entangled in its functionality. This of course is precisely the confusion O'Gorman is hoping to avoid, when he insists that one must choose between aesthetics and function, that it is impossible to have both: "O se sacrifica el máximo de eficiencia por el mínimo de gasto o se sacrifica la arquitectura como expresión estética. A escoger" (124). [Either you sacrifice maximum efficiency for minimum cost, or you sacrifice architecture as aesthetic expression. You choose.]

The technical hygiene of the vision proposed by O'Gorman here emerges in the supposedly fluid reflexivity between function and expression, which should not allow for the intervention of external (in this case, artistic) elements. But the flow is at the same time broken by the suggestion that such elements may indeed be present. As Edward Burian has noted, O'Gorman's built architecture of this period presents metaphors of human biology and hygiene, at times with a similar use of fluidity. A classic example occurs in the studio-houses of Diego Rivera and Frida Kahlo, constructed in 1931. In these houses' interiors and exteriors, as Burian writes, "All pipes were visible, and electrical power runs and connections were used as expressive compositional elements reminiscent of veins and arteries" ("Architecture of Juan O'Gorman," 139). The cables, pipes, water tank, and the structure of reinforced concrete were explicitly revealed, thus inverting the expected relationship between the interior and the surface of a building, or an organism, in accordance with Burian's notion of a "biological metaphor" ("Architecture of Juan O'Gorman," 147). The relationship between interior and exterior in this case becomes part of a singular continuity, since all aspects of the building make themselves visible, and announce their own structural, material necessity. Any element that was not materially necessary to the building would be deemed superfluous, in accordance with O'Gorman's strict interpretation of functionalism during this period. In obeying material necessity, the buildings appear to have opened their entrails to the world, renouncing the need to hide or disguise the practical, functional elements of the construction. Taken to the extreme, this architectural theory eliminates the notion of an interior, and of the division between function and expression that O'Gorman describes in the above-cited passage. Hygiene, in these examples, does not refer only to questions of health or cleanliness in a literal sense, but also to the systematization of a grouping of elements, each one efficient in itself, and together producing a harmonious efficiency. When a system is perfected, and when its construction and function mutually reflect one another, it articulates an absolute control, without the possibility of contamination by elements beyond its own finality.

These instances of rhetorical and built architectural hygiene in O'Gorman's work demonstrate the importance of economic logic as inseparable from the fluidity linking form (or "expression") to function, and at the same time the conflictive aspect of this supposed fluidity. The conflict is epitomized in the insistence that true functionalism is completely incompatible with attention to human or aesthetic expression, combined with the idea that in this architecture, function and expression should be faithful, unadulterated reflections of one another. The notion of expression in O'Gorman's work, which sometimes refers to artistic expression, and elsewhere just to the physical form manifesting a given concept, thus occupies an uncertain space; it is crucial to the fluid logic of functionalist architecture, yet at the same time is constantly under threat of erasure from the functionalist equation as superfluous.

In a classic 1933 lecture, O'Gorman further underscores the economic basis for his argument in favor of functionalism, or what he calls in this case, "technical architecture." He describes the example of two men standing before a waterfall, one an engineer and the other an architect. The engineer, not surprisingly, views the waterfall in terms of the energy that could be harnessed from it for human benefit, "fulfilling general human necessity" (*Conferencia* 114). The architect, in contrast, imagines decorations that might be added to the waterfall, for the enjoyment of a few select people. O'Gorman links these two cases directly to economics, as he states, "Las condiciones económicas actuales producen estos dos fenómenos en la arquitectura. El primero consiste en la necesidad que tiene el capital de producir un interés y de gastar este interés en nuevas inversiones y, por lo tanto, de emplear los medios técnicos para obtener esto, y el segundo, el de invertir el superávit de los intereses en lo que podría llamarse diversiones" (114–15). [Today's economic conditions produce these two phenomena in architecture. The first consists of capital's need to produce interest and to reinvest it, and therefore to use technical means in order to achieve this; and the second is the investment of surplus interest in what might be called enjoyment.] In this passage, capital is useful for the good of the people when it is employed for investment through technical means. Capital is at its best when it functions smoothly, reinvesting itself and maximizing its own production; as O'Gorman states, "the technical [. . .] makes capital productive" (115). Problems emerge when instead profits are spent on enjoyment. As O'Gorman concludes, "El arte se vuelve entonces un parásito que vive de la técnica y chupa la savia que había de fortalecer y aumentar la capacidad productora humana" (115). [Art then becomes a parasite that lives off the technical and sucks the sap that should have strengthened and increased human productive capacity.] One might imagine in this case that O'Gorman is referring to the contrast between money that is spent frivolously by elites for their own exclusive benefit, and money that is instead used to respond to the needs of the majority, as in the earlier example of the construction of schools for working-class children, in which each and every cent must be used efficiently. Yet here the architect refers only to the reinvestment of capital with the more abstract goal of increasing human productive capacity. Capitalism, as exemplary of the technical in this case, appears to operate for its own benefit, responding to its own needs for investment and reinvestment, and creating an effective, hygienic circuit of production linking present to future. This text, though published before O'Gorman's disillusion with functionalist architecture, already makes explicit how functionalism paradoxically dovetails with the goals of capitalism, so that the needs of capital correspond to the needs of the masses, in opposition to the whimsical desires of the elite. O'Gorman's example of the waterfall thus appears to sustain both classic Marxist discourse in which capital is an anthropomorphic subject with its own particular needs, and a celebration of the technical and of capital, as mutually beneficial to one another, and to the masses. "Human productive capacity" defines the center of this troubled hygienic logic.

Through use of the metaphor of art as a "parasite," sucking and weakening the circuit of human productive capacity, O'Gorman returns to his emphasis on biology and hygiene, as seen in Burian's discussion of the houses of Diego Rivera and Frida Kahlo. Hygienic capitalism, within this rhetoric, suggests the smooth functioning of an organism, in this case a tree, whose sap both nourishes the body as a whole, and is produced by it—in conjunction with necessary elements of the tree's ecosystem, such as water and sunlight.[24] The self-sufficient organism of capitalism is contaminated by parasitic art, which interferes in its feedback loop, both corrupting and diminishing the supply of nutrients, or funds. For O'Gorman, the basis of this capitalist circuit of production and investment is the human population, expressed here in the abstract as human productive capacity, yet the nature of the connection between the population and the capitalist model is not explained in detail. Instead, O'Gorman resorts to another metaphor, a description of a continuum of household objects running from the absolutely useful to the completely useless. Useful objects include stoves, bathtubs, and sewing machines, while useless ones are, for example, decorative vases and embroidery, with an in-between category containing items such as chairs and tables, depending on how elaborate they are. These categories suggest, for O'Gorman, the division of human activity into two basic manifestations: the technical, which serves everyone and makes capital productive, and the artistic or academic, which in contrast serves only a minority, and uses the surplus of interest produced by the technical, as was also the case in the example of the architect's vision of the waterfall. The parasitic appearance of artistic expression that is not the logical outcome of technical function contaminates the process through which objects are produced and circulated, leading to an asymmetry and a dead end to the fluidity of the feedback loop of capitalist investment and production.

"A Mexican Problem"

Critical descriptions of such corruption are common in O'Gorman's writings on functionalist architecture, and often occur as the culmination or endpoint of the architect's argument, as if to highlight the apex of his frustration with the contemporary state of architecture, with public misinterpretations of functionalism, or with a corrupt economics that benefits only the elite. In this sense, the dead end to the idealized fluidity between function and expression, or to the efficient circulation of technique for the benefit of humanity, frequently corresponds to a rhetorical dead end as well, a pessimistic vision that runs itself into the ground. In some cases, O'Gorman relates his visions of problems and solutions more specifically to the Mexican context, thus showing that his frustrations, as well as his hopeful ideas for the future population, are bound to the particularity of nationalism. This is the case in the following passage, where he describes the needs facing Mexico City schools, while at the same time criticizing those who would call Mexican functionalist architecture "Swedish" or "Nordic": "Higiene del cuerpo y de la inteligencia. Ventanas grandes que den mucha luz y muchos baños de regadera, y a esto se le llama arquitectura sueca o nórdica, sin analizar los problemas y sin conocer el medio. . . . Si analizamos superficialmente el problema veremos que el bautizar con sueca, nórdica o alemana es simplemente porque se vio por fuera la forma, pero no el fondo. Se vieron las fachadas y no se vio el problema, un problema mexicano, perfectamente mexicano y del Distrito Federal" ("Conferencia" 111). [Hygiene of body and mind. Big windows that let in lots of light and lots of bathrooms with showers, and this they call Swedish or Nordic architecture, without analyzing the problems and without knowledge of the context (. . . .) If we analyze the problem superficially we will see that calling this Swedish, Nordic or German only comes from looking at the form but not the content. They saw the façades but not the problem, a Mexican problem, perfectly Mexican, and of Mexico City.]

National specificity in this impassioned discussion is directly tied to O'Gorman's constant refrain regarding the relationship between form and content, external appearance and internal essence, expression and function. He describes the opposition in terms of form and content (*forma* and *fondo*), and also facades and problem, locating Mexicanness as the interior, base, or root of the problem, which might appear to be foreign if viewed superficially from the outside. Knowledge of the consistency between these elements and insistence on their logical continuity becomes a gesture of patriotism, one that is inseparable from the practicality of solving present social problems through projection into a collective national future. And as noted above, a frugal approach to such problem-solving means, for O'Gorman, "being a good Mexican and solving Mexican problems" (112). Mexicanness here is associated with the specific requirements of the situation, the "Mexican problem," which in turn defines functionalism in this case, since the architecture, to be successful, must be as cost-efficient and as commensurate as possible with the problem or needs. "A Mexican solution to a Mexican problem" describes O'Gorman's architecture, and in doing so, unites the problem with the solution, so that the terms start to become indistinguishable from one another. The joining together of the problem with the solution becomes part of O'Gorman's imperative, since understanding the fluidity between problem and solution will allow the viewer to avoid the mistake of looking only superficially at the façade and not seeing the problem. And as the problem becomes part of the continuity of the solution, the present situation is drawn toward the future, of course an emphatically Mexican future. By the same token misreading the building design as "Swedish, Nordic, or German" means misunderstanding the continuity between function and expression, interior and surface, present and future, and hence misinterpreting the role of the national in architecture. This incorrect view of the architecture in question would imagine an asymmetry between local context and built structure, Mexican particularity and foreign, corrupting influence. The misreading works as another case of a rhetorical dead end, a critical interruption to the fluidity of the relationship between function and expression (or *fondo* and *forma*), as also occurs elsewhere when O'Gorman gives his own examples of aesthetics severed from or superfluous to the technical.[25]

This passage occurs in the context of O'Gorman's argument in favor of a more universal Mexico: "La arquitectura tendrá que hacerse internacional, por la simple razón de que el hombre cada día se universaliza más" (112). [Architecture must internationalize itself, for the simple reason that man is becoming every day more international.] Perhaps ironically, this statement appears as the consequence of the imperative to be "good Mexicans and solve Mexican problems." Patriotism, like the relationship between function and expression, seems to operate in fluid terms, articulated at the crossover point between the internal and the external. The fluidity of these elements is hygienic, in that it offers an alternative to the dead-end view of the isolated, decontextualized, and stagnant façade, and instead promotes constant temporal and spatial movement and exchange, in other words between present and future, and between Mexico and the world. The goal here is the improvement of society, yet this future improvement tends to blend with the present problems to be solved.

As critics have noted, O'Gorman's views on architecture would shift quite dramatically in the late 1930s, with his move toward realist painting. His pessimism, particularly with respect to the Mexican cityscape and society, would become increasingly pronounced in later decades, as is made amply evident in many of his paintings and murals, apocalyptic visions in which heavy industry takes on organic, monstrous forms, in bizarre combinations of mechanical and animal representation.[26] The disturbing reciprocity and blurring of lines between the organic and the inorganic, which eventually becomes the hallmark of O'Gorman's work as a painter, would also seem to reflect the relationship between human bodies and the cities they inhabit, and the enigma of whether the built environment exists because of the human population it ostensibly serves, or whether the human population exists to serve the increasingly monstrous built environment. This notable blurring of divisions between human bodies and urban structures in O'Gorman's painting may remind us of a tendency noted in the earlier school-hygiene inspections, in which faulty or damaged school buildings are linked materially and causally to the illnesses, disabilities, and related conditions affecting schoolchildren. In this sense, O'Gorman's troubled expressions of monstrosity in painting, as the industrial cityscape evolves through its appropriation of human and animal forms, echoes the prior work of school physicians, who navigated continuities between buildings and bodies in their pursuit of a hygienic pedagogical universe. In many of O'Gorman's paintings, capitalism, rather than purely state-sponsored initiatives, appears as the source of the destructive and monstrous forces at work, yet the structural paradox of a self-regulating space in which the human and the inorganic operate within the same continuum is nonetheless still present.

Similarly, the authors of *Utopía–no utopía* emphasize that O'Gorman's explicit disenchantment with state ideology, evident in the later paintings, was in fact already present in his earlier architectural work, including his design of primary schools at the beginning of the 1930s. They note, for example, that the school, as a hygienic space controlled by a hierarchy of authorities, resembles a laboratory: "los gérmenes se quedan afuera, con los borrachos y los imbéciles. La escuela es una pequeña fortaleza científica. En este sentido, se asemeja bastante a las violentas anti-utopías que pintó O'Gorman años después: cerrada, autosuficiente, artificial" (25). [Germs stay outside, with the drunkards and imbeciles. The school is a miniature scientific fortress. In this sense, it resembles the violent anti-utopias that O'Gorman painted years later: closed, self-sufficient, artificial.] Viewing O'Gorman's school architecture as troubled precursor to the dystopic scenes of his later paintings underscores the impasse I have discussed here between mechanics and expression, and its evocation of a paradoxical relationship to the hygienic aesthetics of the state.

Along similar lines, Adriana Zavala reads O'Gorman's classic 1949 painting *Landscape of Mexico City* as a critique of the state, and not as a celebration of urban modernity, which has been the more traditional reading of this work. For example, she describes the indigenous laborer featured in the painting, standing next to a masonry wall, trowel in hand, with a blueprint for a modern, steel frame structure in the other hand. Clearly the brick-and-rubble masonry technology evoked by the wall and trowel would be obsolete and unequal to the task of creating the structure featured on the blueprint (495–96). This and other details in the painting, such as the fact that the sixteenth-century map of México-Tenochtitlán, held by two hands in the painting's foreground, is actually upside-down with respect to the cityscape depicted beyond it (504), suggest the artist's pessimistic emphasis on an incommensurability between the rapidly modernizing city in the context of the so-called Mexican miracle, and Mexico's historically grounded, material reality.[27] Although O'Gorman painted this work well after the period in which his functionalist schools were designed and built, the example fits in a larger trajectory of the architect's complex and conflicting relationship to the state-sponsored vision in which he participated.

These critical voices suggest that O'Gorman's pessimism regarding state ideologies, including the projects of hygiene and eugenics, emerges long before his explicitly dystopic paintings of Mexican industrial cityscapes. O'Gorman's conflictive spirit is clearly present in the early 1930s, and in fact tends to reveal itself precisely through a rhetoric of technical hygiene, though paradoxically it is also the discourse of hygiene that most closely allies O'Gorman with the state-sponsored projects, such as the building of schools, in which he played a key role. The importance of this particular location of conflict in O'Gorman's work, and by extension in the politics of architecture and aesthetics in post-revolutionary Mexico, lies not only in the fact that it reveals O'Gorman's relatively early disenchantment with the state, but in the possibility it opens for a reading of hygiene as rhetoric both within and beyond officially sanctioned state discourse, and indeed for a reconsideration of the boundaries of that discourse. In this way, the question of disability, expressed through emphasis on precise problems of incommensurability between bodies and buildings, becomes central to the conditions and limits of state projects in hygiene, architecture, and pedagogy.

In his pessimistic depiction of the modernizing Mexican cityscape, O'Gorman reveals cracks in the metaphorical edifice of a state-sponsored rhetoric of progress as hygiene that would seamlessly tie present to future and human bodies to urban infrastructure. The architect's critical perspective on hygiene highlights the violent and paradoxical qualities of its movement, and its perpetuation of material and social inequalities. Despite offering a highly critical lens on the roles of urban planning and architecture in the development of Mexican cityscapes and society, these texts do not suggest the abandonment of hygiene as a mode of logic and aesthetics. Instead, they reveal the ways in which hygiene itself marks sites of conflict. Rather than disappearing, technical hygiene as rhetoric recurs in O'Gorman's work, insisting on itself as both "Mexican problem" and "Mexican solution." Ultimately, the effect of O'Gorman's skeptical and partial participation in an overarching discourse of building the city for the benefit of a future Mexico is an explosion of the notion of hygiene in the context of this discourse. In this sense, O'Gorman's voice takes hygiene beyond the showcasing of national programs of streamlined health and progress and reveals its dilemmas in the material details of building design and city planning. Although O'Gorman remained in practice until 1936 as a functionalist architect, whose projects generally dovetailed with the government program of building for a modernizing Mexican future, his writings of the 1930s and his abandonment of architecture in 1936 ultimately speak to a more complex and critical relationship with nationalist revolutionary discourse.

The problems and conflicts O'Gorman brings to light in his analyses testify to the asymmetrical quality of hygiene as rhetoric, and by extension to the persistent role of disability in the material and figurative spaces of the built environment. Just as O'Gorman's functionalist designs of the 1930s began to invert and blur expected oppositions between interior and exterior, his critical approach to practical dilemmas of urban planning and building shows that the post-revolutionary nationalist discourse of hygiene and eugenics is prone to unexpected inversion and elasticity. The troubled rhetorical spaces of hygiene, those of schools and of the institutions of psychopedagogy, thus continually reopen themselves, revealing landscapes of bodies and buildings as irreducible to the programmatic eugenicist logic of biological and social improvement.

Disability and the Cityscape

At the time of O'Gorman's writing on the dilemmas of technical hygiene and functionalism and his design of Mexico City primary schools, physicians of the DPH continued to conduct their laborious inspections, filling charts with the documentation of student measurements, health conditions, and buildings in need of repair. The work of these physician-inspectors also included the elaboration of a discourse of hygiene, as we have seen, in which the human body functioned in causal and contiguous relation with its social and material infrastructure. Disability in this context circulates through spatial and temporal coordinates, defined by the paradoxical continuity between problems and their solutions, as would also be the case in the organizational structure of the National Institute of Psychopedagogy. The repetitive nature of the inspection charts suggests compliance with a systematic approach to state-sponsored hygiene. Yet one might wonder how the carefully accumulated documentation of illness, disability, childhood ailments, structural deficiencies in school buildings, and recommended responses could be seamlessly incorporated into a hygienic and aesthetic national future. Perhaps like O'Gorman, the reader may begin to question the apparently harmonious movement between biomechanical problems—with the seemingly endless documentation they require—and the triumph of a modern, hygienic architecture that would stride boldly from present to future.

My attention to the figure of the school physician from the beginning of this chapter focused initially on the contemporary reader's potential surprise on encountering a medical doctor attending interchangeably to both the inspection of buildings and the health of human beings. Emphasis on this moment of surprise is intended to foreground the appearance of incongruity and its failed or successful resolution. As when old furniture or buildings are conventionally termed "rickety," or when the segregation and education of "abnormals" comes to define a central component of state-sponsored research on the Mexican child, here the instance of surprise—or perhaps anger or fear—signals a space of conflict, transition, or asymmetry in the logic of hygiene, much as O'Gorman's discourse would betray his own indignation at the incommensurability between technical problems and aesthetic solutions. Disability emerges within the landscape of school hygiene, not only because physicians are charged with diagnosing differences in students, but because the inevitably imperfect work of diagnosis comes to define and saturate social life, pedagogical methods, and building codes, extending between abstract and material forms, bodies and buildings, problems and solutions. The persistence of disability across this landscape, along with technical attention to human and mechanical flaws, shapes yet ultimately refuses to conform to the broader logic of a national and hygienic pedagogy.

Four

Biotypology and Perception—
The Prose of Statistics

ℭℬℭ

¿Cómo es posible que prohibamos la procreacion cuando no sabemos si en un caso determinado el hijo resultará con la misma condición patológica? Y esto no lo sabemos porque no hemos precisado y fundamentado nuestro análisis del cuadro clínico, en una palabra, no tenemos los datos para una elaboración que favorezca la conclusión fatal de la generación patológica . . . En México no tenemos estadística (6).

[How is it possible that we prohibit procreation when we don't know in a particular case whether a child will have the same pathological condition as the parent? And we don't know this because we haven't sharpened and solidified the analysis of our clinical picture; in a word, we don't have the data for an elaboration that would uphold the fatal conclusion of pathological generation. . . . In Mexico we have no statistics.]

Eugenics and Statistics

Writing in 1933 in the *Bulletin of the Mexican Eugenics Society*, the engineer García de Mendoza took issue with a colleague who had argued that women with tuberculosis should be encouraged to avoid motherhood until fully cured. Here, as was common in debates of the day, much of the dilemma centered on whether conditions were transmitted from parent to child via inheritance, or through contagion. In addition, however, as García de Mendoza underscored in his essay, the problem became one of insufficient clinical knowledge, a simple lack of information. If physicians and eugenicists were to admit that the transmission of an undesirable condition did not occur in every case, or that outcomes were not easily predictable, what could they offer to the public to uphold the validity of the eugenic undertaking? In other words, how could they argue for particular medical and scientific practices if such practices held no clear guarantee of a more desirable future? In a sense, the problem García de Mendoza underscores is not an entirely unfamiliar one. We might wonder here how suspicions or affirmations of doubt, uncertainty, and error have continued to impact our contemporary perceptions of bodies, health, and reproductive futures. How, for example, do public perceptions of autism, schizophrenia, obesity, diabetes, or—especially at the time of completion of this book—contagious respiratory illnesses, shift as new research contests the findings of previous studies, or when cumulative research seems to offer more doubt than certainty? In this chapter I consider perceptions of corporeal difference in the first decades of the Mexican post-revolutionary period as mediated by both quantitative methodologies, such as statistics, and conditions of embodied experience. This mode of disability contingency—or the displacement, mediation, and framing of difference—is in many ways specific to the texts at hand, yet is also offered as a template for broader reflection on the persistent dilemmas of doubt, error, and sociohistorically conditioned observation that continue to mark perceptions of disability as experience, diagnosis, or concept. Disability is thus mediated here by the desire for knowledge and human "improvement," and by the uncertainty regarding what can and cannot be known.

Projects of hygiene in post-revolutionary Mexico were promoted through the enthusiasm and fervor of public-health professionals and educators, who believed that a better national future could be achieved through improved standards in public hygiene, and through instruction in healthful and moral behavior, among other areas. Excessive alcohol consumption, for example, as discussed in chapter 2, was associated with negative reproductive outcomes, hence the energetic promotion of anti-alcohol campaigns by state officials and healthcare workers. As we have seen, however, such associations tend to be marked by contingency, and by an element of the unknown, as reproductive pasts and futures are never fully available for examination. In a related sense, if the National Institute of Psychopedagogy and its predecessor, the Department of Psychopedagogy and Hygiene, insisted on their mission of obtaining complete knowledge of the Mexican child, as discussed in the previous chapter, the copious measurements and charts documenting degrees of abnormality or irregularity in schoolchildren underscored the difficulty of ever capturing a full picture. Similarly, the causal logic structuring explanations of abnormality, as when poor school furniture design is said to cause spinal deformity in children, or when a family history of illness is said to reduce a child's intelligence, tends to serve as conjecture rather than as verifiable evidence of cause and effect.

The paradox of eugenics and hygiene in this context lies in a rhetoric of unwavering certainty in the pursuit of a better future, in combination with admittedly incomplete information. Yet as it turns out, the larger problem was not so much a lack of statistics, as García de Mendoza had suggested, but rather the growing role of chance and uncertainty in statistical developments of the period. This paradox is not unique to post-revolutionary Mexico but can be traced to the nineteenth-century origins of eugenics and its intimate ties to the rise of statistics. Ian Hacking discusses Sir Francis Galton's key role in the development of statistics, as well as his invention of eugenics, noting in particular how Galton observed that the statistical law of error, or regression to the mean, corresponded to a normal curve (186). This law, as Galton would write, "reigns with serenity and in complete effacement amidst the wildest confusion" (ctd. in Hacking, 2), thus underscoring the paradoxical interdependence of apparent determinism and chance. As Galton showed in his studies of human height, measurements of a population over time would reveal a tendency toward average values, or what Galton called "reversion to mediocrity" (regression to the mean). The resulting normal curve, or "bell curve," would emerge, not despite multiple combined elements of chance, but because of them, although Galton persisted in trying to identify the specific influence of heredity on the outcome (Hacking 185; Louçã 659).

Eugenics and statistics, developed through the work of Galton and continued by Karl Pearson and Ronald Fisher, are inextricably bound together in their histories, as evidenced not merely by the scientists' championing of the eugenics cause, but by their research in genetics and heredity, and specifically by the increasing importance ascribed to the roles of error and variation in the study of populations. As Francisco Louçã succinctly puts it, "Eugenics sought to domesticate error. Statistics was a tool that could be used for that purpose since it sought to identify the error and its distribution" (679). Despite the intertwined history and missions of these disciplines, eugenics, in its rhetorical uses, at times reveals points of conflict with the tools of statistics to which it is indebted. This is the case, for example, when nineteenth-century Mexican hygienists sought to apply the statistical work of Adolphe Quetelet to understand and better regulate the Mexican population, specifically by attending to the causes of pathology. As Laura Cházaro has argued, Mexican physicians focused on the distance between statistical principles and the realities of poverty, illness, and infant mortality in the Mexican context, ultimately using statistics not as an objective tool of diagnosis, but as a means to uphold moral sanctions against extramarital sex and other practices viewed as antihygienic (75–76). In this way, the enthusiastic and eugenicist project of the physicians attempts to ground itself in quantitative data, but ultimately exceeds the statistical model, revealing incongruencies between the proposed methodology and a more powerful moral imperative.

Uncertain Encounters

The present chapter reads disability contingency through a series of four inter-related dynamic encounters. In each case corporeal difference animates and impacts cultural and scientific production of the post-revolutionary period. The *first* of these is the encounter between the projects of eugenics and the "prose of statistics," defined here as the communication of mathematical and scientific knowledge to the public. Such communicative efforts take place in the above-cited text by García de Mendoza, and in the work of forensic psychiatrist and biotypologist José Gómez Robleda, which I will analyze at greater length in the second part of the chapter. Biotypology in Mexico was influenced by Italian scientists, including Gómez Robleda's teacher and col-laborator, Ada d'Aloja. It involved the study and measurement of morpho-logical and psychological features, as well as heredity, which together would produce a "biotype." While eugenicists tended to focus on immoral or anti-hygienic practices as the cause of illnesses or "defects," biotypologists often pointed to patterns of socioeconomic causality behind negatively perceived biological outcomes. Yet in both cases, writers emphasized particular indi-vidual or population traits as negative, as well as the desire to somehow avoid or erase those traits. In this sense, projects of biotypology operate within the broader framework of eugenicist thought.[1] As Yolanda Eraso notes, "Types thus became the result of the combination of continuing variables, for which the English Biometric School, cofounded by Francis Galton and his disciple Karl Pearson, largely contributed the statistical methods" (795).[2] Biotypology in this context may also be said to bridge the fields of eugenics and statistics, and serves as the site of both fusion and uneasy crossover between these areas, or between the impetus to "improve" and the uncertainty of knowledge.

Gómez Robleda served as head of the Psychophysiology Service of the National Institute of Psychopedagogy, discussed in chapter 3, but would later shift his focus from urban schoolchildren to rural indigenous populations, in projects stemming from his positions at the Instituto de Investigaciones Sociales, and the Escuela Nacional de Medicina at the Universidad Nacio-nal Autónoma de México (UNAM). Throughout this time span, Gómez Robleda published occasional works of fiction, including both short novels of limited circulation and a lengthier literary textbook intended for sixth-grade classrooms. The juxtaposition of these literary experiments, by turns tongue in cheek and overtly didactic, with technical works of biotypology, grounded in the obligatory accumulation of data and statistical analysis, reveals the close intertwining of the biotypological enterprise and the author's aesthetic interests. The shift between the technical and the literary, or between scientific and aesthetic concerns, thus represents a *second* key encounter in this chapter. Like the projects of eugenics, these literary texts propose a moral message which enlivens the author's technical, scientific emphasis, allowing him to communicate to a potentially diverse readership.

A *third* encounter central to my argument here occurs between the perceptions of disability and of racialization in the texts. In one sense, race and disability frequently appear in parallel representations, for example when both categories are viewed as indices of social oppression or as the cause of negative self-image, as occurs at different points in Gómez Robleda's writing. In another sense, each category may refer to the other, as when Gómez Robleda discusses the Tarasco indigenous people's "autism" as a mode of introversion specific to their worldview and living conditions. Within this framework of mutual referencing, disability and race become co-constitutive, while each category negotiates its constructed or contingent status, in tension with its material embodiment. In this way, perceptions and experiences of racialization and disability enact a dynamic tension, a *fourth* encounter between lived, embodied experience and the contingency of negatively marked corporeal difference. My analysis of this process borrows from Frantz Fanon's phenomenological approach to racialization, to be discussed further in the chapter.

The four encounters approached in this chapter, between eugenics and statistics, literary aesthetics and science, race and disability, and lived embodiment and perceptual, sociohistorical contingency, are not parallel structures, but work in an interwoven fashion. The contingency of disability, as a continuing theme throughout this book, emerges in the present chapter through the complex and at times conflicted dialogue between elements of these encounters, between the definitive and the uncertain, or the intimate and the distant. For example, in the case of eugenics and statistics, the documentation and desire to control human differences coincides with the recognition that differences may be approached indirectly through mathematically derived estimates but never actually measured or captured, due to an inevitable margin of error. In this way, numerical data and other forms of documentation offer a kind of perceptual scaffolding, through which disability only appears to materialize. Or, in the encounter between lived embodiment and sociohistorical contingency, the negative experience or impression of difference may manifest as caused by external factors such as poverty and colonialist oppression, and hence as not fully integral to the individual person. This structure reflects the continuity of a variant of contingency approached in prior chapters. Diego Rivera's sketch on the transgenerational results of alcoholism in a rural setting, discussed in chapter 2, suggests this process, as human subjects are depicted as victims, damaged by a noxious substance and by capitalist exploitation. In the present chapter, I emphasize the specific role of the perception of such differences, as well as the violence inherent in this process, at times linked to the use of statistics and the collection of observable data. Readers may recall that the problem of visual perception in eugenic discourse was also approached in chapter 1, in relation to diverse narrative and readerly positionalities, as when Eduardo Urzaiz notes that "madness" is just a matter of point of view, or when the notions of racial difference and racism are mediated by competing transnational perspectives. In the present chapter, the question of perception, informed by Fanon, focuses on the fluidity between body and world, or skin and sociohistorical determinants. In addition, perception is framed here at key points through the figure of the biotypologist and the work of scientific observation and quantitative measurements.

I consider disability contingency in these encounters through the metaphor of a scaffolding—or supporting structure—that gestures toward and supports the hypothetical weight of a given object. Differences are marked as the result of a perceptual, causal, or quantitative structure, which offers them a tangibility that they might otherwise lack. Disabilities and racial differences thus emerge through signposted historical processes and intersubjective exchanges and acts of observation, in relation to projected numerical data or to one another. Their negative charge works in an ambivalent sense, intermittently merged with or separate from the human subjects that these categories describe. The framework of contingency contributes to the objectification of the racialized or disabled person, while at the same time signaling a tentative escape route from derogatory object-status. This scaffolding model does not deny the materiality of disability, but rather builds on the conditions of its perceptions, at times becoming coterminous with lived embodiment, as when a seemingly provisional structure turns out to be a permanent one.

In the next section of the chapter, I focus on the role of statistics and quantitative data in eugenics projects, returning to the context of the eugenics *Bulletin* in which García de Mendoza decried a lack of statistics in Mexico, to show how eugenic fervor enlivens quantitative methods, which in turn seek to define human differences. From here, I turn to the encounter between racialization and disability, and the ways in which the perceptual and sociohistorical contingency of difference frames and shapes embodied experience, with reference to the work of Fanon. Following this analysis, I consider how Fanon's phenomenological reading of racialized embodiment offers a dialogue with key interventions in disability studies, and inflects my reading of Gómez Robleda's biotypology, both in his scientific research and his fiction writing. My discussion of Gómez Robleda's works begins with his study of the Tarasco indigenous group, which I juxtapose with Leo Kanner's research on autism of the same period. I then move to some of Gómez Robleda's works of fiction, a sixth-grade textbook, and a short novel of criminal sociology. This reading returns to the discussion of Fanon's embodiment of racialized perception, to explore the dilemma of the intertwined facets of skin, psyche, perception, and history. Here I also consider the problem of error in science and its links to the contingency of disability.

The Prose of Statistics

As we have seen, discourses of eugenics and statistics, while at times divergent in their emphases, share a common history. The quantification of human traits based on their assigned differential values, in reference to statistical models, generally tends to devalue and dehumanize disability and racial difference, by operating through the reference point of the "normal." This is particularly the case within a framework of eugenic discourse, based on hierarchies of strength, intelligence, and other measured categories.[3] Yet in addition, the juxtaposition of human differences with the more abstract and indeterminate qualities of statistical data foregrounds other processes. In the present analysis, the rhetorical uses of statistics tend to work through a lively humanization of what otherwise might seem to be cold, numerical data. It is not merely that emphasis on numbers dehumanizes human differences, although this does occur, but that the numbers and related data themselves begin to acquire a more dynamic and human affect through engagement with human bodies and emotive expression. The role of disability and racial difference in these works is often to activate encounters between data and desire, setting in motion processes of measurement and observation in which numbers approach but can never fully account for the bodies to which they refer.

Written presumably for his fellow members of the Mexican Eugenics Society, García de Mendoza's admission that he lacked data, and his expression of uncertainty as in his statement, "in Mexico we have no statistics," were in fact not typical strategies in the texts of the Society's *Bulletin* of the early 1930s. More often, contributors insisted on the clear attainability of this brighter future, echoing the organization's slogan, "para el mejoramiento de

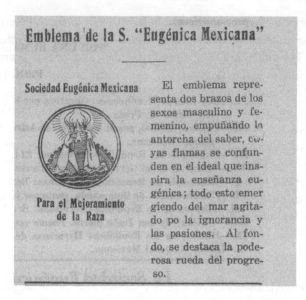

Fig. 17. Emblem from the Mexican Eugenics Society for the Improvement of the Race, published in each edition of the Society's Bulletin. The text on the right reads as follows: "El emblema representa dos brazos de los sexos masculine y femenino, empuñando la antorcha del saber, cuyas flamas se confunden en el ideal que inspira la enseñanza eugénica; todo esto emergiendo del mar agitado por la ignorancia y las pasiones. Al fondo, se destaca la ponderosa rueda del progreso." [The emblem represents two arms of the masculine and feminine sexes, holding up the torch of knowledge, whose flames merge into the ideal that eugenic teaching inspires; all this emerges from the sea, agitated by ignorance and passions. In the background, the powerful wheel of progress stands out.] Sociedad Eugénica Mexicana para el mejoramiento de la raza, Boletín num 8, 6 de oct. de 1932, p. 2. Caja 35505, "educación sexual," Archivo General de la Nación, folio 225 vuelta.

la raza" [for the improvement of the race] and the optimism of its logo, the triumphantly raised male and female arms united in a flame. The first issue of the bulletin from 1932, for example, includes an article on the "Eugenics week" organized by the Ateneo de Ciencias y Artes de México, and opens with a citation from a poem by Horacio Zuñiga: "Era de seda la caricia del ambiente . . . siempre subiendo y penetrando más y más / cual si tendiera el firme vuelo de una flecha. En las entrañas luminosas del cristal." [The atmosphere's silken caress . . . always rising, penetrating more and more / as if it extended an arrow's firm flight. In the crystal's luminous heart.] The author of the article goes on to describe the activities of the eugenicists:

Arriba estaba en un arrobo al infinito, abajo un puñado de seres vivientes ávidos de ver la sombra prodigiosa y en medio de la bruma hacen un paréntesis para también seguir subiendo y penetrando más y más en los estudios de la Eugenesia y así el primer día (lunes 26 de junio) se inician las labores cual si se hundiera el firme vuelo de una flecha en las entrañas luminosas del cristal. (Dr. Anastasio Vergara)[4]

[Above, in rapture to infinity, below a handful of living beings, anxious to see the prodigious shadow, and in the midst of the fog they paused to also continue rising and penetrating more and more in the study of Eugenics and thus the first day (Monday, June 26) begins the work, like the firm flight of an arrow sinking into the crystal's luminous heart.]

From this poetic framework the author proceeds to include details of some of the presentations given by the eugenics specialists, with emphasis on topics such as heredo-syphilis, prostitution, cancer of female reproductive organs, immigration and the role of the state, and love. This striking combination of medical knowledge and dissemination with an exalted and flowery poetics marks the eugenic enterprise with an aesthetic orientation bordering on the spiritual, but nonetheless firmly guided by specific public-health goals. Despite the awkward quality of these lyrical efforts, the juxtaposition does not appear contradictory or strained, perhaps because so often it is the physicians themselves who assume the poetic voice, and because the work of eugenics becomes inseparable from the process through which its ideals and practical measures are disseminated to the general public. The transmission of information must compel the reader to action; hence, in the above example, the somewhat crude metaphor of the arrow reaching its destination doubles to signify both education and the act of sexual reproduction.

Even in cases where authors are less exuberant and absolutist about the promise of eugenics, literary language still serves their purpose. This is the case in a 1933 text from the same bulletin, in which Fernando Ocaranza affirms, "me coloco al margen de la teleología y de la posición finalista . . . después del nacimiento, termina la eugenesia, empieza la higiene y la sociología" (29). [I situate myself at the margins of teleology and the finalist position . . . after birth, eugenics ends; hygiene and sociology begin.] Yet he also describes the process of heredity in explicitly visual terms:

consideremos . . . al individuo mas reciente de un linaje, como si estuviese en pie entre los dos carriles de una vía ferrea, la cual, vista hacia atrás, nos da la ilusión de que los carriles se aproximan, hasta llegar un momento en que se confunden y se pierden, y no en el infinito; sino a una distancia apreciable o próxima; esto quiere decir que el individuo actual de un linaje, sufre principalmente la influencia de sus antepasados inmediatos y que ella misma se atenua en los anteriores y se pierde en los remotos. (28)

[Let us consider . . . the most recent individual of a lineage, as if he were standing between two railroad tracks, which viewed backward, give us the illusion that the tracks come together, until reaching a point where they merge and are lost, not in infinity, but rather at an appreciable or proximate distance. This means that the current individual of the lineage is primarily affected by the influence of his most immediate ancestors, and that this influence lessens in relation to prior ancestors and disappears with respect to remote ones.]

Through this didactic approach, Ocaranza balances the rather poignant image of human genealogy on a railroad track with a sense of caution against projecting theories of influence too far back in history. Ultimately, the passage reassures the reader that heredity, correctly understood, does influence biology. In addition, use of the railroad metaphor lends a sense of certainty to the discussion at hand; even if hereditary influence is not said to continue indefinitely, the familiar, visual representation of the past links explicitly to the human body of the present. Strangely, despite the solidity and symmetry of railroad tracks extending into the past, the writer suggests that our perceptual illusion of their fusion and disappearance offers a more accurate metaphor for heredity than do the tracks themselves.

The engineer García de Mendoza's tone reflects less certainty regarding the eugenicists' scientific knowledge and the ways it should be applied to human populations. His viewpoint differs from those of many of his colleagues, both because of his self-reflexive, critical tone, and because unlike the arguments put forward by other authors in the *Bulletin*, his focuses directly on the question of statistics and on the problems of unavailable data and insufficient methodological tools. His emphasis on statistics reflects the growing importance of this field at the time, and inevitably, its impact in the area of eugenic thinking. Statistics, understood simply as the collection of information, was not new in 1930s Mexico. Yet important developments in mathematical statistics, as exemplified in the work of Ronald Fisher, who published the highly influential *Statistical Methods for Research Workers* in

1925, were rapidly changing the field. It is likely that García de Mendoza's emphasis on a lack of statistics in Mexico was a reference to a discrepancy between such international advances in statistics, and Mexicans' relative lack of access to the new methods of data analysis.[5] As David Salzburg explains, a key aspect of new developments in statistics in the 1920s and '30s was Fisher's approach, which held that a statistical distribution is an abstract formula, and not an actual collection of data.[6]

Although García de Mendoza recommends a properly calculated, statistics-based approach to the eugenic enterprise, he nonetheless shares his colleagues' energy and enthusiasm for the work at hand, simply transferring his attention from human bodies and hygiene policies to a quantitative methodological framework. He grows exultant when describing the promise of statistics as a model through which to overcome the current state of insufficient data. In his opinion, "en México no tenemos estadística" [in Mexico we have no statistics], yet from here, the passage suddenly veers toward an exuberant crescendo:

> Al lado de la estadística es necesario emplear la teoría de las probabilidades que, juntamente con el azar y su eliminación, nos podrá dar las bases necesarias para poder averiguar las medidas tanto aritméticas como ponderadas, como geométricas; la mediana y el modo; así como nos podrá servir para conocer las variaciones o desviaciones estadísticas, las razones, índices y tasas, y aprovechando estos elementos podamos llegar al cálculo de las probabilidades a fijar con exacta claridad las curvas de frecuencia, el error probable, el error medio cuadrático; así como por medio del cálculo de correlación, podemos determinar los coeficientes de dependencia y de correlación así como el índice de dependencia. Por supuesto que todos estos datos nos servirán para llevar a la práctica los diagramas y los índices de diagramas. (7)

> [Along with statistics it is necessary to employ probability theory, which, together with chance and its elimination, will provide us with the necessary basis from which to determine the mathematical, geometric and weighted measurements, the mean and the mode, just as it will allow us to determine statistical variations or divergences, ratios, indices and rates, and taking advantage of these elements we will be able to achieve the calculation of probabilities, precisely identifying frequency curves, probable error, mean square error; just as by calculating the "correlation" we can determine the dependency and correlation

coefficients, and the dependency index. Of course, all of this data will help us to put the diagrams and indices of diagrams into practice.]

The author's rhetorical strategy centers on two crucial elements: an insistence on a lack of evidence, that is, on what is not (yet) known, and an enthusiasm based not on the desire for the reproduction of strong and healthy bodies, as would be typical in the prose of many eugenicists, but instead on the techniques of probability and statistics themselves. This enthusiasm materializes through the protracted extension of the text's longest sentence, its multiple clauses creating a chain of methodological steps that carry the reader from uncertainty toward the promise of quantifiable data. The sentence concludes with only the abstract expression of this data, "coefficients" and "index." The "exact clarity" upon which the author insists contrasts here with the proliferation of elements in the text, including the notion of probable error.

García de Mendoza's technique of squeezing as much statistical terminology as possible into a few lines without actually applying the terms to any data creates a strangely self-referential process. Here, the author grows increasingly delighted by the tools of probability that approach but do not finally provide numerical answers. The text offers us the possibility of graphic images, curves and other diagrams, as a response to the desire to contain all possible errors. This desire, however, becomes self-sustaining as it produces further indices; in the spirit of the new statistics, the author moves away from the measurement of actual objects in the world, and toward mathematical formulas that might only approach such measurements.

Reading this narrative from a twenty-first-century perspective, one might be struck by the combination of dense statistical terminology and the sheer enthusiasm of the author. Statistics, after all, are not generally known for generating much excitement beyond the realm of specialists in the field. Moreover, the written discussion of statistics is typically accompanied by charts or numerically expressed formulas, which offer a more concrete expression, either of actual data or of how a particular method may be put into practice. In the above-cited text, however, the narrator's emotion appeals directly to the reader, and saturates the discussion, underscoring the incongruity between precision of technique and lack of data, while appearing to compensate for the presumed insufficiencies of this model. The style of García de Mendoza's "statistical" prose works through its transmission of enthusiasm, which supersedes the promised numerical content of the indices to which it refers. The apparent novelty of such references to probability and statistics in the Mexican context of the early 1930s, in combination with the author's enthusiastic and accelerated tone, highlight the ephemeral quality of the data in question. Statistical data, in this model, remain out of reach, yet provoke emotional responses, and thus become inseparable from the affective operations and the bodies through which they circulate.

The emotional exuberance of García de Mendoza's statistical prose finds its echo in the writing of some of his colleagues in the eugenics *Bulletin*. As we have seen, other articles in the same publication applied enthusiastic and even poetically inspired language to the eugenic endeavor, generally centering their arguments on sexual reproductive practices and dangers. In focusing primarily on the work of statistics itself, and not as much on the human subjects to which such methods might be applied, García de Mendoza retains the inspired energy of his colleagues but frames his argument through the abstraction of quantitative processes. The human bodies themselves have largely disappeared from the page, but the fervor of improvement they inspire remains, now contained through statistical methods. In this way, what might otherwise appear as dry data and methodology is enlivened by human differences and the desire to "improve the race." In its drive to document and contain human differences, eugenic energy sparks the animation of statistical data, while statistical methods promise to circumscribe the chaos of proliferating error in human populations, though without ever fully defining the objects of their analysis. In this context, disability turns out to be tightly bound to a range of public-health practices and their discursive manifestations, in both numerical and verbalized forms.

Racialization, Disability, Perception

As discussed in prior chapters, disability is produced and experienced in close correlation with the racial categories of *mestizaje* and indigeneity in the Mexican post-revolutionary context. I now return to a closer look at the mechanisms of this connection, in relation to the contingency and framing of differences. The intertwining of racialization and disability suggests not only a cross-referencing of stereotypes, whereby one category of human difference comes to be associated with another, but also a more deeply rooted cross-fertilization, through which the structure of causality used to explain the origins and qualities of a given category of difference acts in turn to produce the logic and representations of another such category. In this sense, race and disability become co-constitutive, and give further form to the prose of statistics.

We have seen that emphasis on quantitative data, and on formulas that do not refer to specific objects but only to estimates, ranges, or indices, produces a kind of animated numerical scaffolding through which human differences appear in an abstract and indirect sense, contingent on statistical methods. Yet also key here is the moment of perception, whether of bodies or of the data referring to them. Reading the data, or reading the body, often in combination with the recognition that particular conditions and histories have produced what appears as corporeal difference, creates a related form of contingency, in which the difference emerges as the outcome of those readings and histories, congealed in a visual encounter. Frantz Fanon's phenomenological approach to the perception and experience of racial difference will further inform this framework, revealing additional nuance as well as potential pitfalls to this structure of contingency.

Perhaps the most frequently cited portion of Fanon's text refers to an episode in which the author finds himself the object of a white child's gaze, made evident through the repeated phrase, "Look, a Negro!" (111). In his narration of this episode, Fanon makes explicit the violent shift from the personal "corporeal schema" of Merleau-Ponty's phenomenology, to a "historico-racial schema," in which his body and self are relocated as objects through a partially external frame of reference. As he writes: "On that day, completely dislocated, unable to be abroad with the other, the white man who unmercifully imprisoned me, I took myself far off from my own presence, far indeed, and made myself an object" (112). The process at work here may be described, to borrow from Fanon himself, as an "epidermalization of inferiority" (11), in which racism manifests through both the accumulated experience of personal and collective history, and through immediate perception at the level of the skin.[7] Fanon's engagement with and critique of Merleau-Ponty's *Phenomenology of Perception* builds on the centrality of corporeality to show that the experience of racism as violent othering is already written into black embodiment at key moments. "The corporeal schema crumbled, its place taken by a racial epidermal schema" (112) writes Fanon, thus revealing racial othering and objectification as integral to the experience of the black body. As Dilan Mahendran has noted, the racial epidermal schema takes precedence here over Merleau-Ponty's notion of body image as an implicitly universal experience of perceiving and being in the world (201).[8]

The structure of othering through which Fanon comes to perceive himself as object depends on a specific moment of perception, one that builds on the accumulated weight of violent history. At the same time, this perception takes place on and through the skin of the othered subject, and in this sense remains integral to his primordial self. Racialization is thus contingent on a historically determined act of perception, but at the same time turns out to be inseparable from the skin. It is interesting to note in Fanon that the role of contingency works to create a strange distance between the subject and his self-perception. The violence of racialization is both intimate, at the level of the skin, and sharply removed through the othering gaze. This distance, a contingency that might in some contexts be read as a line of flight from denigrated subjectivity, also paradoxically fragments the self and the experience of being in the world.

If this reading of Fanon allows for a closer look at the dilemma of contingency that structures racialization and corporeality, it may also remind us that Fanon's work offers important insight into disability studies scholarship. As Dan Goodley suggests, for example, the experiences of disabled people in the contemporary world are constructed through the reference point of the able-bodied; the "abled self" constructs the disabled subject as deficient, and perhaps more significantly, as Other. Goodley writes, "Our task then is, as Frantz Fanon would have it, to recapture the self from its position as Other" (640). However, attending to the points of contact between racialization and disability is a complex process. In the US context, as well as in Mexico and elsewhere, critiques of racism have been predetermined by the need to disassociate ethnic or racial difference from disability. Such critical operations may salvage ethnic or racial identities, or abandon them altogether, but in either case, they tend to retain a basic notion of humanism as inseparable from the unquestioned privileging of normality (Erevelles, *Disability and Difference* 31). For this reason, the work of disability studies includes rethinking the material-discursive sites of human qualification and disqualification, both mental and physical, through which normality has come to be located. Tobin Siebers's concept of human disqualification, through which disabled or other minority populations appear as biologically or naturally inferior, is useful here (24).[9] According to this reading, oppression is justified through the idea of natural inferiority, which involves glossing over the troping of differences. Approaching disability and untangling human disqualification through Fanon and Siebers includes negotiating corporeality and perception, and specifically the conundrum of the body itself as "natural." This is not only because, as Siebers suggests, the idea of inferiority construed as natural proves to be a trope of oppression that must be unpacked, but also because as we learn with Fanon, such tropes at certain moments of perception have become integral to the embodied self. The problem of contingency here, whether in perceptions of racial difference or disability, is both the sense of alienation it may produce, as Fanon shows, and paradoxically, the intimate self-awareness it enables.

In the context of scholarship on eugenics in Mexico, generally from the field of the history of science, the notion of racial improvement emerges frequently in relation to the use of statistics. "Race" is necessarily central, in the double sense of the population in general (*el pueblo* as *la raza* as in the nationalist discourse of *mestizaje*), and the series of phenotypic traits that supposedly reflect genetic continuity within particular ethnic groups. Disability, however, is not frequently mentioned, despite the prevalence in documents of the period of references to conditions that today would be called disabilities. Studies of the roles of eugenics, anthropometrics, and biotypology in Mexico have considered, for example, how tests of mental and physical capacity, as well as photographs, were used to describe and explain differences between ethnic groups, and to discuss the larger issue of "national character" (Urías Horcasitas, *Historias secretas* 56; Dorotinsky 332). We may recognize here how, within a racist agenda, markers of pathology have historically been associated with racialized groups. What is still missing, following Siebers, would be the recognition, in the same context, that particular human traits have been marked as undesirable, and that this undesirability has been posited as natural, given, and self-explanatory. As Fanon's engagement with the problem of perception and contingency shows us, however, it is not enough to denounce the constructed quality of corporeal markers. In considering the intertwined sites of disability and racialization, in the analysis of the work of Gómez Robleda to follow, it will also be necessary to consider more closely the intimate, material embodiments and perceptions of race and disability. In some cases, the materiality of one category—disability or race—may work as foil for the contingent, constructed, or imaginary quality of the other. At other moments, the constructed qualities of each category appear to build on one another, as mutually producing and inseparable differences.

The Face of the Tarascos

Associations between disability and racial difference are sometimes, but not always, present or explicit in documentation of eugenicist discourse in the Mexican context. In many cases in the 1920s and '30s, studies of schoolchildren and other population groups use no direct racial terminology. This is the case in José Gómez Robleda's 1937 study of the biological characteristics of proletariat schoolchildren, and in general in many DPH references to data on Mexico City schoolchildren, in which the mestizo category is implicit but not specified. In other instances, indigenous students are compared to groups of urban, proletariat schoolchildren through tests and anthropometric studies, with the possible implication that the children not specifically described as indigenous serve as control groups devoid of racial marking, or in other words, implicitly designated as mestizo.[10] Gómez Robleda's study of the indigenous Tarascos, in contrast, provides an intriguing example of the mutually producing relations between supposed racial and mental characteristics.

The biotypological study of the Tarasco, which Gómez Robleda undertook as head of a team of researchers from the Instituto de Investigaciones Sociales of the UNAM, included a number of photographs. These were taken by Raúl Estrada Discua, as part of a larger project with the goal of creating a photographic archive of the various indigenous groups throughout Mexico.[11] This initiative may in turn be read as part of a tendency that gained momentum in the late nineteenth century, through which photography became a privileged tool to document and represent human diversity, particularly through categories of racial and ethnic difference, criminality, and illness.[12] Gómez Robleda's study participates in this expansive photographic archive, yet as Deborah Dorotinsky notes, the biotypologist's approach to race is specifically geared toward social and environmental influence (359). As I will suggest further in my analysis of Gómez Robleda's study of the Tarasco, this contingency of racial difference expressed through a combined use of photographic archive, quantitative data, and verbal description, imbues the text with a somewhat open-ended set of meanings. As a result, categories of race and disability in this text refer indirectly to one another, while differences tend to be ambivalently suspended between numerical data, the visible body, and acts of perception.

In Gómez Robleda's 1941 article, "La cara de los Tarascos" [The Face of the Tarascos], which represents a fragment of his broader study of the Tarasco population, there is a photograph of a Tarasco man with the subtitle, "indiferencia, apatía, autismo," [indifference, apathy, autism.][13] The text includes the explanation that because of bodily measurements of the Tarasco people, and of their sensory, auditory, and visual capacities, for which the author includes numerical data, the Tarascos tend toward introversion and a lack of contact or openness toward the world around them, a reduced communicative capacity, and what the author terms "autism." Use of this term in particular as part of a racial and visual classification of human subjects may be surprising to the contemporary reader, especially considering its increasingly common mainstream usage as a designator of mental condition.[14] The definition of "autism" as a form of introversion dates to 1911, yet in the late 1930s and 1940s, the

Fig. 18. Photograph of a Tarasco man with the subtitle "indiferencia, apatía, autism" [indifference, apathy, autism]. José Gómez Robleda, "La cara de los Tarascos" *Revista Mexicana de Sociología*, vol. 3, no. 2, 1941, pp. 83–91, between pages 90 and 91. Universidad Nacional Autónoma de México, Hemeroteca Nacional de México.

Indiferencia, apatía, autismo

psychiatrist Leo Kanner was involved in the first systematic study of "autistic" children, whom he described in terms of their repeated acts, lack of human interaction, and limited verbal skills. Both Kanner and Gómez Robleda focus on the overarching, hypothetical causality of the conditions they observe, and speculate on the relationship between innate condition and environmental influence; both point out that "autism" is not an indication of a lack of intelligence. Kanner's seminal paper on autistic children was published in 1943, two years after Gómez Robleda's article on the Tarasco. Although there is no evidence that the two were aware of one another's work, their research in each case occurs in a context of evolving approaches to cognitive difference and to hereditary causality in medical science. In this sense, the role of "autism" and its shifting meanings represents a potential meeting point between these texts, and merits further scrutiny.

At the time of Gómez Robleda's writing, an earlier notion of autism as a "mode of thinking" associated with schizophrenia (McGuire 29) arguably still predominated in the Mexican context. As Andrés Ríos Molina describes in his approach to the history of schizophrenia in Mexico, Eugen Bleuler's 1911 concept of schizophrenia, which would extend to impact psychiatric theory and treatment in Mexico, included autism as one of its symptoms. A 1944 medical thesis on schizophrenia by Ignacio Sierra reiterates this association, describing schizophrenia primarily as a problem of perception and emotional indifference, with autism again listed as one of its symptoms (Ríos Molina, "Esquizofrenia" 90).[15] The "autism" to which Gómez Robleda refers may be said to correspond primarily to the notion of introversion as a symptom of nonnormative (or schizophrenic) thinking, rather than to Kanner's novel definition of a distinct disorder marked by a series of traits. Yet use of the term in each text, over a time period marked by transition and overlap in the meanings and applications of psychiatric terminology, nonetheless allows for reflection on potentially comparable factors between the work of psychiatric and racial classifications of the time.

Before delving further into structural links between Kanner's text on autism and Gómez Robleda's study of the Tarasco, it is worth attending briefly to contextual elements surrounding the publication of the two works. Anne McGuire notes that Kanner was an Austrian Jew whose mother and three of his siblings were murdered in the Holocaust (33). As she writes, "It is important to understand that Kanner and Asperger were living in and touched by a social context where diagnostic lines were often lines separating life and death" (34). On the other hand, Gómez Robleda's earlier work in psychopedagogy and hygiene included emphasis on the diagnosis and measurement of schoolchildren, and the identification of abnormal traits, in adherence to the broader eugenicist context of public-health and education endeavors in this period. The study of indigenous groups such as the Tarasco operates both within this context and as part of a longer history of the photographic and anthropometric documentation of racialized groups. In this sense, the work of both researchers is ultimately framed by the high stakes of worlds in which some individuals and populations are marked for potential exclusion or disappearance.

In a study of the history of research into autism, with extensive reference to Kanner's pioneering work, S. Wolff comments on previously held ideas about the condition: "The first, and most malignant was that autism is caused by poor parenting, when now we know that the unusual features of parents of autistic children are due to shared genes" (205). This correction of earlier theories of autism still emphasizes the parental role and the question of transmission, thus maintaining a framework in which autism appears as a mystery to be solved within a familial and hereditary context. Although in both arguments, children's autism comes from their parents, the earlier model suggests that parents could have done something to avoid the autism, and dovetails with some aspects of Latin American "soft" eugenics, still prevalent in Mexico of the 1940s. Kanner himself concluded that autism was an innate condition, yet certain moments in his text leave space for speculation on contributing causal factors.[16]

Other contemporary scholars have noted Kanner's negative portrayal of the parents of autistic children, in one example highlighting Kanner's observation that "parents 'stuffed' [the children] with facts, songs or poems," and citing from Kanner, "It is difficult to know whether the stuffing as such contributed essentially to the course of the psychopathological condition" (Kanner 243, qtd. in Blacher and Christensen 186). While the "autism" observed by Kanner in his study of eleven children remains somewhat suspended in its causality, the children themselves appear at an ambivalent distance from the negative charge of psychopathology. This is achieved by distinguishing autism from other conditions, such as "idiocy" or schizophrenia, and by including undesirable parental (or environmental) characteristics and actions as determinants of autistic features. The child, ostensibly the object of Kanner's study, is carefully observed, described, and evaluated in terms of the presence of characteristic traits that are ultimately associated with autism. Yet it is autism itself, newly defined by Kanner, that emerges here as the primary subject under scrutiny, a shifting and uncertain collection of causal factors, a dynamic but still undetermined process of transmission from parent to child. In Kanner's reading, and notwithstanding his conclusion that autism must be attributed to biological, innate qualities, the question of causality and transmission continues to pose an enigma, and thus opens toward future research and new interpretations. In a comparable sense, Gómez Robleda focuses on the physical characteristics of his subjects, but continues to emphasize the structure of socioeconomic causality that has tended to produce these physical results.[17]

Despite clear differences between the work of Kanner and that of Gómez Robleda, the innovative and central function of "autism" in each text highlights in both cases an intriguing ambivalence between innate or physically embodied attributes, and a more fluid process of causality in continuous, potential transition. The juxtaposition suggests that disability and racial difference, the central topics of Kanner and Gómez Robleda's respective arguments, both navigate the uncertain balance between absolute and contingent categories of undesirability, or pathology. The approach thus frames undesirable difference in each case as partially dependent on specific external factors. Reading the two texts together also offers additional ways to think through points of contact and reciprocity between the classifications of disability and racial difference.

Unlike Gómez Robleda's work, Kanner's text is at first glance not about race at all. The author notes only "two of the children are Jewish, the others are all of Anglo-Saxon descent." He also highlights his observation that "*They all come of highly intelligent families*" (248). These two points appear close together toward the last section of the paper, and the author's final lines include the comment, "One other fact stands out prominently. In the whole group there are very few really warm-hearted fathers and mothers" (250). These observations suggest the author's speculation regarding characteristics that might point toward notions of heredity, but that work equally well to underscore an argument that privileges cultural influence. As Mitzi Waltz has written, the demographics of Kanner's study helped to create an association between autism and Jewishness, while at once coding the condition as specific to a white, upper-middle-class, and highly intelligent population sector (68).[18] Ultimately, the children in Kanner's study would probably have appeared to readers as predominantly light-skinned, but via a whiteness that was necessarily ambivalent, or not quite guaranteed. This is because, as Sander Gilman has argued, from the eighteenth century, Jews were culturally coded as black (172). Although by the twentieth century and the period of Kanner's research, representations of Jewishness had whitened, the Jew remained racially codified, often through references to the shape of the "Jewish nose" (Gilman 179). In Kanner's text, the combined classification of "Jewish" and "of Anglo-Saxon descent" serves to complicate the possibility of racial or hereditary categorization, by delineating a combined terrain of hypothetical cultural and genetic continuities. Jewishness—like autism—shifts uncertainly between cultural and racial (or genetic) categories here, as well as between white and non-white. Within this terrain, autism emerges as a unique rubric, its ambiguity parallel to that of racial classification; by refusing to adhere to familiar categories it itself behaves like a newly discovered "race."

In Gómez Robleda's text the question of race works in a far more explicit sense. The juxtaposition of categories of difference in the above-mentioned photograph (autism and indigenous race) illuminates the process by which each is constructed, as well as the importance of numerical body measurements for the conclusions the researchers obtain.[19] The term the author uses consistently throughout his essay is *facies*, which refers to facial expressions, and which in its technical definition is generally associated with some form of pathological condition.[20] The word *facies* in itself implies a certain degree of ambivalence in this text, as it indicates the specific measurements and appearance of a face, but at the same time suggests a facial expression, the reflection of an internal condition, and therefore the possibility of change. On one hand, Gómez Robleda provides indices of quantitative measurements he takes of the Tarasco bodies and from these determines that "Aparecen los indios como personas distraidas, vueltas hacia el interior, indiferentes frente a la realidad exterior, autistas, indolentes y apáticos" [the Indians appear as distracted people, inward looking, indifferent to external reality, autistic, indolent and apathetic]. The index of the head is greater than that of the face and of other members, which means for the biotypologist that the functions of introspection predominate over those of perception. "Es, por consecuencia, un tipo de predominio de las funciones centrales de síntesis sobre las periféricas de recepción y efección." [It is, as a result, a kind of dominance of the central functions of synthesis over the peripheral ones of reception and effection.] But on the other hand, he reaches the same conclusions by basing his analysis on his personal observations of the Tarasco "facies." As he writes, "Encontramos en la facies la expresión de una reacción psicológica de situación de los indios que brevemente puede caracterizarse por su modo de ser indiferente, reprimido y simbólico." [We find in the facies the expression of a psychological reaction to the Indians' situation that might be briefly characterized as indifferent, repressed and symbolic.] The facies is explicitly differentiated here from what the author refers to as the physical, but it is also distinguished from "las manifestaciones de la reacción de situación" [manifestations of a reaction to a situation]. In other words, to situate the facies, one would have to imagine a face suspended somewhere in between the immediate situation of expression and observation—as in the instant of the anthropological gaze—and a more permanent physicality. Despite his insistence on data and specific numbers, and his use of statistics to determine the correct indices of body measurements, Gómez Robleda is somewhat tentative in his use and situation of the facies. He begins his text in the following manner:

> Algún santo dijo en estos, o parecidos términos, que la cara es el espejo del alma y, efectivamente, en la cara es donde se encuentra la mejor expresión de los estados de ánimo. Lógicamente, la facies cambia en cada momento, y si la cara tiene algo de permanente o constante, esto debe referirse a lo que de fijo tiene también la personalidad del individuo.

[Some saint said in these, or similar terms, that the face is the mirror of the soul and, effectively, it is in the face that one finds the most accurate expression of mood. Logically, the facies changes at each moment, and if the face has anything permanent or constant about it, this must refer to what are also permanent qualities of the individual's personality.][21]

The facies indicates change but at the same time seems to offer the possibility of something conclusive, images that can be captured in verbal description or in photographs. The facies, by the same token, is not the face, nor is it equivalent to the indices of its measurements, expressed in numbers. Instead it refers to the intangible quality of the information under study. When the author notes the "symbolic" aspect of the Indians' supposed way of being, he seems to be referring literally to this function of the facies, the ability to gesture toward the face's ephemeral or absent, underlying truth.

The facies' ambivalence in this text is resolved through two visual means, via the inclusion of photographs of human subjects, and photographs of masks made by Tarasco artists. The photos of human faces are said to present evidence of what the author affirms regarding the characteristic immobility of the Tarascos' facial expression, which he describes as "una cara uniforme, indiferente e inmovil" [a uniform, indifferent and immobile face]. The masks, on the other hand, as the author tells us, express everything that the indigenous people repress in their daily lives. It is for this reason that he affirms that the mask is the true face of the Tarascos, and that their faces are actually masks. But he also notes the limits of this observation when he states, "pocas personas, realmente, han podido observar a los indios durante el curso de su vida íntima, cuando seguramente ríen o se encolerizan con toda libertad . . . sin la preocupación de ser observados" [few people, in fact, have been able to observe the Indians during the course of their intimate lives, when they surely laugh or get angry freely . . . without the concern of being observed]. This troubling statement clearly refers to people from outside the Tarasco community, negating the possibility that the Tarasco might actually observe one another.

In general, the search for the real "facies" in the text is at once the search for the inner life of the Tarasco, his "Indian" features, which are in this case his autism, his introversion, and indifference. It is the face that the anthropologist seeks but with which he necessarily fails to establish communication. The facies is constructed on unavailable information; it is created in the act of observation, and its role is always to signal something more. Autism, like

Diablo.—Máscara tarasca de frente estrecha, sin pelo, pómulos prominentes, nariz abultada y dientes con anomalías de implantación.

Fig. 19. Photograph of a Tarasco mask, from the article "La cara de los Tarascos." The caption reads: "Máscara tarasca de frente estrecha, sin pelo, pómulos prominentes, nariz abultada y dientes con anomalías de implantación" [Tarasco mask with broad forehead, no hair, prominent cheeks, bulging nose, and dental anomalies]. José Gómez Robleda, "La cara de los Tarascos." *Revista Mexicana de Sociología*, vol. 3, no. 2, 1941, pp. 83–91, between pages 88 and 89. Universidad Nacional Autónoma de México, Hemeroteca Nacional de México.

the condition of being Tarasco in this configuration, is not defined so much by precise or empirical characteristics, but instead by the function of the gaze and its representation within a delimited cultural space. The act of looking and of photographing the subject who knows he is under observation, framing the seemingly static facial features within a discourse of dynamic symbolism, tends to create an image that can only refer back to itself: the photograph of the so-called autistic Indian.

In the same text the author purports to base his conclusions about the Tarascos' typical features on numerical data, obtained through a method he calls "statistics." Gómez Robleda's indices are always derived from a dynamic of relations, first, between "normal" values—such as for the measurement of the skull—and values found in the indigenous population. Next, he derives a relation between measurements of one part of the body and those of another, to compare, for example, the index of head measurements with that of the face and limbs. In each case, what is compared is the deviation between the index measured in the indigenous population and that of the so-called normotype, taken from standard Italian texts on biotypology.[22]

"La cara de los Tarascos" thus employs a discourse that oscillates constantly between the psychological interpretation of the "facies" and the elaboration of a biotypology based on numerical relations. The work of the facies, that of moving between visible evidence and volatile or cryptic symbology— the impossibility of seeing under the skin—parallels the activity of numbers, expressed as measurements and indices, noted by the author. This numerical data always makes indirect contact with the individual body, thus describing a complex network of relations, not only between the parts of the body, but between the numbers that these parts produce, derived from a chain of relative comparisons both internal and external to the body and to the population in question. The indices, like the facies, adhere to and separate from the described or photographed bodies, without ever revealing the actual "face of the Tarascos." Gómez Robleda mentions and explains his notion of statistics in the text, clarifying that one should not compare "concrete and absolute" numbers, but rather "relative units," or indices, which are in fact percentages of deviation in relation to values deemed normal. In this sense, the essence of the tool of statistics here derives from its rejection of a simplistic literalism; the numbers reveal the body through relations of calculated distances. In this process, the author reminds the nonspecialist reader that the methods of achieving these results are not direct or obvious but require the careful and precise technique that only the biotypologist can bring to the field and to the body of the Tarasco. In other words, it is a body that cannot be taken literally.

The use of a strict, quantitative methodology to document the particularities of human traits, ascribed to a specific ethnic group, may suggest in some sense the model of a "fantasy of identification," to borrow from Ellen Samuels, grounded in the belief that "identity can be easily read upon the body" (17). Gómez Robleda and his colleagues undoubtedly depend at times on such a fantasy, as when numerical data are offered as a means to uphold the researchers' argument. However, the model of statistics and biotypology at work here relies primarily on the suspension of such literality. As we have seen elsewhere, the differences of disability and ethnicity are contingent on modes of perception, sociohistorical causality, and inevitable margins of error.[23] The photographs of the faces included in the text do not ultimately work to inscribe the body with a fixed identity. Instead, they set the biotypologist's technique in motion, signal the always ephemeral facies, and grant liveliness to the numerical indices, in a continuous, self-referential dialogue, one that the author—paradoxically—might himself describe as "autistic."

In this text, the concepts of "autism," as a category of disability, and racial difference, defined here as "Indian," tend to circulate in an intimate relationship, each giving life to the other, though generally it is the issue of racial difference that takes center stage. In a parallel sense, the numerical data come to life thanks to their association with aesthetics and the symbolism of the faces and masks photographed and discussed in the text. The categories of difference—indigeneity and autism—also suggest uncertainty regarding their perceived characteristics, and whether they originate from within or without, from environmental or hereditary factors, or a combination of these. In other words, these categories are delineated primarily through their contingency and mutual dependency, the ongoing possibility of a shift in the explanation of their causality, their origins, and their potential futures.

In Kanner's work and its reception, as we have seen, the enigma that is autism resists racial classifications, and in this way comes to function in the text as a strange new kind of "race," one that both reflects and exceeds cultural anxieties toward Jewishness and notions of heredity. In Gómez Robleda's analysis, on the other hand, the indigeneity of the Tarasco remains the primary mystery, and autism its structuring feature. The inward and self-referential gaze that Gómez Robleda projects onto his Tarasco subjects and describes as autistic also defines the relationship between bodies and numerical data, as well as between the observed, physical body and the fleeting expressions of the facies. The facies in turn is said to hold the Tarasco's ephemeral, inner truth, marked by the effects of colonialism, poverty, and related forms of oppression. In this way, disability and racial difference continue to suspend one another, deferring causal explanation even as the texts point repeatedly to the precision of their methodologies and data.

Gómez Robleda clearly intends to present a scientific project both in his described methodology and in his conclusions. At the same time his writing demonstrates a keen interest in aesthetic questions, as in his discussions of the face as the mirror of the soul, and the mask as the true face, pointing toward diverse possible fields of application for the author's ideas. This tendency reflects a writerly didacticism, present here and in other texts, particularly in the explanation of basic concepts. The bridge between statistics and aesthetics works to further enliven numerical data, making them relevant and attractive to the general reader, literally giving the numbers a face, and offering a means of translation between the technical and the humanistic.

Regarding the dissemination of his notions of statistics, one can read in another of his works, coauthored with Ada d'Aloja, *La familia y la casa* (The family and the house):

> El modo, esencialmente, es el dato sobre el cual se observa la máxima frecuencia; por lo mismo ha sido llamado, también, promedio típico. Lo más frecuente, sin duda, es lo que atrae la atención con mayor intensidad en un fenómeno colectivo. (El fenómeno social de "la moda"—en el vestido, por ejemplo—corresponde, justamente, al modo de la Estadística). (23)

> [The mode essentially is the figure for which the maximum frequency is observed; for the same reason it has also been called typical average. The most frequent is undoubtedly that which attracts attention with maximum intensity in a collective phenomenon. (The social phenomenon of "fashion" (*la moda*)—in clothing, for example—corresponds, in fact, to the mode of Statistics.)]

Here too, the illustration of a technical concept through a popular and accessible example shifts the discussion from the abstract function of the numbers in question toward their more tangible, colorful enactment. This strangely successful example appears to make even a dry discussion of basic concepts from statistics both entertaining and attractive, like the latest fashions to which it refers.

Diagnostic Fictions

In his numerous studies in the field of biotypology, his work in psychopeda-gogy and in juridical psychiatry, a range of activities that demonstrate what today might be called interdisciplinarity, Gómez Robleda frequently employs a shift in register from the technical to the humanistic, thus inviting a broader readership to appreciate his insights, and continuously drawing numerical data toward the emotions they elicit. Given the variety of his interests, it is perhaps not surprising to find that Gómez Robleda was also the author of several short works of fiction, which tend to reveal the same themes and con-cerns noted in his ostensibly more technical works. Reading these works of fiction does not simply reveal another side of the author's personality, or his interests. These books, mainly short novels published in the 1930s and early 1940s, juxtapose clinical and technical work with Gómez Robleda's ideas regarding morality and aesthetics in a more literal sense, giving life and per-sonality to theoretical concepts in medicine and statistics. His fiction writing and its links to his technical works underscore the complexity and breadth of action of medico-scientific practices and concepts of the day, through which numerical data and related tools acquire dynamic and passionate affect. A similar paradigm of transdisciplinary movement underpins the work of José Vasconcelos, discussed in chapter 2, as when the author, though not himself a scientist, incorporates his own notions of Mendelian genetics and Lamarck-ian evolution into a political and aesthetic project. And the physician Edu-ardo Urzaiz's science fiction novel of 1919, *Eugenia*, analyzed in chapter 1, is a key earlier example of medico-scientific thinking acquiring a literary voice. Gómez Robleda's transition between medical and literary realms illustrates a particular mode of didactic writing, through which the discursive movement between data and bodies—as between science and literature (or what is, and what could be)—both enlivens the subject matter and reflects the structure of contingency that is crucial to the role of disability in eugenicist thought. Although the situations and characters appearing in his fictional works do not represent real cases, they offer moral impulse and the impression of fleshly embodiment to the problems of human difference that the author's research sought to quantify. Fiction, like eugenic desire, thus achieves what quantitative measurements and statistical formulas cannot.

Gómez Robleda's fiction writing emerges in the context of the increas-ingly influential trend of criminal sociology in Mexico. As Beatriz Urías Horcasitas describes, debates in this area, derived in part from the ongoing influence of nineteenth-century Italian positivism, emphasized links between crimes and the biological characteristics of criminals, as well as the importance of social environment in the study of crime (160–61).[24] The association between crime and notions of physical and moral degeneracy also appears explicitly in the late-nineteenth-century Mexican context, as displayed in Carlos Roumagnac's popular 1904 *Los criminales en México*. Robert Buffington analyzes the narrative discourse of this work, underscoring the entertaining qualities of the text and noting a structure in which family and medical history situate each accused subject, followed by a more dramatic description of the crime itself (68–71). Roumagnac's emphasis on medical and biological causality, along with his ability to engage a popular audience, suggests continuity between his work and Gómez Robleda's fiction, as well as a possible source for the biotypologist's inspiration.[25]

Gómez Robleda was the author of a textbook for sixth-year primary-school students, titled *Don Justo*, published in 1948. In this work, through a process of didactic translation, many of his ideas regarding the association between moral vices and physical characteristics take on a life of their own through fictional narrative.[26] For example, in one chapter of the textbook, a student is trying to knock down a bird's nest by throwing stones at it. When another student witnesses this and protests to the teacher, don Justo, he responds, "Déjalo; no logrará lo que se propone, porque tiene muy mala puntería. Julio padece de un vicio de refracción en los ojos y precisamente, porque su visión es defectuosa, se empeña en hacer lo que jamás podrá lograr." [Leave him; he won't be able to do what he's trying, because he has very bad aim. Julio suffers from a defect of refraction in his eyes and precisely, because his vision is defective, he insists on trying things that he will never be able to do (35).] In this description, don Justo's view of Julio's problem is not simply that due to poor vision he is unable to aim properly. The idea of defective vision is taken a step further, with the suggestion that defects actually come to impact character and behavior. The final passages of the textbook include short descriptions of don Justo's students as adults, years later. Some are married, some have careers, yet of Julio, significantly, the author affirms he knows nothing. In this way, defective bodies and characters are ultimately erased from the future.

However, when a student asks don Justo, at another point in the text, whether illness and vice are the same thing, the teacher is careful to avoid blaming the sufferer: "Los alcohólicos crónicos, tan repugnantes, comúnmente, al principio sólo fueron individuos amargados o desilusionados de la vida . . . decir, despectivamente, de estos desafortunados, que son viciosos, equivale a no haberlos comprendido." [Chronic alcoholics, so repugnant, usually at the beginning were just embittered or disillusioned by life . . . to say, despectively of these unfortunates, that they are depraved, is the same as not having understood them.] Similarly, when Tiburcia, a student described as mentally ill, bites a substitute teacher's hand and is sent away to an asylum, don Justo expresses pity, tempered with faith in medical treatment: ¡Pobre niña! Algún día, era inevitable, tendría que haber sido trasladada al Manicomio; allí estará bien atendida" (337). [Poor child! One day, it was inevitable, she would have to be transferred to the Asylum; she will be treated well there.] In this text, students described as defective have no future, and as don Justo seems to suggest, it is perhaps through no fault of their own. Similarly, his indigenous Tarasco subjects, discussed above, are said to reflect only the outcome of inherited histories of oppression. Yet the framing of these subjects depends on an affective exchange between the so-called defects and those who observe them. Just as the Tarasco facies, suspended between momentary expression and physical body, gestures toward the ephemeral "true" face, in a comparable sense, the so-called vices or defects of fictional characters emerge through the interplay between their described appearance and other characters' reactions to them. The messages on human physical and mental flaws that underpin the many academic lessons on topics of science and history imparted throughout the textbook are revealed through this tension. For Gómez Robleda, the dilemma of bringing academic topics to life for young readers becomes an occasion to work through an ambivalence between absolute and contingent qualities of human difference, or in other words, between specific differences that might be expressed in numerical data, and those registered by emotive expression—the visceral reactions of others.

Two of Gómez Robleda's short novels from the early 1930s, *El güero* and *Un ladrón*, are fictional accounts of criminal cases in which medical knowledge turns out to be key to solving the mystery. In these novels too, as was the case in *Don Justo*, the author's ideas regarding associations between human behavior and physical pathology take shape through literary characters, the criminals who inhabit the pages of these works. In other works, specifically his *Esquizofrénico* of 1933 and *Noúmeno*, published in 1942, however, the writer's exploration of philosophical dilemmas regarding the existence and status of the self in relation to the world, language, and thought become the central concern.

In the short novel *El güero*, to which I now turn to conclude the present chapter, the author achieves an explicitly didactic tone. This means a marked separation between the voices of the specialists who diagnose the pathology, and the pathologized subject in question, as described in the text. Yet the reader nonetheless learns that the experience or apprehension of physical or psychic difference depends on a fluid relationship between body and surroundings, one that may continually redefine the differences in question. In addition, in this text the question of race turns out to be a crucial and unavoidable aspect of the story, without which the plot would be unsustainable.

Written on the Skin

The novel, *El güero*, includes the following ruminations from a doctor who is discussing the topic of albinism:

> Ahora recuerdo una feliz expresión de Guillaume . . . "la piel es el espejo del simpático . . ." solo que la teoría nerviosa simpática para explicar la pigmentación melanordérmica en los addisonianos hoy está en desuso. (35–36)

> [Now I remember Guillaume's apt expression . . . "The skin is the mirror of the sympathetic nervous system . . ." except that the theory of the sympathetic nervous system as explanation for the melanodermic pigmentation of those with Addison's disease has fallen out of use.][27]

These thoughts appear within a conversation about the case of an albino man, son of a mestizo father and an indigenous mother. The son has been accused of having attacked and wounded his father, and a major part of the investigation into the crime involves analysis of medical data. The dialogue in the novel is sustained throughout between a doctor who is chief of social services and investigator of the case, and a second, senior doctor and former professor of the first.

As in other novels by the same author, the plot is structured through the subordination of the juridical to the medical, for the answers to the pressing questions that guide the narrative are always revealed through the analysis of clinical observation. Why did the albino character, named Margarito, attack his father? This is the central mystery that readers, as well as characters in the novel, including doctors, students, and lawyers, all wish to solve. The final answer here, as in another of Gómez Robleda's novels, *Un ladrón*, about a thief who turns out to also be a diabetic, will be clear and definitive, yet the story allows for the exploration of unresolved relations between medical diagnosis, embodied experience, and racialized perception.

The enigma of the crime becomes an occasion for the writer-scientist to showcase particular features of his thinking in relation to medical theories of the day. In the above-cited passage, the senior doctor wishes to argue for a causal relationship between the skin, an organ visible to the outside world, and the sympathetic nervous system. Use of the term "mirror" suggests that part of the function of the skin is actually to show the hidden action of an internal system, to literally reflect it and not simply to mimic it. The doctor's observation that this idea is no longer current as an explanation for Addison's disease seems curious, given that albinism, rather than Addison's disease, is the topic under scrutiny. Yet here the issue of perceptions of racial difference turns out to be the link between the two conditions. Addison's disease, or "bronze skin disease" as it has sometimes been called, may cause a darkening of the skin, while the most recognized characteristic of albinism is lack of skin pigmentation. Both conditions affect skin color, and each suggests the potential for racial ambiguity, through darkening of the skin in one case and lightening in the other, although there is no clinical relationship between the two. The doctor's reflection thus ties the dilemma of diagnosis and physiological description to the social significance of the condition, including disparate opinions and possible errors regarding the appearance and explanation of albinism. The passage includes a notable increase in use of technical language with terms that would not be familiar to the general reader. We may imagine that the intended audience here was both an inner circle of Gómez Robleda's fellow physicians, and a nonspecialist readership for whom unrecognizable medical terminology would lend a sense of realistic clinical complexity to the narrative.

The proposed link between skin and nervous system becomes, in turn, according to the physicians' logic, a link to the endocrine system, and from there to the alcoholism of the albino's father. Here, the doctors discuss the case:

El padre del albino fue un alcohólico inveterado.—¡Eso es! La acción tóxica que principalmente se hace sentir sobre el sistema endocrino–simpático, por igual mecanismo las enfermedades infecciosas que lesionan las glandulas endocrinas acarrean la rápida desaparición de una pigmentación solar, y se ha dicho por gentes dignas de crédito, que aun hacen palidecer a los negros. (36)

[The albino's father was an inveterate alcoholic. —That's it! The toxic action that mainly impacts the sympathetic-endocrine system; infectious diseases that damage endocrine glands lead to the rapid disappearance of solar pigmentation by the same mechanism, and credit-worthy people have said that they even make blacks go pale.]

At this point, the question of race, previously included in the technical reference to Addison's disease, becomes unavoidable and obvious. If infectious diseases can "make blacks go pale" by damaging endocrine glands, the doctor reasons, alcohol can do the same to the offspring of the alcoholic, perhaps both weakening him and whitening his appearance. The skin, in these passages, turns out to be more than a useful mirror of internal conditions available to the physician for quick diagnosis. In addition, it reminds the viewer that race remains an irrevocable factor within this diagnosis, linking the subject to his genealogy and to the social significance of his physical appearance. The relationship between parent and child, as in other texts pertinent to the pursuit of eugenics in this period, establishes both a presumed racial—or genetic—continuity, and a contaminating distortion to this bloodline. Albinism—purportedly caused by the parent's alcoholism in this case—works as an ideal contaminant in the narrative, since it appears to erase the skin color that would (supposedly) otherwise define racial continuity. However, lest the reader believe the text to be a celebration of darker, hence uncontaminated skin tone, the chapter concludes with side dialogue between the two doctors who are discussing the case. The younger physician refers to an attractive woman, with brown skin, green eyes, and blond hair. His senior colleague responds that he prefers the combination of white skin, green eyes, and black hair. And he notes, in a final punchline, that in any case the brown-skinned woman in question dyes her hair (38). This conclusion resituates the narrative firmly in a social context of preference for whiter, lighter features, as a necessary backdrop to the unfolding of the story.

The dialogue in the novel is further dramatized through verbal illustrations of how the albino character perceives and interacts with the world around him. The main dilemma, one which is not entirely resolved in the dialogue, has to do with how the character receives information, how his physical characteristics—including his perceived racial identity—influence this process of reception, and how others react to his differences, which in turn influences his personality and experience of the world.

For example, as the younger doctor says of the albino,

Si se le observa de cerca, se comprueba que padece de nistagmus, ese incómodo movimiento de los globos oculares en sentido horizontal, que parece una sacudida constante y rápida y que hace la mirada incierta. Pero esto no es todo; su ojo izquierdo es víctima de estrabismo interno. El estrabismo ha sido muy cruel con 'El Güero' pues en los momentos mas inoportunos, cuando atiende con la mejor de las intenciones, su fisonomía toma un aspecto ridículo, lamentablemente cómico y por ello ha tenido múltiples disgustos. (17)

[If one observes him at close range, one will see that he suffers from nistagmus, that awkward horizontal movement of the ocular globes, which appears as a rapid and constant shaking and which makes his gaze uncertain. But this is not all; his left eye is victim of an internal strabismus. The strabismus has been very cruel to "the blond" for in the most inopportune moments, when he responds with the best of intentions, his physiognomy takes on a ridiculous, sadly comical aspect, and for this reason he has suffered many upsets.]

This description of Margarito, the albino character, highlights a particular separation between physiognomy and the character himself, indicated by the phrase, "the best of intentions." If others laugh at Margarito or mistreat him, the guilty party is his strabismus, which "has been very cruel." In this sense, physical difference becomes one more character in the story, an inherent part of the albino's body, but at the same time distinct, and capable of creating particular effects in other subjects.

Eyes and visual sensibility are crucial to this story, partly because of the clinical associations, as discussed by the doctors, between albinism and specific vision pathologies, such as strabismus. But in addition, the text connects the sense of vision, and other senses, to the sensorial function of the skin, thus in turn suggesting a link to the visibility of albinism, as one may note in the following portion of the dialogue:

—Estamos en relación con el mundo exterior por medio de los órganos de los sentidos, los ojos, los oídos, la nariz, la lengua . . . y la piel.
—Margarito es bizco.
—Sí y también míope, pero no olvide que lo que llega a su interior por su piel, también se modifica . . . . Me refiero a algunas de sus sensaciones . . . porque . . . su piel está enferma. Su mundo es otro y él es diferente y lo siente así. (44)

DOCTOR 1: [Our relationship to the outside world is mediated by our sense organs, the eyes, the ears, the nose, the tongue . . . and the skin.

DOCTOR 2: Margarito is cross-eyed.

DOCTOR 1: Yes, and also short-sighted, but don't forget that what reaches him through his skin is also modified . . . I am referring to some of his sensations . . . because . . . his skin is sick. His world is other, and he is different, and feels it that way.]

Sense organs here are said to function as a border separating inside and outside, between the subject and his world, but also as conductors that link the two spaces, creating some degree of continuity between the character, his perceptions and feelings, and his surroundings. Disability is not limited to a physical representation of specific bodily traits or of illness, but rather extends to encompass a totalizing context of body, person, sensations, and world. In these textual examples, disability is contingent on a causal structure, through which negatively perceived qualities come to appear as ambivalently separate from and continuous with the rest of the person. In "The Face of the Tarasco," similarly, the so-called autism of the indigenous subject is the result of his socioeconomic situation and colonialist history, but also emerges through perceptual processes.

The figure of the albino character here, like that of the "autistic" person in the text on the Tarasco, points directly toward the question of race through disability, and disability through race. As it turns out, the social problems suffered by Margarito are rooted in a misunderstanding of his genealogy, for both father and son suspect that the real father was another man—a white man. What else could explain Margarito's pale skin color to those unfamiliar with the condition of albinism? Gómez Robleda's narrative ruse of his darker-skinned characters confusing disability with racial difference works in a blatantly obvious way to showcase an intertwined relationship between race and disability, while at once insisting that the confusion can be resolved through recourse to medical and scientific precision. The doctors' clarification, which serves to define albinism as distinct from racialized understandings of difference in skin pigmentation, cannot ultimately remove the issue of race from the story, since it is the idea of racial difference that provides the link between physical features and characters' experience of the world. The key to this history is found in the skin itself, in constant engagement with its environment, as the author affirms in his description of Margarito's situation: "His world is other, and he is different and feels it that way." The doctors' conclusion, achieved in consultation with experts in law and sociology, and based on a collection of diverse data, is in the final instance an insistence on this sensorial organ, the skin, and the relation it continually produces between the subject and his surroundings.

The role of the skin as link between sensorial, perceptual, and historically determined experience, both in this text and in the figure of the Tarasco "facies," returns my analysis to the work of Fanon. As in the case of Fanon's frequently cited description of himself through the perspective of an externally determined, "historical-racial schema," Gómez Robleda's albino character comes to read himself and his world through an external and racialized view of his skin. Lighter skin signifies racial superiority over a father figure, whose biological paternity is thus called into question. In the article on the Tarasco, in a related sense, the biotypologist diagnoses the Tarasco as shaped by a particular, interiorized way of looking that is in turn informed by a history of inequality and exploitation. Indices of bodily measurements, photographed appearance, and gaze congeal together to produce an "autism" that is at once a mode of perception and of being perceived, in historical and present time.[28]

In *El güero*, the criminal sociologist unpacks the trope linking skin pigmentation to racial difference, but not surprisingly, fails to further unpack tropes associating racial difference and disability with inferiority. In the Tarasco text, the author also partially unpacks the notion of innate racial inferiority, by explaining difference as the outcome of socioeconomic conditions and modes of perception. Yet he seems to take for granted the undesirability of this racialized difference. In each of these texts, racial difference and disability, named as albinism or autism, thus produce one another as contingent categories, through which the subject in question is perceived, or perceives himself, as other. In each case as well, the skin, as surface of the body, becomes the site of quantitative and qualitative diagnosis, observation and sensation, linking the subject's experience (and perhaps his soul, as the author suggests) to the diagnostic act, and congealing ephemeral expression into seemingly permanent data.

For the engineer, García de Mendoza, whose lament at the lack of statistics in Mexico marked the opening of this chapter, the absence of both data and appropriate methodology becomes the occasion to celebrate the potential power of quantitative analysis. Statistical formulas gesture toward the bodies and populations they measure through the mediation of indices and estimates, and in the process affirm their own methodological triumph. Such gestures mark García de Mendoza's text, and are also a key feature of biotypology present in the work of Gómez Robleda and his contemporaries. The efficacy of these modern statistical approaches stems from their insistence on formulas and estimates rather than on literal measurements of objects in the world. In this way, the body remains at a distance, calculated by a necessary and ephemeral margin of error, in accordance with the "new statistics" pioneered by Fisher and Pearson. At the same time, the body in its array of potential differences grants purpose, shape, and energy to the data of the statistical enterprise, in a sense bringing the numbers to life.

The observation and diagnosis of the body by the statistician, the biotypologist, or within the same framework, by the subject himself, occurs through the mechanism of indirect calculation and the assumption of possible error. The distance of mediated observation is the space of error and of the correction of prior error, as well as the space of self-alienation, in the recognition that the body is perhaps not what it seems or cannot be known as such. In the case of *El güero*, the error in perception is integral to the linkage between disability, racial difference, and crime, and of course to the narrative tension and resolution. Disability is always potential error in this context, both because it serves to mark a departure from measured normative frameworks, and because it emerges through the contingency of perception, measurement, and sociohistorical causality.

In the study of the Tarascos, as part of a longer trend in the documentation of indigenous populations and bodies, the disability of the othered subject is also construed as a problem of perception, hovering between permanent and changing features, and between quantitative evidence and distance from the body at hand. The persistent dilemma of the impossibility of truly knowing the racialized subject also becomes a feature of that subject's gaze; in this case an inward and self-referential focus works to reaffirm the statistical methodology of indirect perception.

The structures of perceptual, quantitative, and sociohistorical scaffolding observed in these cases appear to offer a degree of separation between the othered subject and the presumed negativity of attributes ascribed to him. Yet, paradoxically, the contingent circumstances adhere so closely to the subject that they become virtually indistinguishable from his skin, and ultimately his psyche. The albino's physical appearance, like the Tarasco's "facies," becomes a site of encounter between medical or numerical data and emotive expression, as well as between bodily expressions and the responses they elicit. It is at once a site of error, the expression of a method that refuses literality, of a body that cannot be known and is therefore not congruent with itself. This affective zone, in which the lived body animates the prose of statistics, encompasses both the continuing violence of epidermalization, to use Fanon's term, and an indifferent storehouse of technical information, an enigma written on the skin. Reading the violence of this contingent embodiment might compel us to seek to further correct the errors we inevitably observe, perhaps to find a truer body or self beneath the scaffolded layers. Yet it may also allow us to recognize, beyond this corrective impulse, that these quantitative indices and conditioned, perceptual frames have become strangely integral to a flesh they still cannot quite contain. Rather than the promise of an underlying truth, this reading insists on the troubled encounter with these cumulative frames, on the witnessing of each surface in its imperfect sedimentation.

Five

Asymmetries—Injury, History, and Revolution

Time Frames

Toward the beginning of Martín Luis Guzmán's classic novel of the Mexican Revolution, *La sombra del caudillo* (*Shadow of the Tyrant*), the car in which the protagonist is traveling suddenly takes on the characteristics of a horse. In this scene, Ignacio Aguirre sees Rosario, object of his affection, through the window of his Cadillac, and his driver speeds up to meet the young woman:

> para que el auto detuviera allí emulando la dinámica—viril, aparatosa— del caballo que el jinete raya en la culminación de la carrera. Trepidó la carrocería, se cimbraron los ejes, rechinaron las ruedas y se ahondaron en el suelo, negruzcos y olorosos, los surcos de los neumáticos (7).

> [so that the car would stop there, imitating the virile, showy dynamic of the horse that the rider halts at the end of the race. The coach trembled, the axles rocked, the wheels screeched and the tire treads, blackish and smelly, dug into the ground.]

The rapid transformation of car to horse is in fact spurred on by the impulsive emotions of the passenger, experienced as bodily affect as he contemplates Rosario: "sintió, conforme se acercaba, un transporte vital, algo impulsivo, arrebatado, que de su cuerpo se comunicó al *Cadillac*" [he felt, as he approached, a vital transport, something impulsive, attracted, that his body communicated to the Cadillac]. Yet perhaps there is more to this scene than seduction and animal instinct. The novel's account of violent political transformation effectively begins here, between the city and its outskirts, where streets give way to a picturesque landscape of the Mexico Valley and the volcanoes beyond. The transitional space, similar to the backdrop of the novel's penultimate chapter, in which Aguirre and his political allies are assassinated, offers the reader a mediated perspective, through a spatially rendered distance from the described events. As Rosario and Aguirre move from the streets to more open terrain that allows for contemplation of the faraway mountains, the two characters themselves appear to recede into the distance, as the reader follows their gaze to the background landscape.

The car that suddenly becomes a horse, and the driver a rider, suggest a related, temporal distancing mechanism, through which the modern and urbanizing political context of the revolution's aftermath, played out on city streets and in government buildings, may give way at any moment to a violence that evokes the mythologized rural battlefields of the recent past. The fictional mechanism that allows a car to appear, momentarily, as a horse, complicates the literary evocation of the revolution as history, by showing that movement in time and space does not necessarily proceed in one direction only. In such cases, the literary narration of history, whether fictional or otherwise, may interrupt or explode historical continuity, or blur the notion of progress with an affective and critical distancing.[1]

The dilemma of the revolution as literary narration implies a refusal to move forward in a temporally or spatially straightforward manner, or perhaps the impossibility of doing so. The problem suggests an echo of my discussion in chapter 2, of Alfonso Reyes's view, according to Gareth Williams, of the revolution as "historical aberration" (105). For Reyes, within Williams's analysis, the revolution itself, and the exploited population it foregrounded, was "abnormal," and therefore destined for historiographical bracketing. But in my approach to this episode from Guzmán's novel, and to the work of Rafael F. Muñoz, to be taken up further in the present chapter, aberration emerges instead through narration of the affective experience of the body, and the distance such narrated experience allows from lived events, or what might pass as objective history.

In this chapter I consider the literary narration of the revolution, with attention to the novels of Rafael F. Muñoz. In the first section I focus on the 1941 novel *Se llevaron el cañón para Bachimba*, as a pedagogical project.[2] I then turn to Muñoz's earlier and more popular 1935 work, *¡Vámonos con Pancho Villa!* and the film based on it, as well as to particular links between the texts. The implied processes of learning, progress, and individual or collective maturation or transformation that the pedagogical project would suggest are continually mediated through the bodies of characters—that is, through the violent changes these bodies may experience, and through bodies' relative (in) ability or refusal to assimilate the lessons they receive within the contexts of the revolution and its aftermath. The injuries and traumas of war represented in these texts of the revolution contribute to what Tobin Siebers has called "disability aesthetics," identified through attention to "beauty that seems by traditional standards to be broken, and yet it is not less beautiful, but more so, as a result" (3). As Siebers also notes, "The capacity to be wounded, injured, or traumatized is not always considered a feature of disability, but it should be" (102). Disability, affectively experienced as corporeal difference and non-conformity, mediates the pedagogical project of the narrated revolution. This form of corporeal mediation and its asymmetry with respect to the revolution as political, pedagogical, or social project, results in certain instances in the novel's critical distance from its own overall narrative arc, and the ongoing renegotiation of the revolution as literary form. In a structurally similar sense, in the scene from *La sombra del caudillo*, discussed above, affective bodily sensation creates the transformation of car to horse, and hence disrupts conventional notions of historical chronology and progress.

Before delving further into the temporality of wounding and the disability aesthetics of Muñoz's novels, it may be useful to briefly situate these works as part of the larger genre of the novel of the Mexican Revolution, though without pretending to encompass the vastness and complexity of the literary works sometimes included under this banner. *Se llevaron el cañón para Bachimba* is narrated from the perspective of a young teenager, Álvaro Abasolo, and recounts his departure from his family home and his participation in a series of battles as part of the rebellion led by Pascual Orozco against Francisco Madero's government. Events in the novel correspond to the years 1912 to 1913, ending in the defeat of Orozco's forces known as the Colorados. Abasolo, having learned and grown through the violent and traumatic experiences of war, nevertheless concludes his narration on a seemingly optimistic tone. *¡Vámonos con Pancho Villa!*, the more widely studied of the two novels, centers on the Leones de San Pablo, a group of friends who decide to take up arms and join Pancho Villa's troops. Initial revolutionary fervor and bravado soon shift toward repeated instances of wounding and death that punctuate the narrative. The latter half of the novel focuses on the figure of Tiburcio Maya, the group's leader and last remaining survivor, as he navigates the violent trajectory of his own unwavering and ultimately fatal allegiance to Villa.

Both novels employ commonly cited tropes of the literature of the Mexican Revolution, including the celebration of patriotic virility transmitted through literary realism (Sánchez Prado 36–37), detailed attention to a vast and specifically Mexican national landscape (Legrás 25; Fornoff 96), and the affirmation of a popular subjectivity, the unruly alterity of a (semi) anonymous multitude (Aguilar Mora, *El silencio* 14). Yet, as Aguilar Mora also notes, such novels also necessarily fail to truly convey "el lenguaje, el comportamiento, el cuerpo mismo del *otro*, de la alteridad social y racial" (18) [the language, the behavior, the very body of the *other*, of social and racial alterity]. For Legrás as well, discontinuity and asynchronicity are key to cultural productions of the revolution, because culture cannot fully represent popular revolutionary agency, but nonetheless "reveals the popular pressure upon the formal apparatus of representation" (12). In both of the novels to be discussed in the present chapter, popular resistance, as well as forms of disability, whether depicted through dramatic and massive battle scenes or through the silently endured, excruciating pain of wounding, generally emerge through processes of distancing and deferral, and in particular in ways that disrupt the experience of temporal chronology.

As discussed in the previous chapter in relation to statistics and eugenic discourse, disability frequently emerges as contingent on factors external to a given body. This is the case, for example, when human characteristics are portrayed as the result of past and present oppressive living conditions, and as mediated through quantitative analysis, as in Gómez Robleda's study of the Tarasco. In other cases, disability is said to appear as the result of an unhygienic environment, as when children's compromised health is read as the result of improper school infrastructure, as analyzed in chapter 3. In the present chapter, the literary texts in question still tend to represent disability as contingent on external causes or on transparent epistemologies. Yet more than in previous chapters, I emphasize a reversal of the phenomenon. In this case, history and progress in the literary text are also conditioned by disability and the corporeal affects with which it associates. It is in this sense, as the work of Muñoz demonstrates, that disability as literary representation and lived experience impacts the pedagogical and temporal progression of the revolution in the narrative.

The discussion of Muñoz's literary work to be taken up here may appear as a departure from the work of previous chapters, with their emphasis on state-sponsored projects of public education and health. Rather than incorporating archival materials pertaining to issues of hygiene and eugenics, this chapter focuses more consistently on literature. In addition, the idea of the revolution in the present chapter refers to battle scenes and to the impact of war on the body, rather than to a post-revolutionary imperative shaping collective ideals of embodiment and future. However, the connection between war and its protracted aftermath is a necessary one, particularly because of the ways in which narratives of violence repeat and are popularized through cultural production, as part of a process of solidifying a nationalist identity.[3] The body, wounded or in some cases killed in battle, and continuously evoked in literature, music, and film, makes visible specific forms of fragility, while necessarily engaging with and negotiating a field, or frame of recognition. As Judith Butler notes, "there is no life and no death without a relation to some frame" (7), suggesting that our perception of bodies subjected to violence "takes place" through the precondition of a field of recognition, even when the bodies and forms of violence depicted call the borders of the frame or field into question.

In the contemporary context of the so-called war on terror that is the setting for Butler's discussion—to which we might add the "war on drugs"—the frame of recognition of subjects of violence is determined primarily by the nation-state, conditioning both their visibility and precarity. In the context of the Mexican Revolution, an evolving nation-state similarly shapes the recognition of bodies—that is, which ones appear, and which remain implicitly somewhere outside the frame. Borrowing from Tobin Siebers's notion of fragility, or the capacity to be wounded as a feature of disability, I read the disability aesthetics of these war narratives as engaged in the continuous redefinition of the framing of human subjects over time. Through this reframing process, the revolution makes particular forms of embodiment and affect visible, even as the conditions of visibility themselves are being transformed. The disability and racialization we have encountered in archival and literary documents of the post-revolutionary decades similarly work through a framing process, in which the documentation of anatomical, physiological, and cognitive differences, for example, offers both the recognition of the shifting parameters of corporeal visibility, and a desire to define and contain the apparent proliferation of difference. In this way, the bodies of the revolution's (literary) battlefields give birth to new subjects of state recognition. These are not only the hypothetical sons of the *soldaderas* (female combatants or camp followers) as evoked in the conclusion to Eisenstein's classic film *¡Qué viva México!*, but also new forms of fragility and of potential allegiance or threat to a vast and modernizing state.

The problem of the framing and reframing of the body and its recognition, as potential contribution or as drain on resources, as figure of allegiance to a larger cause or as threat to national unity, as continuous over time or indicative of uncertain pasts and futures, links the narratives of revolutionary battlefields to the documentation of health and hygiene in later decades. In addition, like the pedagogical projects of public health and education that inspired the work of healthcare professionals, eugenicists, and reformers, the narratives of war to be taken up here also operate through a pedagogical imperative, shaping the experience of emblematic survivors toward the construction of a national future. However, this future does not simply appear as more desirable and optimistic than prior situations, but is complicated by experiences of suffering, by temporal distancing, as noted above in the example from *La sombra del caudillo*, in which chronology may appear to shift or reverse unexpectedly, and by uncertainty or partial nonconformity with the revolutionary project.

Wounds and Witnesses

Wounds and scars are recurring figures in the works discussed here and play an important role in my approach to the temporal chronology of the narrative. Gilles Deleuze and Félix Guattari's analyses of these figures as central to the structure of the event and of temporality are a key resource, one that has been taken up previously by disability studies scholars within distinct critical projects. Petra Kuppers reads the scar as generative of complex and creative possibilities: "The scar moves matter into the future of a new flesh: a different subject emerges, a recreation of the old into the new, into a repetition that holds onto its history even as it projects itself into an unpredictable future" (Kuppers 19, qtd. in Garoian 146, *Prosthetic Pedagogy of Art*).[4] Charles Garoian emphasizes the temporal element of Kupper's reading through "repetition and difference," linking this scar in turn to Deleuze's analysis of time as "out-of-joint" (Garoian 146). Here he cites from Deleuze's *Logic of Sense* on the concept of the event, often figured as a wound: "always and at the same time something which has just happened and something about to happen; never something which is happening" (146). For both Kuppers and Garoian, the scar, though a mark of violence and loss, also works as a site of creative and performative possibilities. For Jasbir Puar, in contrast, wounds and scars refer primarily to a temporality conditioned by state imperatives; wounding is necessarily predetermined rather than accidental, occurring through a logic of inexorable repetition that violently binds bodies and subjects to a national—and often, colonialist—project. The difference between these readings may be explained in part by the fact that Puar focuses more closely on the role of the state apparatus through reference to Deleuze and Guattari's *A Thousand Plateaus*.

Deleuzian structures also figure in the critical work of Jorge Aguilar Mora, a leading scholar of Muñoz, Nellie Campobello, and other authors of the Mexican Revolution.[5] For Aguilar Mora, referring to Deleuze's *Differ-ence and Repetition*, repetition is part of an affirmative project through which literature becomes collective memory, and through which the histories and events of the revolution, in their repetition, define the salvation of the father-land (*patria*) for those who lived and died (*Una muerte sencilla*, 13). Elsewhere in the same work, citing Nicola Chiaromonte, Aguilar Mora refers to battle as "the event in its very essence," describing it as "always in the future and already past" (142).[6] In the context of the Mexican Revolution, Aguilar Mora is concerned with the dichotomy between the event and the more abstract theoretical formula, and in turn with the division between history and his-toriography. The critic expresses these dichotomies in terms of a race- and class-based division between those who fight in the revolution and are often depicted as ignorant of its logic or context, and those who read, write, and theorize the revolution and its politics. The event, battle, or wound, which for Aguilar Mora is often a mortal wound, is embodied by soldiers of the racialized multitude. At stake is the question of whether or not the recipient of this wound, neutralized within abstract temporality, remains caught in the "vicious cycle" (142) of historicized life, the inexorable hierarchy of violence that demands subordination and predetermines mutilation and destruction, as in Puar's reading, above. Alternatively, Aguilar Mora ultimately argues that the soldier defies this political structure by refusing to explain his allegiance in a conventional manner, thus freeing death from the confines of its rela-tional logic (Aguilar Mora 144).

In each of these readings, the scar or wound, mortal or otherwise, suggests a time "out of joint," as well as forms of embodiment that impact the tem-porality of narrated history, issues I return to in greater detail in the present chapter. Yet key differences lie in how this paradoxical temporality may—or may not—leave open possibilities for various modes of critique, resistance, creative productivity or denunciation. Scars and wounds in my discussion of war narratives build on these interpretive possibilities, though I do not claim to resolve the differences between them. My analysis, following Puar, fore-grounds the temporal structure of exploitative violence through which the post-revolutionary state frames the inexorable repetition of the wound. Yet I also insist, borrowing from Kuppers, on the active and affective role of the narrated body, on "the scar, the trauma and the cut" as "sites of fleshly (and skinly) productivity, if productivity at a price" (18–19), and in particular on the body's mediation of temporal unfolding. I recognize, with Aguilar Mora, the racist paradigm underpinning the division between nationalist ideology and the multitudinous wounded bodies of anonymous soldiers—between

History and Event. However, I approach with caution his celebration of an inherently seductive patriotic repetition, and of violent death in its moment of supposed liberation from hierarchical political structures.

In his *Logic of Sense*, Deleuze describes the Stoic philosophy of time according to the paradoxical coexistence of two temporal models, *Aion* and *Chronos*. *Aion* is infinitely divisible into pasts and futures, as in the above-cited example of a wounding that is never present, but instead has just happened, or is about to happen. *Chronos* refers in contrast to the embodied present, and to the contraction of all pasts and futures into a perpetual present, hence to a cyclical eternal return.[7] The event as sign of something that just happened or will happen is abstract, impersonal, and disembodied, expressed through *Aion* as a pure, straight, and infinite line (62). The impersonal and abstract authority of *Aion* subjects the individual to the Event as wound, a neutral and pre-existing truth that s/he embodies (148). In *Capitalism and Schizophrenia*, cited by Puar, above, the wound or disability as effect of war suggests the embodied effect of this authority, of *Aion* as state apparatus. The repetition of violence that is no accident, always both private and socially determined, abstract, predetermined, and impersonal, nonetheless leaves space for denunciation, or witnessing, in Deleuze and Guattari's reading, as well as in Deleuze's *Logic of Sense*: "All forms of violence and oppression gather together in this single event which denounces all by denouncing one" (153). Such denunciations occur in particular through the work of poetry and in the reclaiming of psychopathology, in which what appear as accidents to the body are in fact the infinite repetitions of emblematic histories of violent oppression.[8]

The question of wounding in the context of political revolt acquired particular relevance at the time of writing this chapter. In Santiago, Chile, during an increased government crackdown against political protests in October and November of 2019, numerous instances of eye injuries by pellet guns, leading to partial blindness, were documented.[9] The practice of shooting rubber pellets at the face, while not generally lethal, causes high rates of such injuries, evoking Puar's argument from *The Right to Maim* on the state's a priori demand for injured bodies as the multiple embodiment of its continuous and authoritarian logic. Wounding here links as well to a mode of witnessing, as the bandaged eye becomes a familiar symbol of protest and of unwavering determination in the face of brutal oppression (McDonald). Such horrific images and experiences cannot be celebrated, however; they remind us, instead, of an impersonal state structure in which multiple repeating "accidents" congeal into an implacable singularity. They underscore as well the sites of denunciation that have yet to fully unfold.

The time of the wound in these Deleuzian readings seems to hover between forced submission to an impersonal authority and a mode of resistance that is difficult to capture, based as it is on the embodiment of violence, on singular instants of suffering that are said to each denounce a violent totality, but might also simply serve to repeat and cement this logic of violence. In the context of debates in disability studies, this dilemma might be understood in terms of a similar tension, simplified here, between materialist critiques of disablement, particularly in its asymmetrical, racialized global distribution, and readings of corporeal difference as generative of creative productivity, of lines of flight from normativist paradigms, although these positions need not be mutually exclusive. In my approach to narratives of the revolution, and to processes of wounding in these texts, I focus in particular on the temporal disadjustments enacted by corporeal difference and wounding. These instances problematize the tension between authority and resistance, or predetermined repetition and creative generation, although without resolving it, by shifting emphasis toward the roles of witnessing and of bodily affect in mediating temporal and historical progression. In altering experiences of time, wounding and witnessing reframe the progression of the revolution as history, offering moments of distance from its narrative arc, gesturing not only toward bodies that history has not captured, but toward the need for other ways of registering embodiment and injustice.

The issue of a distanced and critical perspective within the narrative arc, as achieved by disruptions to the temporal flow or the pedagogical project, is perhaps inevitable in approaches to literature of this period, because much of the criticism on the novel of the revolution sooner or later confronts the same general question: whether the work offers a celebratory vision of the struggle and its heroes, or if it repeats the theme of disillusionment as a response to violence and cyclical tyranny. It is in this spirit, for example, that John Hall concludes his article on Muñoz's *Se llevaron el cañón para Bachimba*, noting that, "the ending does not suggest the pointlessness of a closed circle of continuing violence and oppression as in *Los de abajo*; a better analogy would be with the return of Ulysses—not so triumphant, but at least a reasonably positive homecoming" (95). For his part, Jorge Aguilar Mora offers a reading of the same novel, but emphasizing what he reads as a purely triumphant conclusion, based on the protagonist's discovery of a pure and unconditional happiness.

As Max Parra has described, Muñoz was a central figure in the formation of Mexican revolutionary ideology, and a founding member of the Partido Nacional Revolucionario (100). His literary production, including short stories published in *El Universal* and later anthologized, and the novels *Se llevaron el cañón para Bachimba* and *¡Vámonos con Pancho Villa!* reflect adherence to revolutionary ideals of manliness, the celebration of violence, and allegiance to the figure of Villa as national legend (101).[10] Yet as Parra also states, in reference to *¡Vámonos con Pancho Villa!*, "the author takes a critical and ironic distance from the legend by contriving scenes in which a shrewd and manipulative Villa deliberately fosters the construction of his own mythology" (116). The space of this kind of "critical and ironic distance" ultimately allows for a nuanced reading of Muñoz's work, and for the recognition that despite an overall fidelity to specific revolutionary ideals embodied by generals such as Villa, these novels also complicate the notion and rendition of allegiance.[11] Rather than an explicit critique of revolutionary exploits, corporeal affect and violence in these novels register a space of mediated unsettling, through which particular bodies, disabled or marked by other differences, impact the narrated revolution and alter its temporal progression. The question of allegiance to the military leader and the revolution he embodies becomes inseparable from the narrations of wounding in the novels, a point to be taken up further in this chapter.[12]

In my approach to *Se llevaron el cañón para Bachimba* and to the question of the revolution as historical process, I consider the degree of distance that separates the narrating subject from the bildungsroman-style chronology he witnesses. Such a distance cannot be measured directly, but emerges through affective tonalities, or in other words, in the material and corporeal impact that the narrative registers, and that gives form and sensibility to the judgment and experience of events in the (fictional) history. The body as witness carries the marks of individual experience, which at the same time record the distance that separates this body from lived or narrated events. It is most notably through the body and its sensations that the measurement of distance is encoded, and sometimes revealed.

Corporeal Pedagogy

In a course I taught a few years ago on literature of the Mexican Revolution, I received the final essay of one student who offered an analysis of Muñoz's text. The student affirmed that, unlike in the argument sustained by Jorge Aguilar Mora in his article, "Novela sin joroba" ("Novel without a Hump"), Muñoz's novel effectively did have a *joroba*, or hump, like the *jorobados* or "hunchbacks" to which the novel refers in a brief anecdote. Without using these exact words, the student, Juliana Ramírez, referring to Roland Barthes's text, "Myth Today," demonstrated how the novel, rather than representing the positive, transformative journey of a child to fulfilled consciousness, actually expressed a cynical and ironic view of this journey. The apparent joy of the young man at the end of the text belies the function of language; words (artificially) express a natural and poetic authenticity so as to better dissimulate language's instrumental and symbolic efficacy. In this sense, for Ramírez, Muñoz's text witnesses and documents the social, economic, and political transformative process that leads from the battlefield to the postrevolutionary Mexican state, and implicitly, to the foreclosure of many of the revolution's promises.

For Aguilar Mora, as for my student, the central axis of the novel and of the critical argument occurs in an initial episode, one that the narrator references again at the end of the novel. The novel's protagonist and narrator, a child named Álvaro Abasolo, describes a servant, Aniceto, who worked at his home: "La viruela había dejado en su cara hoyos semejantes a los de la piel del cerdo" (9) [smallpox had left holes in his face that resembled those of pig skin]. Abasolo remembers a story about witches that Aniceto once told him. The witches would sing, "Lunes y martes y miércoles tres; lunes y martes y miércoles tres" [Monday and Tuesday and Wednesday three; Monday and Tuesday and Wednesday three]. A hunchback who heard them in the woods added to the verse: "jueves y viernes y sábado seis" [Thursday and Friday and Saturday six]. The witches, happy with the new arrangement of the verse, rewarded the hunchback by removing his hump and hanging it from a tree. In the same village lived another hunchback, who was jealous, and on seeing what had happened, decided to follow the example of the first hunchback. He went to the forest and when he heard the witches sing, "Lunes y martes y miércoles tres; jueves y viernes y sábado seis" he added with a shout, "y domingo siete" [and Sunday seven]. The witches, angry this time that the verse was ruined, punished the jealous hunchback, and instead of removing his hump, they placed the hump of the first hunchback on top of his own (9–10). At the end of the novel, Abasolo, having lived through bloody episodes of battle and the defeat of the followers of Pascual Orozco by federal troops, finds himself alone in a forest, walking along, when he realizes his own maturity, "¡Ah, qué alegría! Yo soy un hombre completo desde hace mucho tiempo. Yo sé luchar, yo sé resistir, yo sé perder. Yo tengo ya las enseñanzas de una vida y un propósito muy alto para el futuro" (205). [Oh, what happiness! I have become a complete man since some time ago. I know how to fight; I know how to resist, and I know how to lose. I already have the lessons of a lifetime and great goals for the future.] Here the novel ends with the protagonist's repeated chant, "Lunes y martes y miércoles tres! Jueves y viernes y sábado seis." According to Muñoz, whose 2008 article (also printed as the introduction to an edition of the book) is titled "Novela sin joroba," the end of the novel celebrates the loss of the hump, the symmetry and beauty of the verse, and the eternal and innocent life of the virtual child, full of possibilities before an open future. "El verdadero destino es vivir sin joroba" (248) [True destiny is to live without a hump] writes Muñoz at the conclusion to his text.

As Ramírez notes, however, the language of the first hunchback with its symmetrical verse, when placed in contrast to that of the second, is an example of metalanguage, depoliticized and intransitive, which allows reality to appear as eternal and natural, as an unchanging and normative body. Metalanguage, in Barthes, and in Ramírez's reading, serves to celebrate the objects it designates, to "speak of things" (Barthes 17). In contrast, the added verse of the second hunchback, "y domingo siete!" [and Sunday seven!] is political language, for it expresses a transitive relationship between man and the days of the week. As Ramírez explains, "uno no habla de los días sino que los cuenta y los vive" (Ramírez 11) [one doesn't speak of days but rather counts them and lives them].

In this reading, Abasolo's apparent innocence and happiness at the end of the novel does not indicate a fulfilling and unmediated encounter with the natural world, as Aguilar Mora would have it, but instead the assimilation of a language constructed as if it were natural, so as to dissimulate the ideology sustaining it. For Barthes, the work of language as myth is to dissimulate the historical contingency of modern bourgeois (French) life, to make it appear inevitable and natural. As he writes, "The status of the bourgeoisie is particular, historical: man as represented by it is universal, eternal" (16). In the context of Muñoz's writing, the repeating refrain instead points to an urge to naturalize and dissimulate the historical contingency of the young revolutionary soldier, between one battle and the next, between subservience to a specific general and eventual subservience to the more abstract power of the State. As Abasolo repeats the refrain, he thus reveals his own desire to live outside of historical contingency, as if the repetition would erase the specific conditions of his lived present and historical situation, as easily as the witches could remove the first hunchback's hump. The irony of the repeated verse at the end of the novel gestures toward the violence that this refrain attempts to conceal.

Aguilar Mora's text offers a rigorous, detailed literary analysis of Muñoz's novel, which inserts it in the trajectory of Latin American literature, thus productively questioning the limitations of the category, "the novel of the Mexican Revolution." This is, after all, a category that risks insinuating a reductive and simplistic version of history through literature. Muñoz's narrative, as Aguilar Mora describes, is not historical because of its representation of battles and heroes, but instead because it narrates History, and in this way creates a "Historia como fuerza secreta, la Historia como potencia moduladora de la visión, de los objetos, de los hechos narrados. La historia como gemela de la Naturaleza" ("Novela sin joroba," 236). [History as a secret force, History as modulating power of vision, of objects, of narrated facts. History as the twin of Nature.] But it is perhaps in this notion of History and Nature that asymmetries paradoxically emerge, as when the author affirms, "La Naturaleza no se niega, nunca se entrega a un proceso dialéctico: su condición última de azar es la afirmación pura." [Nature does not negate itself; it never gives in to a dialectical process: its ultimate condition of chance is pure affirmation.] Affirmation, freedom, reconciliation, innocence, and above all, a lack of symbolic distance, are the predominating terms in Aguilar Mora's argument, and which in turn serve as the basis of Ramírez's counterargument. The second hunchback, who cannot be written out of the story, always insists on adding an additional term to the verse, upsetting the balance of the world so as to reveal that its presumed "nature" was never natural. How one reads the extra term, and the asymmetry of the body, has everything to do with the role of disability and its political possibilities in the narrated revolution, which is in turn central to the broader politics of narration and history.

Aguilar Mora's reading insists on bodies, texts and stories that are "bien hechos" [well-made], or "sin joroba" [without a hump]. In a sense the fusion he postulates between subject and history implies the full realization of nature as aesthetically adequate and in harmony with literary aesthetics. Removing the hump in this case means getting rid of the verse that is "literalmente cojo" [literally lame], the second hunchback's "y domingo siete" [and Sunday seven] that leads to a corporal punishment by the witches. However, this interpretation does not account for the disability aesthetics of the novel, the persistence of the hump that is never fully removed. Nor does Aguilar Mora consider that the double hump does more than signify the supposed sin of an asymmetrical verse and body. It also serves as a reminder that in the witches' universe, humps may be added and removed in accordance with one's obedience to the apparent laws of nature and history. In other words, the mechanism of the hump as double or singular, present or absent, underscores its own contingency. In the story of the hunchbacks, neither the hump (singular or double) nor its lack is "natural." Rather, these bodily forms offer language a means to express and dissimulate material conditions as natural and desirable, or just the opposite.

I propose an approach to texts of the revolution such as the work of Muñoz that allows for further attention to bodily affect as part of narrated history, but more importantly, as irreducible to a totalizing project within that history. Disability becomes central here when it is read within the literary text in terms of a nonconformity between the material body and the broader narrative project, or between corporeal experience and historical chronology. In Muñoz's *Se llevaron el cañón para Bachimba*, specific bodies and elements of the landscape bear emphatic marks that create such a sense of nonconformity.[13] In these bodies and objects, history and our critical distance from it is thus rendered affective. The story of the witches and the hunchbacks that frames the novel is more than a refrain and infantile memory, as it connects intimately with the life story and memory of the protagonist.

The episode emerges in the second chapter, just after the speedy departure of Abasolo's father. Aniceto, the servant of the house, is described here in physical terms, in reference to smallpox marks on his face, as cited above. The mention of smallpox finds an echo in Muñoz's previous novel *¡Vámonos con Pancho Villa!* in which a character infected with smallpox is sacrificed to avoid further contagion among the troops. In *Bachimba*, the narrator describes Aniceto as a father figure, and as a permanent part of his memories of his childhood home: "Llegué a imaginar alguna vez que también había sido plantado por mi bisabuelo" (9). [I came to imagine at one point that he had also been planted by my great grandfather.] The servant is therefore animal, through reference to pig skin, vegetable, like a tree on the property, and inseparable from the family lineage. He is also a surviving victim of a smallpox infection prior to the history represented in the novel, the marks of which now define his image and identity forever. In *¡Vámonos con Pancho Villa!* smallpox obeys a more practical, causal logic, allowing for the sacrifice of the individual for the good of the group. In the case of *Bachimba*, on the other hand, the illness functions in a more nuanced fashion because the holes in Aniceto's face prefigure his death, which occurs shortly afterward when Marcos Ruiz (Abasolo's symbolic father, and revolutionary general) fires on him by accident, but without remorse. As the narrator describes, "Y sobre el cadáver de Aniceto pasaron las balas que Marcos Ruiz siguió disparando, hasta marcar media docena de agujeros en el cartón clavado en los adobes pajizos de la pared" (20). [And the bullets that Marcos Ruiz kept shooting passed over Aniceto's corpse, marking half a dozen holes in the cardboard hanging from the straw adobe wall.]

Smallpox does not produce death in a direct manner in either of the novels. Instead, it insists on its own morbid signification, which ultimately makes it literal, with death the inevitable outcome. At the risk of an unfashionably semiotic rendering of this process, one might say that the sign becomes its referent at the same time that it underscores the separation between the two. The reiteration of death, as when a bullet perforates a body already marked with smallpox holes, inscribes this death as pre-determined, but also cruelly unnecessary, a punishment based on a logic of aesthetics. The logic of the double hunchback works in the same sense, for when the second hump is added to the first it emphasizes the symbolic, literalized quality of the punishment for an aesthetic wrongdoing. The hunchback, guilty of disrupting the symmetry of the witches' verse, is in fact always already guilty for his physical difference. The punishment of the double hump affirms this, by equating literary with corporeal aesthetics; it is the repetition of a predetermined and physical identity.

In this sense, the representation of smallpox also refers to the story of the hunchbacks. Aniceto does not simply tell the anecdote about the witches with its refrain, but in fact claims to have heard and seen these witches himself, every night, when they sang their song of the days of the week. As witness to the witches' song, Aniceto occupies the role of the hunchbacks in the story, while also functioning as a link between myth and reality in the narrator's infantile cosmovision. The second hunchback fails to understand the poetic function of the verse and tries to assimilate it to a literal notion of time, and of the chronological sequence of the days of the week. He reveals the awkward and uncomfortable link between the world and language, and for this reason the witches punish him. In a similar sense, Aniceto represents the problematic eruption of literality in the target practice scene. On one hand, his death is accidental, and on the other, necessary and prefigured, as his skin already bore the marks of smallpox holes that would become bullet holes. In this practice scene, Marcos Ruiz and Abasolo use a piece of cardboard, "fijado a la altura de la cabeza de un hombre, en la pared" (19) [fixed at the level of a man's head, on the wall]. Aniceto suddenly appears behind the cardboard, turning the practice session into a literal killing, the novel's first death and first blood. Aniceto inserts his body into what was a theatrical, symbolic space, created by the cardboard that was to receive the bullets. He is punished by death for having literalized the scene, and for putting an end to Abasolo's innocence, which occurs as soon as he witnesses the accident. The logic of the novel is fulfilled from this moment, in which cause and effect, or sign and body, are fused in a singular horizon.

When Abasolo walks along at the end of the novel, to the rhythm of the witches' song that he repeats, he insists on this same logic, to the point of making it into a bodily practice. But far from being a purely celebratory march, the ongoing repetition of the song at once embodies the violence it has produced. The fact that this refrain, repetition, and symbolization of childhood has instantaneously fused with the present body of the narrator does not indicate that the text has produced a harmonious universe, free of symbolic or critical distances. Instead it suggests that the body contains and repeats its own history, which is in turn inseparable from the asymmetries and injustices of a past in continuous movement. This is the repetition of a scene of refusal, a refusal to see the effects of war as mere holes in cardboard, and a reminder that human bodies, too, have wounds and the scars of those wounds.

The joint dilemmas of time and causality in these scenes of repeated wounding suggest the structure of the event, as discussed by Deleuze as both eternal present, and as continually divided into past and future. The impersonal authority of time as *Aion* ensures that the body submits to its predetermined role in a linear temporality. Accidental death is no accident here, but instead the re-inscription of a necessary victimization, repetition as the literalization of symbolic function. At the same time, the wound or scar requires a body, a material embodiment of the event as present, personal moment, in accordance with Deleuze's reading of time as *Chronos*.[14] In this case, too, the scene depends on a witnessing of that body, a repeated, traumatic wounding that continues to move forward and refer back in narrative time while still retaining the intensified present time of the wound as corporeal moment. The fact of witnessing suggests a space of affective response to scenes of wounding, the extension and multiplication of the time of those scenes, gesturing toward both suffering and implicit denunciation.

The experience and representation of disability in the novel, through the images of smallpox marks as bullet holes, the hunchbacks' humps and their removal and replacement, and the story that links these figures, impact the life of the protagonist-narrator and shape the novel's portrayal of temporal progression. Abasolo's repetition of the witches' refrain at the conclusion of the novel functions not only as a return to the scene of a prior wounding, but also as an insistent reminder that this earlier wounding too inhabits an uncertain temporality, always paradoxically both happening now, and projected into the past and the future. The refrain triumphantly omits reference to the "y domingo siete" [and Sunday seven], which would disrupt its aesthetic form. Yet as Abasolo marches to the rhythm of the verse, his body seemingly disciplined by its symmetry, this omission remains crucial for readers who recognize the refrain from its origin story earlier in the novel, and for the narrator himself, whose experience is marked by a prior asymmetry that is both corporeal and temporal. The extra term in the verse—literalized as an extra "hump"—like the temporal asymmetry of the bullet-perforated scar, suggests that the wounded body exists, but does not take place only at a singular, definitive time. This multiplied time that defines the wounded body and its wounding inscribes the body into a relentlessly authoritarian history. Yet the witnessing of these divergent times, and of the absent or present "hump" by the reader and the protagonist, inserts a critical separation from the event and underscores its contingency, the possibility that it might be otherwise. This process of witnessing as affective experience thus defies the triumphantly symmetrical refrain and distorts the narrator's progress through the revolution to ostensible maturity and liberation from his past.

A Duty to Die

The representation of disability in *Se llevaron el cañón para Bachimba* is closely linked to that of death, as is clear in the figure of Aniceto, whose smallpox marks are reiterated through the bullet holes that perforate both his body and the cardboard used for target practice. In Muñoz's earlier novel, *¡Vámonos con Pancho Villa!*, a similar mode of representation emerges repeatedly, as several characters are killed shortly after their violent wounding. This association raises the question of whether these texts represent disability as significantly separate from death. The issue of temporal continuity versus separation between disability, or wounding, and death relates to a separate tension, discussed previously, between the abstract violence of repetition of the event as an always predetermined (mortal) wound, and moments of resistance, denunciation, or creative generation, through which wounds and scars, whether or not they are in some way linked to death in the narrative, offer an affective mediation or disruption of temporal progression. These two forms of tension operate contiguously, because both work through the problem of temporality, and depend on the degree of determinism structuring the unfolding of events over time, on the sense of repetition as abstract equivalence or as conditioned by embodied, affective specificity. Framing disability as distinct and separate from death, despite the novels' insistence on a relentless sequence of mortal wounds, and despite Deleuze's effective analysis of the event as mortal wound, underscores not only the value of disabled lives, whether marked by wounds, scars, trauma, or other conditions, but also the complex connection between disability, with its narrative affects, and the temporal structures it necessarily engages and shapes.

In the case of *Bachimba*, it is the narrator's aural and visual witnessing of physical difference, through the story of the hunchbacks and Aniceto's pock-marked face, that ultimately structures his experience and narration through disability. Aniceto's death within this narration, and the temporal conundrum of his repeated scarring at the moment of death, impact the narrator's experience of temporal continuity; if disability is irrevocably linked to death in this initiating scene of war, it nonetheless also transcends the representation of death through an extended web of meaning that becomes crucial to the narrative arc of the novel as a whole. In the next section of this chapter, I turn more specifically to the novel, and to a lesser extent, the film, *¡Vámonos con Pancho Villa!*, in which the relationship between disability and death punctuates the narrative repeatedly. The graphic representation of violence throughout these popular works helps to sustain the fluidity of action from one battle scene to the next. Yet in addition, detailed textual focus on bodily injuries and their emotional effects becomes central to the novel's aesthetic project and its marked engagement with the problem of chronology, in which trauma and disability play important roles.

The dilemma of disability representation as partially continuous with representations of the process of dying may seem in some ways unique to literature and film of war, with its battlefield accelerations of time between wounding and death. Yet this structure of continuity or equivalence also gestures toward a logic of eugenics as discussed in previous chapters, in which the future for individuals or groups deemed undesirable or marked by circumstances such as poverty, alcoholism, or disease, may be radically foreclosed. A similar structure appears in contemporary debates on physician-assisted suicide. As Alison Davis argues, "the supposed 'right to die' is a subterfuge for what is really a 'duty to die'" (DSQ); in this way, choosing euthanasia potentially acquires a moral quality for the supposed greater benefit of society, just as war narratives may underscore the heroism of death as the ultimate sacrifice, particularly when other lives are saved in the process. In addition, literary and cinematic portrayals of war, injury, and death often work through a narrative logic in which wounding is the necessary precursor to death, so that wounding and death are partially collapsed into a singular process. In a related sense, those on both sides of the contemporary euthanasia debate have expressed, in distinct ways, that concern about this issue stems in part from a socially perceived collapsing of the separation between disability and dying, so that disabled people may be marked as not fully living and not valued.[15] In many war narratives, the dead are monumentalized through the fact of their death, while the affective charge of the text often relies on moments of blurring between the wounded and the dead. This is the case in narratives of the Mexican Revolution as well as those of other wars, in which blurred distinctions between disability and processes of dying, as between death and survival from injury, become inevitable plot features, and contribute to the value of particular bodies, body parts, and personal objects. Partial or ambivalent continuity between disability and death in such narratives of war contributes to the disability aesthetics of the text in question and does not necessarily imply a denigrating depiction of disability. Such representations nonetheless raise questions regarding the symbolic function and human value of characters depicted as both veterans and casualties of war. As Robert Goler asks, in reference to histories of disabled US Civil War veterans, "To what extent does the wounded veteran retain individual personhood in the eyes of the viewer—and of the nation . . . ?" (167). This question becomes increasingly urgent when wounding is depicted in close or uncertain proximity to death. For Elaine Scarry, cited by Goler, injury is the purpose, rather than an incidental outcome of war (Scarry 73). Yet Scarry's language suggests that death is a form of injury: "on the road to injuring soldiers, some civilians were massacred; on the road to injuring civilians, some children were accidentally killed" (75). In the context of war within Scarry's reading, injury as distinct from death is difficult to identify, again raising the question of the status and value of wounded survivors, and of disabled humanity more generally.

In her analysis of literary and cinematic representations of the Mexican military, Elia Hatfield similarly suggests some degree of ambiguity in the separation of disability from death. She writes: "tanto en las novelas como en la pintura y las publicaciones periodísticas, se incluye la temática de los veteranos de guerra, esto es, soldados caídos en batalla o los que quedaron mutilados" (139) [in novels as well as in painting and journalism, the theme of war veterans is included, that is, soldiers fallen in battle or wounded]. The language in this citation itself underscores the difficulty of categorizing subjects as strangely both living and dead, fallen or wounded.[16] Hatfield refers to examples of such "mutilados" in the murals of David Alfaro Siqueiros, in unidentified newspapers, and in the novels *Campamento*, by Gregorio López y Fuentes, and *Tropa vieja*, by Francisco Urquizo (138). She notes that in the case of *Campamento*, the narrative is ambiguous regarding the death or survival of a soldier whose leg is amputated, while in *Tropa vieja*, the wounding of a soldier becomes a form of figurative death. Perhaps the most explicit and lyrical depictions of proximity between wounding and death occur in Nellie Campobello's *Cartucho. Relatos de la lucha en el Norte de México* [*Tales of the*

Struggle in Northern Mexico]. Yet Campobello's text offers not so much a col-lapsing of wounding into death as momentary revitalizations of the dead, and startling temporal reversals that project death into living bodies.

If these works reiterate close associations between disability and death, they also pry open a time and space between these representations, without which they would arguably lose narrative interest. It is this time and space of interrogation that requires further attention in order to appreciate the criti-cal roles of disability in these texts of the revolution. In literary depictions of war, authorial choices regarding the use or omission of graphic imagery or pathos bear a range of aesthetic effects. As Max Parra describes, Muñoz's style in *¡Vámonos con Pancho Villa!* was largely a response to his male, urban readership's demand for graphic, violent depictions of war (98–99). In this sense, detailed descriptions of living wounded bodies and corpses provide a thrill to the reader and sustain fascination with the sensationalized figure of Villa. Parra writes, "The novelist resorts to hyperbole to offer the urban reader a thrilling glimpse of the Other, the 'uncivilized' world, of what is free and unrestrained, along with the morbid and the cruel" (118). Wounded bodies, particularly in the thick of battle scenes, are a key aspect of this otherness, as many violent episodes in *¡Vámonos con Pancho Villa!* make clear. The thrill of otherness also operates here by engagement with temporal continuity and disruption, for the violence of wounding achieves its narrative effects through abrupt shifts in pace, repetition, and the betrayal of readerly expectations—and through the witnessing of death and survival.

Otherness, it may be noted here, also connotes a degree of racial differ-ence in some texts of the Mexican Revolution. This is the case, for example, in Mariano Azuela's *Los de abajo*, in which the protagonist, Demetrio, is explicitly described with indigenous features. In *¡Vámonos con Pancho Villa!* as well, Tiburcio Maya, the central character, is figured as indigenous. Vio-lent wounding and racial difference thus come to participate in processes of mutual signification that remain radically unresolved. This dynamic poten-tially exacerbates a sense of "disidentification" between the urban—hence whitened—reader and the racialized subject of the narrative. Jennifer James uses this term in her discussion of African American war literature, and in reference to the work of Rosemarie Garland Thompson, arguing that realistic depictions of disability may ultimately distance the reader or viewer from the other (248). For James, moreover, the relative absence of graphically repre-sented wounded black male bodies in much of the literature she analyzes is due to black writers' concerns that "war damage and 'congenital' racial dam-age could be conflated" (247–48). Although in *¡Vámonos con Pancho Villa!*, as in other novels of the Mexican Revolution, the question of race is far less explicitly foregrounded than in the African American works in James's study, her insight nonetheless underscores how witnessing doubly marked otherness in these texts may risk congealing the dehumanization of disabled, racialized bodies, even as these narrative ruptures also potentially initiate a denunciatory or radically empathic critical perspective.[17]

¡Vámonos con Pancho Villa!

The first chapters of the novel are punctuated by a series of violent deaths of the Leones de San Pablo, as the group of followers of Pancho Villa call themselves. The youngest of the rebels is the first to go, wounded in the jaw by a grenade. The text suggests that death is inevitable, yet not immediate. The bleeding cannot be contained because the Leones "no entendían nada de cirugía" (22) [knew nothing of surgery], with the implication that proper medical intervention could have saved their comrade's life. Tiburcio, the oldest of the Leones, shoots Miguel Angel del Toro (Becerrillo) to end his suffering. The narrative implies this ending, but never makes it explicit, instead describing in detail the emotional exchange of glances between the Leones, and Becerrillo's final gift of his pistol to Tiburcio. The postponement of death in this episode provides the narrative with an opportunity for gruesome detail, including depictions of what remains of the soldier's mouth and tongue. At the same time, the interstitial space after the wounding allows for the elaboration of affective relations between the soldiers, as well as an emotionally charged depiction of the landscape as the sun sets.

The transformation of the youngest León de San Pablo from brave but innocent rebel soldier to casualty of war takes place through an emotive and grotesque interlude, in which Becerrillo embodies the Other, as referenced by Parra. Here the narrative offers a window onto the soldier's wounded body, the horrific pain he experiences, and onto a visceral encounter with death. The episode also sets the stage for the violent scenes of wounding and death to come, repetitions that replay the inevitability of each prior and subsequent scene and cement the camaraderie of the group members through a collective victimization that this first casualty seems to foretell. Becerrillo's death is the first in a chain of traumatic deaths that ultimately defines the sacrificial honor of the Leones de San Pablo, and their allegiance to the ideal of the revolution as embodied in Pancho Villa. The subsequent chapter includes two additional deaths, so that in these first pages of the novel the Leones are quickly reduced from six to three.

Wounding and death in these pages become a means through which characters are sealed into a common destiny, paradoxically also allowing each to
acquire a particular identity, distinguished from the rest of the group. This
is especially clear in the case of Martín Espinosa, as shown in the following
dialogue: "—¿A qué hora llegaremos, Tiburcio?—preguntó uno de aquellos
hombres, el que tenía cercenado, a la altura del hombro, el brazo izquierdo.—
Lueguito te digo, Espinosa–contestó el viejo" (26) ["What time will we arrive,
Tiburcio?" asked one of those men, the one who had his left arm cut off at the
shoulder. "I'll tell you soon, Espinosa," the old man answered.] Prior to this
chapter the text includes only the mention of the name, Martín Espinosa,
when the men first present themselves to Pancho Villa. But in this chapter
there are five references to Espinosa's one-armed condition, in two cases with
the mention that Victoriano Huerta had ordered the amputation in unspeci-
fied circumstances.[18] It is the first time the reader learns that one of the Leones
de San Pablo had lost an arm, a fact that becomes the character's distinguishing feature, and central to the subsequent descriptions of his heroic death on
the battlefield. References to the one-armed Espinosa throughout the lead-up
to the dramatic battle scene are part of the evocation of a wartime landscape.
Other elements of disability also contribute to these scenes, as in the following passage: "Toma de agua en Jiménez, dónde unos cuantos revolucionarios
heridos reposan, con las piernas extendidas, en el pórtico de la estación, pre-
guntando cómo va la batalla. No se mueve ni una locomotora, que todas han
rodado hacia el sur; ni un hombre, pues todos los útiles se han ido a la guerra"
(27). [They stop for water in Jiménez, where a few wounded revolutionaries
are resting, their legs stretched out, at the station entry, asking how the battle
is going. No engines are moving, for they've all gone south, nor any men, for
all the useful ones have left for the war.] It is a landscape of desolation and
waiting, with the clear implication that the action is taking place elsewhere.
Wounded soldiers are not useful to the war, the passage states explicitly, yet
their representation undoubtedly helps to set the tone of the scene, in combination with other key descriptions: "osamentas de animales perdidos por la
sequía, perros fantasmas . . . Ni un alma. La guerra, la Guerra . . ." (27) [bones
of animals lost to the drought, ghostly dogs . . . Not a soul. War, war . . .] or "un
montón de piedras con una crucecita de brazos torcidos, desiguales, que parece
el esqueleto de un abandonado espantapájaros" [a pile of stones and a little
cross with twisted uneven arms, that looks like the skeleton of an abandoned
scarecrow]. Human and animal remains or their symbols populate the deso-
late landscape, in which even the makeshift grave sites with their asymmetrical humanoid crucifixes contribute to the disability aesthetics of the scene.

If wounded soldiers are left at the sidelines of the battlefield, the same is not true for Espinosa, whose clearly referenced wounding necessarily affects his activity. We learn that he carries a backpack full of dynamite by hanging it around his neck, while others in his group also carry pistols and 30-30 rifles. In the final, dramatic nighttime sequence of the chapter, written as if for film adaptation,[19] Espinosa appears in action, this time after sustaining another major injury:

> Cerca de un tercer fortín no conquistado aún, entre dos rocas que hacían un ángulo obtuso, el manco Espinosa, a quien Victoriano Huerta había mandado cortar un brazo, estaba sentado en el suelo. El fuego de una ametralladora que le disparó casi a tres metros de distancia, le había clareado ambas piernas. Fumaba un largo puro, en cuyo fuego encendía las mechas de las bombas, y con su brazo único las tiraba a rebotar en los muros del fortín. (32)

> [Near a third, still unconquered fortress, in the obtuse angle between two rocks, the one-armed Espinosa, whose arm had been amputated under the orders of Victoriano Huerta, was sitting on the ground. A machine-gun that had fired on him from nearly three metres distance had destroyed both of his legs. He was smoking a long cigar and using its tip to light the fuses of the bombs, which with his only arm he threw at the walls of the fortress.]

Unlike the wounded revolutionary soldiers seated and waiting at the railway station, deemed useless to the war effort, Espinosa emerges here as a strikingly active figure. He too is seated on the ground, as if to evoke the earlier image of the wounded with their outstretched legs, yet rather than resting he uses his one remaining limb to continually strike blows to the enemy. The image effectively contrasts an active, heroic style of aggression with the relative immobility caused by a double wounding. Espinosa's sudden loss of both legs reiterates and enhances his prior physical asymmetry. As in the case of Aniceto's smallpox marks that a fatal bullet hole reiterates in *Bachimba*, here too the destruction of the soldier's legs appears to fulfill the logic of his previous condition. The double wounding situates the scene within a temporal trajectory, in which each injury refers to the other as future or past. Similarly, as Espinosa throws his grenades, he cites prior wrongdoings: "¡Ahí les va por Rodrigo Perea!" (33) [Take that for Rodrigo Perea!], or "¡Por Becerrillo!" [for Becerrillo!] in reference to his recently fallen comrades. One injury demands another within the logic of warfare, but in this case, Espinosa's body also showcases this symmetry in a self-referential sense, embodying and containing its own self-destructive aesthetics.

The cigar that the character smokes, and with which he lights his bombs, adds to the hypnotic violence of the scene, for in combining the casual pleasure of smoking with the purposeful work of the soldier, Espinosa appears to be strangely separate from the deadly situation he occupies, as well as from the pain of his recent wound. At this point in the narrative, the soldier comes to inhabit an interstitial space; his comrades have taken shelter, waiting for additional troops, while only he remains exposed to enemy fire. With one arm and now two legs destroyed, his future activity in the revolution has been radically redetermined. The image is one of hypermasculinity, in which an apparent indifference to pain combines with unwavering adherence to the task at hand, and in which even the nearly complete destruction of bodily capability does not appear to reduce the soldier's display of force. The destructive power of the body is present up until the final seconds of the scene: "De pronto, el rayo de luz de la linterna iluminó entre dos piedras a un medio hombre, contorsionado y sangriento, con los sudorosos cabellos pegados a la frente, manco, con las piernas torcidas hacia afuera, que con el puro en la boca y el costal de bombas colgado del cuello, encendía en la punta de su tabaco la mecha gris de una granada enorme, más grande que el puño" (33). [Suddenly, a ray of the lantern's light shone on a half-man, between two rocks, contorted and bleeding, with sweaty hair stuck to his forehead, one-armed, with his legs bent out to the sides, and with a cigar in his mouth and a sack of bombs hanging from his neck. He was lighting the gray fuse of a huge grenade, bigger than a fist, with the tip of his cigar.]

Because Espinosa throws his final, giant grenade at the same moment that the Federal soldiers shoot him, the force of the destruction he exerts on the enemy extends beyond the life of his body, creating the impression of a transcendent and superhuman power. The last that the reader witnesses of Espinosa is his cigar, which slowly goes out, still held in his clenched jaw, adding to the sense that the power of the revolutionary soldier as instrument of warfare is not reducible to that of a conventional human body, but is continually rearticulated through the prosthetic functions of the grenade and the cigar. The crux of Espinosa's heroism is nonetheless the evident fragility of the body, its injurability, or what allows it to sustain repeated wounds.

In each of these cases, the graphically displayed wounding of the body leads to eventual death and satisfies the voyeuristic desires of Muñoz's readership. At the same time, these scenes, along with the wounding and deaths of the other Leones de San Pablo, build on one another to suggest an ordered continuum in which the logic of each injury ultimately stems from its relation to both prior and subsequent injuries. This progression of violence impacts the chronological sense of the text, as the effects of each wound are determined by those to follow, as well as those that precede it. In this way, Espinosa's destroyed legs in his final battle scene fulfill the aesthetic logic that previously linked his lost arm to the image of the seated, wounded soldiers that the Leones passed en route, while in subsequent cases, this breach will expand and take on distinct forms.

In the iconic scene I have just described, disability becomes specifically visible and determines the overarching aesthetics of the chapter, from the lead-up to the culmination of the battle. It also serves to complicate the temporal division between battles, between the loss of an arm and the subsequent loss of legs, and death. As in the previously discussed case of Aniceto's scarring and death in *Bachimba*, here too the process of injury appears to paradoxically both contract events into a singular present, and separate them out as before and after, as through a Deleuzian temporality of scars and wounding. The repeatedly wounded body confronts and troubles the temporal progression of the narrative, continually gesturing toward the abandoned bodies and injured soldiers that remain both within the landscape of the revolution, yet beyond the parameters of its projected future. The disabled body of the soldier offers a unique mode of witnessing and fragility within the broader narrative arc, for its differences refer to prior battles or other scenes beyond the reader's focus, as well as to continuing survival and to a corporeal memory linking one history to another. To witness these scenes is to sustain injury, this body tells us, to recognize mortality but also to engage in an alternative temporal aesthetics, in which narrative continuity depends on forms of disability as the intertwining of fragility and survival.

The conclusion to the first half of the novel is marked by another emotionally charged death, this time as the consequence of a smallpox infection. The episode repeats the structure of earlier scenes, creating an ambivalent disjuncture between illness and death, while also anticipating the symbolic role of smallpox in Muñoz's later novel, *Se llevaron el cañón para Bachimba*. Tiburcio, following the orders of General Urbina, under Villa, must incinerate Máximo Perea's body (whether dead or alive), along with his belongings, to prevent an epidemic among the troops. In this case, a final and brutal action finishes off the injured victim, completing the logic of wounding but at the same time negotiating the affectively charged difference between the living, wounded body and its annihilation. The disturbing sequence of repeated violence sets the stage for the injuries to come in the second part of the novel, in which Villa himself plays a more central role.[20]

The chapter following this episode includes graphic descriptions of the numerous gravely wounded soldiers, who fill the train cars to overflowing or are carried by others; in many cases the bodies appear to be bordering on death: "inmóviles como cadáveres" (78) [immobile as corpses], "un cargamento de carne destrozada" [a cargo of destroyed flesh], "unos encima de otros, como troncos de árbol, como haces de paja" (80) [some on top of others, like tree trunks, like bundles of straw]. Tiburcio, witness of these scenes, declares to himself, "Si supieron el pago que les tocaba. . . . Pelean como leones, arriesgan diez veces la vida, les agujeran el pellejo, y cuando no sirvan más, les darán una patada en el asiento . . ." (83) [If they knew what reward was coming . . . They fight like lions, risk their lives ten times, get their skin pierced by bullets, and when they're of no further use, they give them a kick in the rear. . . .] This reaction to the collective injustice he perceives suggests continuity with his angry response to the order to burn his former comrade, Perea. Here Tiburcio asks, "¿Éste es el premio a un soldado de la Revolución? ¿Es éste un ejército de hombres o una tropa de perros?" (71) [Is this the reward for a soldier of the Revolution? Is this an army of men or a troop of dogs?]. Attention to the plight of the revolutionary soldiers as collective and exploited body leads to a graphic interrogation of the limits between living and dead—as well as human and animal—bodies. The descriptions, clearly elaborated from Tiburcio's perspective, ask the reader to share in the old soldier's horror at the dehumanization and devaluation of life that is the outcome of battle. These representations, as well as the episode of Perea's death, suggest a dual perspective on the ambiguous divide between injury and death. General Urbina's implicit view that individual lives have value only in relation to their ongoing ability to contribute to military goals contrasts with Tiburcio's emotionally charged reactions to the horrors of war and the devaluation of human life. This duality is exemplified in Tiburcio's refusal to determine whether Perea is alive or dead, after learning from Urbina that from his viewpoint, the question is irrelevant. Urbina states, "Hay que incinerar el cuerpo" (71). [The body must be incinerated.]

These graphic depictions of wounding and death, of both individual and multiple bodies, displayed through an ambivalent, dual framework that emphasizes both the practical worthlessness of men whose status as either dead or close to death becomes irrelevant, and the affectively charged horror as a response to this proximity to death and its cruel circumstances, mark a crucial turning point in the novel. It is at once an echo of the tensions, discussed previously, between the impersonal authority of time as *Aion* and the corporeal denunciation of the Event. This moment also draws our attention to the troubled proximity—and separation—between disability and death.

Embodied Allegiance

The duality between submission to the authority of necessary, inevitable death, and the individual embodiment and witnessing of valued fragility, mediates a key issue in the novel overall, specifically, the question of allegiance to Villa and to the revolutionary cause. Having witnessed the untimely deaths of all five of Tiburcio's comrades in the first half of the novel, all for the cause of Villa's revolution, the reader will now observe the further development of Tiburcio's relationship with Villa at closer quarters—and through multiple episodes of injury—hinging on the issue of whether the soldier will ultimately maintain his allegiance to the general. If Tiburcio's allegiance to Villa or to the abstract revolution is at stake here, so too is Villa's role as embodiment of a post-revolutionary nationalist ideal. Following in Tiburcio's tracks as witness to horror, the reader must determine as well how much her own allegiance can stomach, and whether the nationalist revolutionary cause will retain or reject Villa as its ideal incarnation.

This model of allegiance is further complicated by Villa's unique and shifting role in Mexican post-revolutionary culture. Denigrated in official history but celebrated in popular arts and music (Gilly 136), Villa nonetheless achieves heroic stature in Nellie Campobello's *Cartucho*, published in the same year as *¡Vámonos con Pancho Villa!* As Campobello would later note in reference to her own work, "Mi tema era despreciado, mis héroes estaban proscritos. A Francisco Villa lo consideraban peor que al propio Atila." [My topic was despised; my heroes were banned. Francisco Villa was considered worse than Attila himself.] (Campobello, *Mis libros*, qtd. in Aguilar Mora, *El silencio de la revolución*, 87). Jorge Aguilar Mora reads the differences between the novel and film versions of *¡Vámonos con Pancho Villa!* as suggestive of a divide between the novelist's allegiance to *Villismo* and the state-sponsored film project's apparently more critical view of the general (*El silencio*, 140–41). Horacio Legrás, in contrast, notes a "splitting" of *Villismo* in the film (172), in which the work celebrates the abstract "loyalty and bravery" of Villa's followers but ultimately seeks to remove Villa himself from the equation. These distinct perspectives reveal the complexity of Villa's role in both post-Revolutionary cultural production and in more recent criticism. Moreover, in complicating the structure and scope of allegiance in these works, the critical panorama reframes the position of the body and its injuries in the narrative as relatively separate from or continuous with national and revolutionary ideals. At stake, then, is not merely the question of whether Villa is celebrated or despised, but also the fleshly specificity that allegiance either rejects or retains.

At the end of the episode described here, which marks the conclusion of the film version, Tiburcio walks away, just after Villa snubs him. Although Tiburcio abandons Villa, he retains the formality of military discipline, saluting, as Legrás suggests, "the ideal subsumption of revolutionary force into a nationalist discipline that Villa fails to incarnate" (173). The novel, however, extends the dynamic much further, showing a Tiburcio who returns to fight with Villa, undergoes extreme loss, hardship, injury, and death, all to avoid betraying his general. Both Max Parra and Jorge Aguilar Mora pay particular attention to the issue of Tiburcio's allegiance to Villa in the novel, even in the face of extreme circumstances, each suggesting that the novel ultimately represents a radical form of masculine honor and fidelity to the revolutionary ideal, embodied by Villa.[21]

Whether or not readers respond enthusiastically to Tiburcio's perpetual allegiance and self-sacrifice, it is interesting to note that the pivotal question of the soldier's fidelity, and by extension of the figure of Villa as continuous with the revolution as a collectively affirmed, just cause, derives directly from representations of wounded bodies, in some cases suspended between injury and death. Although the novel represents a seemingly endless proliferation of deaths, and most incidents of violence depicted end either in death or suggest its inevitability, it is in fact wounding rather than death that sustains the novel's central tension. The wounded body in the text offers witnesses the opportunity to focus either on an inevitable and necessary proximity to death, or on the wounding itself and its continuity with the life of the human subject in question. The textual space of wounding and the questions it poses correspond to the more explicitly crucial question of allegiance to Villa and the extremes to which such allegiance may extend. Yet this allegiance, rather than an absolute position, emerges through the experiences of wounding and its uncertain temporality, and is ultimately inscribed on the bodies of both Tiburcio and Villa. As noted, the issue is not simply whether Tiburcio remains faithful to Villa, but as a corollary, to what extent Villa himself will continue to embody the abstract ideals of revolution and nation. This is why the specificity of Villa's body and the injuries it sustains become the central focus in the concluding pages of the novel.

The repeated insistence on wounding in the novel, as continuous with the issue of allegiance to Villa, reaches its apex toward the conclusion of the text. Villa, himself wounded by a bullet in his knee, has fallen ill and takes refuge in a cave, accompanied by just a handful of his soldiers, including Tiburcio. When Tiburcio leaves the cave to look for two of his comrades who failed to return one day, he falls into a trap and is captured by American soldiers looking for Villa. The Americans, part of the Punitive Expedition following Villa's incursion into Texas, are accompanied by Apache guides, who are the ones to inflict physical punishment on their victim in an effort to make him reveal Villa's whereabouts, in this case skinning the soles of Tiburcio's feet with a knife. The descriptions of Tiburcio's torture, suffering, convalescence, and execution, extend through the final two chapters of the novel, prolonging the timing and details of wounding as physical experience and as mode of engagement between conflicting parties.

The extension of Tiburcio's trauma has dramatic appeal as a conclusion to the novel and as an apex of the suffering to which Villa's followers must commit. It turns out, however, that Tiburcio's extreme wounding, followed by his death at the hands of the Carrancistas to whom the Americans finally abandon him, is not the end of the novel. Following a break in the text, an extended quotation appears, attributed to "Nicolás Fernández, compañero de Francisco Villa por más de trece años" [Francisco Villa's companion for more than thirteen years]. The initials, R. F. M. (Rafael Felipe Muñoz) function to assert that the quoted passage was conveyed directly to the author of the novel. The words ascribed to Nicolás Fernández, with which the novel concludes, describe Villa's eventual escape from the cave where he had been hidden, and the aftermath of the injury to his leg. The narrative pays particular attention to the details of a crude operation, through which a bullet is removed from Villa's leg, with no anesthesia, and with a jackknife and horseshoe pliers as the only available instruments. As the passage concludes, "[se] sacó la bala, que estaba chueca, porque antes de metérsele al jefe había tocado una piedra" (222) [[they] took out the bullet, which was bent, because before entering the commander it had hit a rock].

The explicit asymmetry of this final image, with its curious focus on the extracted bullet, distorted in its path, portrays Villa's injury as an unexpected accident, a divergence from the central narratives of war and battle, just as the bullet itself was diverted in its path by the rock, and subsequently by Villa's body. Similarly, this final injury and surgical cure present a distorted mirroring of the previous episode featuring Tiburcio's wounding and aftermath, for the two narrative sequences reflect and oppose one another in multiple senses. While Villa's wound is featured as a partial accident, a form of collateral damage during battle, Tiburcio's feet are deliberately skinned as a means of torture in order to extract information, and his treatment by the Americans and the Carrancistas is purposeful, leading to an outcome that follows the inexorable narrative logic through which other characters in the novel have suffered. Tiburcio's experience of wounding is drawn out in painful detail and includes shifts in the soldier's sense of material reality and body image. In contrast, the description of Villa's injury suggests extreme pain, but is relatively short and direct, obeying the laws of mechanical physics, and in this sense conforming to material reality as conventionally understood. And while the episode of Tiburcio's wounding forms part of the fictional universe of the novel, the final anecdote about Villa is set apart from the text as a quotation of words ostensibly communicated to the author, as if beyond the realm of fiction. Through this narrative strategy, Villa's body—wounded and healed—acquires additional material weight, in contrast with Tiburcio's more ephemeral representation. The final description of Tiburcio's hanging dead body enhances its fictional qualities: "todavía sangraban los pies de Tiburcio Maya cuando los besaron las aguas sollozantes del Papiogóchic" (221) [Tiburcio Maya's feet were still bleeding when the sobbing waters of the Papiogóchic River kissed them]. The lyricism of this description ascribes active, lifelike emotions and actions to the river water, while emphasizing the fluidity and suspension between the states of life and death of the body. Metaphors of flowing and hanging ambivalently between these two states become literal in the figure of Tiburcio's body, strung above the water. In contrast, Villa's wound and subsequent surgical intervention, complete with mechanical explanation, appear as the answer and counterpart to the painful, prolonged and fluidly uncertain suspension through which Tiburcio, the last and most faithful of the Leones de San Pablo, is finally displayed.

The distorted mirror image of wounding with which *¡Vámonos con Pancho Villa!* concludes underscores the explicitly corporeal nature of allegiance as central to the project of the narrated revolution, as well as the asymmetries of this project. The lessons of allegiance occur through their graphic inscriptions on the body, which in turn describe tenuous separations between wounding and death, faith and betrayal. Even in the final scene of Villa's bullet removal, Villa must agree to hand over his pistol, lest extreme pain cause him to fire on the man operating on him. The asymmetry of this dual scene of wounding and allegiance, with its deadly consequences for Tiburcio and brief convalescence for Villa, once again foregrounds a temporal disjuncture, as occurs in earlier instances of wounding throughout the novel. In the case of Tiburcio, the wound marks a temporal impossibility, his feet expressing the continuous present of having been wounded, which is at once also future and past.

Unlike the narrative progression from Tiburcio's torture, wounding, and eventual death, Villa's convalescence appears in direct relation to calendar time. The text includes specific reference to the number of days and months of each stage of Villa's movements, and in one case an exact date: "exactamente el día primero de julio, a los tres meses exactos de la salida de Guerrero, se nos vino a aparecer en San Juan Bautista, Durango, donde lo estábamos esperando" (221) [on exactly July 1, three exact months since the departure from Guerrero, he arrived in San Juan Bautista, Durango, where we had been waiting for him]. Villa moves according to standard measured time, a time that is both predetermined and historically specific in retrospect. This conclusion, with its seemingly historical depiction of Villa and his actions within the chronology of the revolution, nonetheless continues to gesture toward its immediate and asymmetrical counterpart, the episode of Tiburcio's wounding and its aftermath, thus incorporating scenes beyond the framework of historically defined temporality, yet still crucial to the landscape of the revolution and the novel.

The problem of allegiance to the revolution in this conclusion is realized through a double staging. In one sense, Tiburcio's wounding and death confirm an unwavering fidelity to both leader and cause, inseparable as the body from its mortality, as each event from the totality of repetition, even while suggesting that Tiburcio could have saved himself at any moment by choosing to betray Villa. In a second sense, the question shifts to encompass Villa himself, as authoritarian figure and abstract ideal, who nonetheless turns out to sustain his own physical injuries. Villa's embodiment and relative fragility may remind the reader that the general, too, is replaceable, and that the ideals of nation and revolution transcend the materiality of a given body. This recognition suggests that allegiance, enacted through repeated wounding, does not always leave its symbols intact, and that abstract authority may shatter to reveal—and even to abandon—its own vulnerable, fleshly content. The seemingly inexorable structure of authoritarian temporal continuity begins to waver as we realize, witnessing injury, that even the authority itself must submit to embodiment and its repeating logic.

As I have emphasized throughout this chapter, representations of disability and wounding mediate the functions of time and temporal progression in these narrations of the revolution. Time, and the events that may serve to define it, are in turn experienced through forms of wounding, borrowing from Deleuze's notion of events in time as wounds or scars. In slightly different terms, time in these novels may be said to appear in key instances as "out of joint,"[22] a figure of speech that serves effectively to bridge the use of time in language to the corporeal expression of disability, for conventionally it is a limb or a bone, not time, that is out of joint, or dislocated. Taking note of instances of wounding in relation to disrupted time, and to the dilemma of allegiance in the narrative of the revolution, as I have proposed, means focusing on the roles of corporeal asymmetry and disability and their potential, transformative impact on the politics of narration and history. Such a focus, however, does not necessarily lead to the conclusion that disability functions as a radical disruption in these texts, for repetitions of violent injury may also work to congeal an authoritarian temporal logic. Yet the question of whether such repetitions ultimately solidify the power of a prior authority, or whether they potentially offer a space for some form of resistance, could be reconfigured through specific attention to the act of witnessing injury and the transformations this entails. Here, we might consider Derrida's formulation of a related temporal asymmetry, or what he calls a disadjustment:

> It is easy to go from disadjusted to unjust. That is our problem: how to justify this passage from disadjustment (with its rather more technico-ontological value affecting a presence) to an injustice that would no longer be ontological? And what if disadjustment were on the contrary the condition of justice? And what if this double register condensed its enigma, precisely [justement], and potentialized its superpower in that which gives its unheard-of force to Hamlet's words: "The time is out of joint"? (Derrida, 22)

The "double register" to which Derrida refers here comprises both disadjustment, for example, in the sense of an asymmetry or incongruity in narrative temporality, and an injustice—paradoxically continuous with a potential demand for justice—that is inseparable from such an incongruity. The demand, in this case, depends as well on the witnessing and subsequent articulation of the injustice. In the novels discussed in this chapter, wounding enacts and defines temporal disadjustments, while at once negotiating sites of injustice, drawing attention to a devaluation of life, to a projected, eugenic erasure of future wounded or disabled life, and to the ongoing exploitation of racialization and disability. Throughout this book, we have observed related articulations of disability, often expressed through the hygienic and generally uncritical projection of undesirable difference toward uncertain pasts and futures. Here, however, temporal continuity is itself ruptured through the emergence of disability, thus foregrounding the dilemma of an asymmetry that shapes our sense of chronology and cannot be simply delayed or postponed.

This reading recognizes a demand for justice in Muñoz's novels—precariously threaded into the repeating structures of authority and allegiance—through the refusal of definitive conclusions, and through the continual reconfiguration of wounds and the time they express. The narrative leaves evidence of highly charged asymmetries, returning again to scenes of wounding and the bodies they continually recreate, evoking an aesthetics of allegiance that is always corporeal, and a lesson that is brutally unresolved. As physical evidence, the spent bullet from Villa's leg, impacted and bent by a rock, a time-stamped text, remains available and demands another investigation, another test of our allegiance, and perhaps, an inevitable submission to its authority. But for the evidence of Tiburcio Maya's feet bleeding into the river, of the many wounded, suspended bodies, still marked by past and future fragilities, we will have to find other ways of witnessing.

Epilogue

In 2001, Dr. Julio Frenk, who served at the time as Minister of Health, gave a presentation at a conference on genomic medicine in Mexico. Discussing the contemporary situation of public health in Mexico from a historical perspective, Frenk stated the following:

> Hemos pasado una situación donde predominaban las muertes derivadas de eventos agudos, donde el tiempo entre la aparición de la enfermedad y su resolución era corto, la resolución era ya fuera por la curación o por muerte. Ahora pasamos una situación donde el tiempo con que una persona pasa enferma es largo, donde el tiempo en que aparece la enfermedad y ocurre un desenlace es muy largo. Y este predominio de la discapacidad en el panorama de la salud es una de las características importantes de la transición epidemiológica: cada vez más, hay personas que, sin estar enteramente sanas o enteramente muertas, viven con grados distintos de discapacidad y nuestras medidas tienen que tomar en cuenta que la salud no es un estado binario de vida o muerte, sino que es un estado con múltiples grados de discapacidad.

> [We have been in a situation in which deaths caused by acute events predominated, in which the time between the onset of illness and its resolution was short, resolution being either through cure or death. We are now in a situation in which the time that a person experiences illness is long, in which the time from when illness appears to its resolution is very long. And this predominance of disability in the panorama of health is one of the important characteristics of the epi-

demiological transition: increasingly there are people who, without being entirely healthy or entirely dead, live with various degrees of disability, and our measures must take into account that health is not a binary state of life or death, but rather a state with multiple degrees of disability.]

Frenk juxtaposes two partially overlapping health models here, contrasting his twenty-first-century moment with a prior period exemplified by data from 1940. The transition, though gradual and incomplete, corresponds to improvements in public health and the availability of newer vaccines over the latter half of the twentieth century. This temporal juxtaposition also corresponds roughly to the encounter enacted throughout this book, between archival and literary documents of the early post-revolution, and the present-day moment of our reading, in which these texts come to participate in shaping a disability genealogy. Frenk's focus, however, is on the disability of our contemporary times, understood, in a troubling sense, as embodied by those who are neither "entirely healthy" nor "entirely dead." This devaluation of disabled life, which Frenk situates predominantly in the poorer, southern—and hence racialized—regions of the country, works through the categorization of humans as not fully alive, or as indefinitely suspended between life and death through an extended, uncertain prognosis.

This state-centered discourse is noteworthy for its radical othering of disabled people, but also for the temporal dilemmas it performs. First, the suggested overlap between states of life and death creates a rupture with conventional chronology, strangely evocative of the disadjustments of wounding and death in Rafael F. Muñoz's novels, discussed in chapter 5. Second, the incomplete transition between public-health standards of the earlier twentieth century and those of the twenty-first means, as Frenk further notes, that patients may experience illnesses commonly ascribed to the earlier period, such as tuberculosis, at the same time that they live with conditions generally associated with more recent history, such as diabetes. In a sense, such patients come to inhabit a dual time, embodying the simultaneity of past and present health histories. Third, the perspective of the health official who observes and accounts for these trends over time suggests a position that is partially outside the temporal progression of life and death, illness and prognosis. While the public-health phenomenon of extended or delayed prognosis occurs in Frenk's contemporary moment, it is at once mainly situated elsewhere, as if from another time, though touching on and threatening to overflow the limits of a collective national self. Disability and illness, as evoked in this perspective, seem perpetually bound up with the troubled flows of time and history. The precarity of human life described here becomes inseparable from a precariously experienced temporality, and from unsettled histories that refuse the conventions of singular linearity.

In this book, my focus has been on reading disability in the early post-revolutionary decades, and not on the high mortality rates due to infectious illnesses to which Frenk refers in this period. The disability that emerges in my readings is shaped by diagnoses of developmental delay, by notions of abnormality stemming from the influences of statistics, eugenics, and racism, and by projected fears or suspicions of past and future causes and effects, or what I have referred to as temporal contingencies. I also consider the role of disability as injury and its capacity to transform or distort the experience of temporal progression. The archival encounters discussed in the pages of this book enact uncertain temporal and causal horizons, in which disability is often difficult to locate in a precise manner, mediated by diverse perspectives, diagnostic frameworks, unknown pasts and futures, or other conditioning factors.

A twenty-first-century viewpoint also mediates these readings; similarly, as Frenk reflects on historical changes in paradigms of health, illness, and disability, he perhaps unwittingly reminds us that a contemporary perspective necessarily transforms the shape of the prior history to which it is juxtaposed. At the present-day moment in which I conclude the writing of this book, a global pandemic, unimaginable just six months earlier, has thoroughly saturated our collective attention, superimposing another lens onto these accumulated histories. As in Frenk's configuration of certain populations as strangely suspended between life and death, contemporary statistical projections on the impacts of Covid-19 in various global regions also suggest a prolonged suspension, in which precarity and potential risk mark bodies in accordance with their perceived chances of survival. In this case too, racialization, socioeconomic inequity, and disability shape the proliferating data, as well as public impressions of others' proximity to death. From this perspective, instead of seeing bodies or their conditions "as they are," we may tend to focus on what such bodies might become, or on what has happened to them.[1] The statistical data through which we imagine or interpret differences and prognoses today may remind us as well of the perceptual and quantitative frameworks of biotypology and statistics in post-revolutionary Mexico, which approach but never fully define the bodies to which they refer, as discussed in chapter 4.

Disability, from Frenk's contemporary perspective, operates as a conundrum of time and history, but this structure, as it turns out, is not entirely new or unique to the twenty-first century. Notwithstanding undeniable improvements to public health over the last century, as emphasized in Frenk's discussion of the "epidemiological transition," as well as radical social changes, state-sponsored discourses of disability reveal the persistence of familiar dilemmas. Undesirable differences may exist in the past, may soon arrive in the future, can be explained by a set of circumstances or perspectives, are often displaced from the specificity of the here and now, or may in turn displace and reshape experiences of time and history, blurring passage from one moment to the next. In this way, the eugenically perceived, potential birth of an alcoholic's child in 1930s Mexico, as discussed in chapter 2, marks a site of disability as driven by both uncertain causality and morally inflected national history. In a related sense, the extended prognosis of late-twentieth-century and contemporary health conditions situates the disabled person in an indefinite, tentative suspension between life and death, not fully valued as human because not deemed fully alive. In each case, though particularly in the twenty-first century, the suspended location of disability is determined in part by a biopolitical framework in which population tendencies increasingly take precedence over individual lives or stories. Both scenarios, though distinct, imagine disabled life as delimited by indefinite temporal coordinates, potentially stretching into individual or transgenerational futures and pasts. In each case as well, disability becomes curiously identified with both marginal subjects and with an overarching national experience and collective identity. For Frenk, the long time span of disability appears to saturate the public-health horizon, potentially impacting everyone, while at the same time remaining disproportionately present in poorer regions, hence elsewhere. Similarly, discourses of health and pedagogy addressed in this book tend to situate disability in marginal spaces such as special schools or underserviced areas, yet at the same time center the projects of Mexican education and hygiene in direct proximity to notions of abnormality and aberration. This occurs, for example, in the National Institute of Psychopedagogy's impetus to acquire exact knowledge of "the Mexican child" discussed in chapter 3, as inseparable from its emphasis on special education, the "feebleminded," and "cripples."

What has changed significantly over this time span, however, are the centrality and power of the Mexican state, particularly since the defeat of the Partido Revolucionario Institucional (PRI) in the 2000 presidential elections. As Oswaldo Zavala argues, this moment represents the culmination of a gradual process of the weakening of the state, initiated in the neoliberalism of the 1980s (193). When Frenk speaks for the state in 2001, he evokes a dispersed and fragmented power, through reference to bodies that appear increasingly outside the reach of both state care and control, liminally situated in the distance and at the suspended frontier between life and death. Much like the debility to which Jasbir Puar refers, emerging through unequal structures of exposure to illness and injury under colonialism and capitalism (xvii) or Lauren Berlant's notion of slow death as the gradual wearing down of populations (754), Frenk's description of the contemporary disabled population as "not entirely dead" also suggests a mode of biopolitical violence, specific in this case to a transitory splintering of federal power in early-twenty-first-century Mexico. In this contemporary scene of eugenics, projected over a distant southern landscape in prolonged, intimate proximity to death, the state both sustains and relaxes its grip, gesturing toward other, private-sector players that might intervene or collaborate in the administration of survival through biomedical initiatives.

My juxtaposition of Frenk's strangely worded discourse with the archives we have encountered in this book suggests, inevitably, both rupture and continuity over an incomplete twentieth-century time span. The temporal and spatial dispersal of state power and public-health discourse in the era of genomic medicine offers a complex and diluted image of embodied nationalism and mortality, in some ways at odds with earlier configurations of a vigorously centralized post-revolutionary state. At the same time, Frenk's transhistorical perspective, binding the evocation of disability to temporal suspension, ambiguity, and discontinuity, both inflects and echoes prior stories and their repeating dilemmas of time and history. Following the trace of this backward glance thus reveals a disability genealogy, one that is necessarily tentative and unfinished, composed of the ruptured chronologies of human differences, of the contingencies of causality, perspective, and mediation, and the imperative for a witnessing of injustice. Throughout this book, I have aimed to imagine such a genealogy, placing archival and literary encounters in the context of a present-day reading, while reflecting on possible points of contact between disability discourses of our contemporary moment and those of the historical texts. The connections explored here are in part the result of what I term an embodied archive, the fleshly witnessing of documents as a lived and transformative intercorporeal encounter. This reading, though reaching its endpoint within these pages, does not pretend to offer the finality of a conclusion, or a resolution of the repeating dilemmas it has posed. Instead, as the active retracing of incomplete histories, the embodied archive envisions and enacts the dynamic uncertainty of disability. Such a dwelling with uncertainty may risk the reiteration of ongoing, unresolved suspensions of life as death and the troubled bracketing or postponement of undesirable prognosis that the state and its agents still articulate in evolving forms. Yet in recognizing the discursive and literal violence that the archive mirrors back to us, we might instead begin to participate more seriously in a historically grounded witnessing of injustice, and to imagine the unknown ways in which we could yet come to inhabit our differences.

Notes

Introduction

1. According to Chapman, Carey, and Ben-Moshe, "Institutional life, whether in a prison, hospital, mental institution, nursing home, group home, or segregated 'school' has been the reality, not the exception for many disabled people, both throughout North American history since the poorhouse, and globally—again because of concrete impositions of colonialism and neocolonialism, here and the world over" (17).

2. The concept of intercorporeality is borrowed from Gail Weiss, who reads it in a phenomenological and psychoanalytic key. She writes, "The experience of being embodied is never a private affair, but is always already mediated by our continual interaction with other human and nonhuman bodies" (5). Weiss emphasizes the notion of body image through the work of Merleau-Ponty, Schilder, and Lacan (among others), and argues that body images are shaped by fluid exchanges within and beyond each individual (86). The idea of intercorporeality appeared in my previous book, configured in literary terms as "prosthetic relationships between body and text, as well as between one body and another, or a body and itself" (*Carnal Inscriptions* 12). Rebecca Janzen productively takes up intercorporeality in her reading of marginalized literary characters in Mexican fiction, arguing that these figures together form an intercorporeal, collective entity (11–12).

3. Studies of eugenics and hygiene in Mexico do not typically emphasize the concept of disability, nor do they often link this history to contemporary debates in disability studies. A notable exception to this tendency is Adriana Soto Martínez's article on disability and injustice in Mexican history and society. Also see Christian Giorgio Jullian Montañez's outstanding doctoral thesis, "Palos de ciego."

4. See for example Marius Turda, *Eugenics and Modernism*; Alexandra Stern, *Eugenic Nation*; Nancy Leys Stepan; David Mitchell and Sharon Snyder, "The Eugenic Atlantic."

5. See for example Dolmage, 23–30; McLaren, 46–67.

6. As Stepan writes, "In the Lamarckian tradition it was assumed that external

influences on an individual life could permanently alter the germ plasm, so that the distinction between germ plasm and somaplasm was blurred" (25). Dr. Alfredo M. Saavedra, founder of Sociedad Mexicana de Eugenesia para el Mejoramiento de la Raza (Mexican Eugenics Society for the Improvement of the Race), defined eugenics as "a group of rules of social application which has as its goal the transformation of society towards an effective biological improvement" (ctd. in Suárez y López Guazo 146). All translations in this book are mine unless otherwise indicated.

7. López Beltrán writes that figures such as Spencer, Haeckel, Delage, and Le Bon, rather than Lamarck, were influential in Latin American scientific thought. As he states, "La herencia humana a menudo es vista por ello como un proceso complejo, de naturaleza holística y contradictoria, en el que se combinan atavismos (influencias ancestrales retrógradas) y capacidades de creación innovadora (o adaptación) de los organismos" (186). [For this reason human inheritance is often seen as a complex process, of a holistic and contradictory nature, combining atavisms (retrograde ancestral influences) and the capacity for creative innovation (or adaptation) of organisms.]

8. In *Eugenic Nation*, Alexandra Stern discusses the roles of neo-Lamarckism and Mendelianism in eugenics and genetics, 14–16.

9. The coexistence of the two models creates an additional dilemma for historians of science, as may be observed in the divergence between those who read Mexican eugenics as a fluid category with links to nineteenth-century degenerationism and twentieth-century social hygiene, among other fields, and those who mark out a stronger disciplinary separation, in which eugenics is granted a more strictly defined and limited role. Andrés Ríos Molina argues for a degree of division between eugenics and hygiene in Mexico, affirming that unlike in Europe and the US, the eugenics movement in Mexico never acquired strong state support, in part because the Mexican notion of race through *mestizaje* was incongruous with eugenic theories of race (148–49). For Ríos Molina, the issue of race does not play a role in the projects of mental hygiene that are the topic of his study (150).

10. This distinction is also relevant to my discussion of statistics and hygiene in chapter 4.

11. Joshua Lund also notes the importance of Molina Enríquez's contribution to the discourse of *mestizaje* (x, xv). Both Miller and Lund cite the importance of Agustín Basave Benítez's work on Molina Enríquez.

12. See for example Moreno Figueroa and Saldívar Tanaka, and Navarrete.

13. Also see Octavio Paz's classic reading of the foundational union of La Malinche with Hernán Cortés, 86–88.

14. See chapter 2, note 8, for reference to disability as invoking pathos.

15. Oliver and Barnes provide a useful discussion of the social model in the contexts of both academic study and policy implementation. Carolina Ferrante provides a detailed discussion of the social model in international and Latin American contexts. For discussion of the social model in the Mexican context, see Jorge Victoria Maldonado, and Norma Acevés García. Also see Patricia Brogna.

16. See for example Mitchell, Antebi, and Snyder; Barad; and Chen, referenced in chapter 3, notes 3 and 4.

17. Carolina Ferrante discusses the UN Convention and discrepancies between national and international law and implementation, particularly in the Latin American context (41–43). Also see Christian Courtis.

18. The notion of encounter here borrows from V. K. Preston's approach to the archive as "performative," as well as "processual and embodied" (16). Preston in turn draws on Jill Lane's concept of witnessing, and Alanna Thain's theory of the anarchive, in which "potential for the creative entails an ethics of research and performance, even as it discloses fantasies of accumulation and objection nested in the archive" (16).

19. Public welfare would fall within the purview of the state in 1861, thanks to President Benito Juárez's reforms, which sought to reduce ecclesiastical influence in public matters. In the later nineteenth century, conflicts and overlaps between Public Welfare and Public Health led to shifts in their respective jurisdictions, with the latter ultimately taking precedence over the former (Agostoni, *Monuments of Progress* 58–60). In 1915, Beneficencia, including its various hospitals and institutions, became subordinate to the government of the Federal District, to be managed at the municipal level, while the Constitution of 1917 established the Departamento de Salubridad Pública as a federal entity. In 1924, President Obregón established the Junta Directiva de la Beneficencia Pública, increasing its independence from the municipal government, but at the same time subjecting its institutions to norms imposed by the Ministry of Public Education and the Department of Public Health (Jullian Montañez 96). In 1937, the newly created Secretaría de Asistencia Pública (Ministry of Public Assistance) replaced the institution of Beneficencia, and 1943 saw the fusion of health and assistance into a new Ministry of Public Health and Assistance (Alonso Gutiérrez).

20. As Jullian Montañez describes, in reference to the establishment of the Escuela Nacional de Ciegos y Sordomudos in 1928, the notion of abnormality during this period underwent a shift, thanks to the influence of eugenics. No longer strictly defined by the inability to receive education in a conventional manner, abnormality now came to encompass negative or undesirable traits, determined by statistical measurement (116–22).

21. See Torres Puga.

22. "Así, el espacio actúa una lucha en la que pasamos de la administración de los cuerpos inadaptados a la de una forma de traer la memoria, los regímenes de verdad y el carácter de lo público" (Draper 353).

23. See for example Laura Suárez y López Guazo, *Eugenesia y racismo*, 99–101. Alexandra Stern also discusses this point in "Unravelling."

24. Alexandra Stern provides a rich analysis of this history. See "Responsible Mothers."

25. On this point see Titchkosky, referenced in chapter 2, note 4.

26. See chapter 4 for discussion of this structure.

Chapter 1

1. Carranza's 1917 speech in favor of the Ley sobre Relaciones Familiares, in which he argues against the marriage of people with certain illnesses that might be transmitted to their offspring, is exemplary of this tendency; see Suárez, "Evolucionismo y eugenesia," 20. Both Aaron Dziubinskyj and Ermanno Abbondanza discuss the history of the eugenics movement in Mexican and international contexts relevant to the novel. Also see the work of Nancy Leys Stepan and Alexandra Stern on this period in Mexico and in other Latin American countries.

2. On the history of eugenics in Cuba, see Armando García González, who emphasizes 1914 as a key year, thanks in part to the Primer Congreso Médico Nacional (87). On Urzaiz's New York residency, see Ermanno Abbondanza, who discusses Urzaiz's probable exposure to the eugenics movement, as well as its growing international importance in the period.

3. Although I do not address Ortiz's work in detail here, his participation in eugenic discourse through criminological studies such as *Los negros brujos* (1906), published with a prologue by Cesare Lombroso, makes him a key figure for understanding early-twentieth-century Cuban and Latin American debates on race, immigration, and hygiene (Amador 27). I am grateful to Catia Corriveau-Dignard for making the connection between Urzaiz and Ortiz.

4. In her discussion of face-to-face encounters, Rosemarie Garland-Thomson notes that "while staring's form is scripted, its capacity to create meaning is unstable and open-ended" (39). My analysis of the processes of observation at work in these eugenic encounters similarly emphasizes both the codes through which visible differences appear, and the unstable transformations that acts of looking allow.

5. As an example of the centrality of race in Mexican eugenic discourse, see Beatriz Urías Horcasitas's groundbreaking study.

6. I use the term "disability" here as distinct from "pathology" in this case so as to distinguish between Tucker's examples of pathology, which generally indicate morbidity, and the bodies depicted in Urzaiz's work, which present nonnormative characteristics but are not necessarily close to death.

7. For Abbondanza, the reference to sugar is a key indicator of Urzaiz's reference to Cuba.

8. Jorge Quintana Navarrete also makes the argument that the novel offers radical ambiguity regarding whether the world it imagines is a utopia or a dystopia, building on David Dalton's affirmation that the work "blurs the distinction between utopia and dystopia" (Dalton, *Mestizo Modernity* 163). For Quintana Navarrete, this ambiguity has allowed for sharply contrasting interpretations of the work, but also for a reading that is open to creative and transformative fluidity, of "la vida *como* impulso utópico."

9. These lines also fit the context of late-nineteenth-century decadentism.

10. My translation of the passage from Urzaiz's thesis is closely derived from the English translation of the relevant portion of the novel; see page 71 of the English edition.

11. Davis locates the concept of normality as corresponding to the rise of the

novel in the eighteenth and nineteenth centuries, and through reference to Adolphe Quetelet's work in statistics and eugenics (*Bending Over* 92–94).

12. See David Mitchell and Sharon Snyder's classic work on this topic.

13. There were a few sterilization laws in US states prior to 1919, as Urzaiz suggests, but compulsory eugenic sterilization was not widespread in the US until the 1927 *Buck v. Bell* Supreme Court decision. See Paul Lombardo. As Alexandra Stern has shown, the only sterilization law to go into effect in Latin America was enacted in 1932 in Veracruz, but there is no evidence of actual sterilizations performed under this law, "The Hour of Eugenics in Veracruz." Marius Turda and Aaron Gillette note that in the 1920s and '30s eugenic sterilization became more common in Protestant countries but was condemned by the Catholic Church (11).

14. Galton alludes to a distinction between a "positive" and a "negative" eugenics in his 1883 work, *Inquiries into Human Faculty and its Development*, 307.

15. Here Davidson refers to the work of Sherry M. Velasco on male pregnancy in early modern Spain.

16. In his 2014 critical translation of *Eugenia*, written jointly with Sara Kachaluba, Dziubinskyj offers a revised view of the racism in the novel. The authors read the depiction of the African doctors as explicitly racist, and not as a satire or critique.

17. Rachel Haywood Ferreira also offers a detailed and nuanced reading of *Eugenia*, ultimately arguing that if the novel does not offer a satirical or clearly dystopian reading of the eugenic future it portrays, neither does it represent a comfortably resolved utopia (66–79).

18. "The deliberate juxtaposition of distinct racial physiologies is in part a critique of the inherently racist ideologies associated with eugenics" (Dziubinskyj 467). However, annotation to a 2014 English translation of *Eugenia* that Dziubinskyj coauthored with Sara Kachaluba revises this perspective, indicating that the racism expressed in this passage was intrinsic to eugenics and reflected Urzaiz's thinking and that of his colleagues (*Eugenia* 92n14).

19. On the work of the two neurologists and the relation between them, see Siegel. Though not focused on Charcot, Delaporte's *Anatomy of the Passions* offers useful insight on the work of Duchenne and his development of links between physiology and emotions, as well key connections to Darwin's *Expression of the Emotions in Man and Animals*.

20. Kachaluba and Dziubinskyj also make this point in a footnote to this episode in the novel.

21. I am grateful to Néstor Rodríguez for pointing me in the direction of Morán's work on this topic.

22. There were many reproductions of this painting in circulation (Forbes Morlock 135), and it is not unlikely that Urzaiz would have had occasion to see it or a similar image, given his familiarity with the work of Charcot. In addition, Freud (a student of Charcot) owned a lithograph of the painting, which later came to be displayed at the Freud museum in London (Morlock 136). Moreover, as Morlock points out, Brouillet based his image of Charcot on a photograph of the physician,

which was later published, in 1894 (135). This is further evidence that many available images of Charcot would have featured his Legion of Honor badge.

23. Tucker's reading of "racial sight," while strongly grounded in the Enlightenment epistemology of universal human likeness, also extends the long post-Enlightenment as far as the twenty-first century, with her analysis of *The Wire*.

24. Strangely, Goetz's critical reading of the drawing avoids mention of the Jewish identity of the subject, despite the fact that the title makes Jewishness explicit.

Chapter 2

1. During this period, healthcare workers and teachers were encouraged to create and disseminate public messages on the dangers of alcohol and the importance of hygienic practices. As Mary Kay Vaughan has written, the Ministry of Public Education was also particularly active in "action pedagogy" to promote hygiene under the leadership of Minister Narciso Bassols, from 1931 to 1934 (Vaughan 31–32).

2. In a reading more specific to the question of racial difference, Joshua Lund discusses the nineteenth-century Mexican journalist Luis Alva as a "contextualist" thinker, meaning that he understood environmental factors as the cause of human differences. Lund links this position to Kant's theorization of race, and to the work of Franz Boas and its impact on that of Manuel Gamio (Lund 10). In this broader sense, the notion of contingency is not specific only to post-revolutionary Mexico. Beatriz Urías Horcasitas offers a different view of the relationship between Boas's approach to race and that of Gamio; see note 27.

3. Puar emphasizes debility as a disruption to the ability/disability binary. As she writes: "Debility addresses bodily injury and exclusion that are endemic rather than epidemic or exceptional, and reflects a need for rethinking overarching structures of working, schooling, and living, rather than relying on rights frames to provide accommodationist solutions" (xvii).

4. Titchkosky emphasizes "the question of 'how'?" as a means to interrogate the conventional supremacy of "Why?" As she explains, "Asking 'why?' is a legacy of the Enlightenment, with its belief in progress, releasing the power of cause-and-effect rationality that gives rise to explanations that seem to permit people to know, control, and manipulate *what is*" (134).

5. In his 1916 study, "Hygiene in Mexico," Alberto Pani discusses mortality rates in Mexico City over an eighteen-year period, focusing his analysis on physical and social causal factors including temperature, humidity, food, and dwellings. He found that Mexico City in 1911 had a higher mortality coefficient than cities such as Madras and Cairo, and three times higher than US cities of similar population. Pani places responsibility for these stark conclusions on "the administration of our sanitary authorities" (4–5). Claudia Agostoni emphasizes the period from the late nineteenth to the early twentieth century as marked by a transition to a nationally consolidated public-health system with the goal of strengthening the population and producing more hygienic conditions ("Introducción" 7).

6. In this text Santamarina refers to Paul Boncour, and his categorizations appear to borrow heavily from the 1905 text, *Les anomalies mentales chez les écoliers*, by Jean Philippe and Georges-Paul Boncour.

7. See Eunjung Kim's work on this point, as referenced in the introduction.

8. Paul Longmore's work on charity telethons is illustrative in this respect. He writes of US audiences of the telethon and underscores the question of sympathy as linked to the perception of causation: "How did this event happen to this person?" (92). Also see Eli Clare's discussion of "overcoming disability" in popular media (8–10). Sami Schalk's analysis of the figure of the "supercrip" reminds the reader of stereotypes of overcoming and inspirational narratives of disability, and then offers a more nuanced reading of the variety of narrative forms that the "supercrip" figure may take.

9. Elsewhere I discuss Eli Lilly's advertising campaign in greater detail in relation to the Map of the Mexican Genome, a state-sponsored biomedical project geared toward the develop of genomic-specific pharmaceuticals. See Antebi 2014. These images are no longer available online, and unfortunately, I was not able to secure permission to include an image from the campaign in this book. A reference to the advertising campaign, with a related image, may be found at the following site: https://www.merca20.com/eli-lilly-mexico-se-lleva-el-oro-en-los-premios-aspid-2008/

10. The *tarjeta sanitaria* (a student health card including information on academic performance, body measurements, and health data) and the use of IQ testing are discussed in chapter 4.

11. Mitchell and Snyder's reading of T4 is based on the concept of the "low-level agency" of "those who do not perform their opposition openly or even with a working knowledge of themselves as oppressed" (253). In this sense they question the expectation that resistance must work through forms of robust opposition.

12. The Veracruz law of 1932, studied by Alexandra Stern, is the exception, but there is no evidence that it was ever put into practice.

13. See for example Stepan; Stern, "Responsible Mothers"; Suárez y López Guazo, *Eugenesia y racismo*; Saade Granados; and Ríos Molina.

14. Roberto Esposito describes the concept of "racial hygiene" as "the German translation of the eugenic orientation" (128).

15. Those with the documented participation of Mexican scientists included, for example, a 1907 hygiene conference in Berlin, a 1910 school hygiene congress in Paris, a 1925 child congress in Geneva, a 1937 mental hygiene congress in Paris, and a series of Pan-American child congresses in diverse Latin American locations.

16. The Instituto Médico Pedagógico was renamed Servicio de Educación Especial in 1937, as part of the newly founded Instituto Nacional de Psicopedagogía.

17. Suárez y López Guazo also discusses the continuity and influence of eugenic thinking in state-sponsored anthropology, education, and public-health initiatives (*Eugenesia y racismo* 85–140).

18. As Alison Kafer notes as part of her discussion on desire for crip futurity, the notion of the "future" has tended to work in support of heteronormative and ableist paradigms. She writes, for example: "Eugenic histories certainly bear the mark of reproductive futurity" (30).

19. Strong negatively construed associations between indigenous people, drunkenness, and various social ills can be traced to documents of the early colonial period. As William B. Taylor notes in his classic work, colonial Spanish sources regularly describe indigenous people as barbarous, lacking in judgment, and given to excessive drinking, which in turn was described as the cause of social problems (40–42).

20. Gudiño also discusses the journal *El Maestro rural* within the same context of health and hygiene campaigns promoted by the Ministry of Public Education and the Health Department (Departamento de Salubridad) during the 1920s and 1930s. Also see Vaughan 32.

21. Rivera's sketches also illustrated the 1929 textbook for rural schools, *Fermín*, which told the story of a young peasant's ideological coming of age following the revolution. See Vaughan 38–39.

22. Poetic renditions of the myth that include a vulture devouring Prometheus's entrails include Seneca's *Hercules* and Miguel de Unamuno's 1907 "El buitre de Prometeo." In this sense the substitution of vulture for eagle and entrails for liver may be read as continuous with both classical and more recent versions of the mythology.

23. Among such public officials of the period are Narciso Bassols, public education minister from 1931 to 1934 (see note 1), and Moisés Sáenz, who occupied a number of positions including subsecretary of public education from 1925 to 1928, and who was influential over the course of his career in the assimilation of indigenous cultures to a national system of education. See Sáenz, *México íntegro*, a collection of essays on rural Mexico in 1930, focused on the goal of creating a unified Mexico, which incorporates efforts to bridge practical and philosophical projects. Scholarly works as varied as Carlos Alberto Sánchez's *Contingency and Commitment*, Ignacio Sánchez Prado's *Naciones intelectuales*, Claudio Lomnitz's *Deep Mexico, Silent Mexico*, and Pedro Ángel Palou's *El fracaso del mestizo* suggest but do not exhaust the complexity and scope of Mexican nationalism as a political and philosophical project.

24. David Dalton notes that for Vasconcelos, science "plays a key, supporting role in the aesthetic politics of continued human evolution" ("Science and the (Meta)physical Body" 539). Marilyn Miller also discusses the complex relationship between scientific and spiritual discourses in Vasconcelos's work (42).

25. This discourse fits as well with the notion of Latin Americanism described by Julio Ramos in his reading of José Martí as founded on an opposition between Latin American humanist, spiritual values and northern commercial interests (Ramos 190).

26. The notion of orthogenesis, or directed evolutionary change, central in Lamarck's work, emerges here in Vasconcelos's explanation. Henri Bergson's 1907 text, *Creative Evolution*, which borrows from elements of Lamarckism and argues for "an original impetus of life" (*élan vital*) as the cause of evolutionary change, is also a likely influence in Vasconcelos's *Ética* and in *The Cosmic Race*. For Ignacio Sánchez Prado, Vasconcelos's theory of evolution in *The Cosmic Race* is Bergsonian, rather than Darwinian (395).

27. Franz Boas, a major German-American anthropologist who gave a series of conferences in Mexico from 1911 to 1912, and had a significant impact on Mexican anthropology, is often credited with shifting Mexican anthropologists' understanding of racial difference toward emphasis on cultural and historical influences rather than evolutionary determinism. Yet as Urías Horcasitas points out, the Mexican anthropologists of this period tended to retain their nineteenth-century positivist framework (60). For example, clear differences between Boas and Manuel Gamio are evident in Gamio's 1916 *Forjando patria* [*Forging a Nation*], in which the Mexican anthropologist cites Boas yet retains a largely nineteenth-century racial discourse (Urías Horcasitas 80). I discuss the work of Gómez Robleda at length in chapter 4.

28. Vasconcelos here returns briefly to Prometheus, a figure he had explored at greater length in his 1916 play, *Prometeo vencedor*. As David Dalton notes in his rich and extended analysis, this work has been largely neglected by critics.

29. Vasconcelos refers here to quantum physics, but mistakenly writes "cuantas moleculares." The scientifically correct word is "cuantos," as in "la teoría de los cuantos" [quantum theory].

30. I refer here to Walter Benjamin's well-known evocation of fascism as linked to the aestheticization of politics (242).

31. More recently, McRuer has described a notion of generative longing stemming from "crip displacements" in the contexts of neoliberalism and austerity politics. In this reading, disability is subtly imbricated with eviction and other forms of displacement, yet paradoxically generative of spaces of resistance (*Crip Times* 133, 175).

Chapter 3

1. In *Eugenics in the Garden*, Fabiola López-Durán offers an in-depth analysis of continuities between eugenics and architecture in France and Latin America, showing how architecture, infused with theories of Lamarckian eugenics such as the concept of milieu, or the process of struggle and adaptation between living beings and their surroundings, worked to shape both the built environment and human life (6–10). The discourse of school hygiene in Mexico, with emphasis on dynamic continuity between students' bodies and school infrastructure, clearly corresponds to this broader eugenic context.

2. There is a significant body of scholarship on the social model and its history. See for example Oliver, "The Social Model in Action," and Owens.

3. See for example Mitchell, Antebi, and Snyder (1–12) for discussion of new materialism and posthumanist disability theory, and the notion of continuities between the natural and the social, matter and discourse. The work of Karen Barad and her theory of matter as "intra-active" (151–52) is influential in this area.

4. This argument echoes Mel Chen's theory of animacy. See for example Chen's discussion of the global circulation and troping of lead (159–88).

5. Santamarina gave two papers at the 1921 conference, one on the classifica-

tion of schoolchildren, the other on contemporary knowledge of the Mexican child from a medical-pedagogical perspective. The ideas presented in both papers would continue to impact the work of the Department of Psychopedagogy and Hygiene and the mission of the National Institute of Psychopedagogy, founded in 1937.

6. Ximena López Carrillo studies the history of *"retraso mental"* or mental delay in Mexican psychiatry, but focuses more specifically on the population of La Castañeda psychiatric hospital. According to her analysis, during the period from 1910 to 1931, *retraso*, along with alcoholism, epilepsy, and syphilis, is associated with degeneration and primarily diagnosed through physical symptoms (133). Outside the context of the psychiatric hospital, however, the notion of *retraso* when applied to schoolchildren, as in Rafael Santamarina's classification chart, discussed in chapter 2, includes a broad variety of causes and manifestations.

7. The physician's emphasis on indices and on the compilation of measurements here illustrate the impact of biotypology on the work of the Department of Psychopedagogy and Hygiene, an area to be addressed further in chapter 4.

8. Lozano had made similar arguments in a presentation at the 1921 First Congress of the Child, in which he discussed the classification of abnormality in schoolchildren.

9. See Santamarina, "Ensayo de clasificación," 1921.

10. This structure appears to reflect Georges Canguilhem's observations from his reading of Comte: "every conception of pathology must be based on prior knowledge of the corresponding normal state, but conversely, the scientific study of pathological cases becomes an indispensable phase in the overall search for the laws of the normal state" (51). Michel Foucault builds on Canguilhem's work to discuss the process of "normalization," achieved through techniques of intervention and the accumulation of knowledge, using as one example the spatial partition of populations susceptible to the plague (*Abnormal* 46–50).

11. As Elena Jackson Albarrán observes, during the Cárdenas presidency (1934–1940), visual representations of children were increasingly politicized (68–69). Daniel Vargas Parra notes that while the DPH printed statistics and graphs, the INP began to include corporeal images of children (54).

12. Alberto Pani's 1916 text provides empirical data on categories such as illness rates, mortality, education, and sanitation from the immediate prerevolutionary period. For a contemporary analysis of data for the mid-1930s, see Olsen, especially 182–98.

13. For a distinct reading of the notion of a rhetoric of hygiene, in the Colombian context, see Diana Obregón. Also see Beatriz González Stephan on hygiene as rhetoric in nineteenth-century Latin American cities.

14. This argument borrows in part from the critical project of Ignacio Sánchez Prado's *Naciones intelectuales*, in which the author proposes a "reappropriation of literature for the imagination of alternative strategies for understanding the nation, and a revindication of the role of literature as space of functional intellectual articulation even within hegemonic systems" (my translation; 10).

15. Alberto Pérez-Gómez and Edward Burian's discussion of the differences

and links between technical education and the humanities, as well as between the writing of José Vasconcelos and the discourse of technical rationalism (24–37), is useful here.

16. Also see the introduction and chapter 2 for further discussion of hygiene and eugenics.

17. In his text Adorno discusses the impasse of anti-ornamental functionalism, noting, for example, that "The difference between the necessary and the superfluous is inherent in a work, and is not defined by the work's relationship—or the lack of it—to something outside itself" (7). His analysis suggests a conflict similar to that encountered by O'Gorman in his discussion of technical functionalism. Yet Adorno lacks O'Gorman's cynicism here, and ultimately upholds the role of a critically productive "modified aesthetics" (19) in architecture and in all art.

18. Here Foucault is referring to the origins of American neoliberalism, which he contextualizes as beginning in the mid-1930s, as part of a response to Roosevelt's New Deal (216). This historical context corresponds to O'Gorman's period of critical activity in question, as well as to a period of increased urbanization and foreign investment in Mexico, in partial conflict with President Lázaro Cárdenas's mission of collective social justice for the nation.

19. I am grateful to Rosa Sarabia for pointing me to this invaluable reference.

20. O'Gorman's unpublished 1955 essay, "The Degeneration of Architecture in Mexico Today," provides insight into the architect's ongoing conflicts with global architectural trends, and their influence in Mexico. See Eggener, "Juan O'Gorman versus the International Style."

21. Le Corbusier's work also had a major impact in Latin America, and shaped O'Gorman's earlier formation as an architect. As López-Durán shows, Le Corbusier is a key figure for understanding the role of eugenics in Latin American architecture (144–88).

22. It is worth noting here that the history of functionalist architecture reveals varied approaches to the complex relationship between functionality and aesthetics. For example, O'Gorman was influenced by both Le Corbusier and the Mexican architect José Villagrán García, who is famous for his 1929 design of the Tuberculosis Sanatorium in Huipulco, among other structures. Yet as Kathryn E. O'Rourke has argued, Villagrán was in turn heavily influenced by the French architects Julien Guadet and Auguste Perret, and the Beaux Arts tradition of symmetry, proportion (71), and "the projection of authority" (72). According to O'Rourke, Villagrán, unlike O'Gorman in his early work, "did not deny the importance of beauty in architecture" (70), despite participating in the "structural honesty" (69) of modernist architecture. For more on Le Corbusier's influence on O'Gorman, and on the distinctive quality of O'Gorman's Mexican functionalism, see Fraser, 38–41, 55. Also see Burian, "Modernity and Nationalism."

23. Despite this insistence on the elimination of artistic expression, O'Gorman did allow for the inclusion of murals in the primary schools he designed. As Luis Carranza notes, "Anything added to the architecture that appeared to be nonfunctional or ornamental (paint, art, sculpture, and so forth) . . . needed to didactically

express the social aims of the functionalist building" (148). Ariadna Patiño Guadarrama offers a more detailed analysis of the role of Julio Castellanos's tryptic mural in the Escuela Héroes de Churubusco, and suggests that in general, O'Gorman saw the murals in schools as obeying a didactic imperative (147).

24. López-Durán notes that trees were also a frequent metaphor in Le Corbusier's work of the early 1930s, with the role of the architect being to synthesize technique and nature, "to make the tree grow straight" (159–60).

25. For an engaging and useful reading of O'Gorman's architectural nationalism in later decades, in contrast to the vision of Luis Barragán, see Keith Eggener, "Contrasting Images."

26. Examples include "Después del diluvio que nos trajo el arca" (1967) and "Corrupción y polución en nuestra maravillosa civilización" (1975). On this mode of O'Gorman's painting, see for example Rodríguez Prampolini, and Caleb Bach.

27. Also see Keith Eggener's reading of this painting in his "Settings for History and Oblivion."

Chapter 4

1. Joel Vargas makes a similar argument in his reading of José Rulfo's study of the Otomis, noting the ongoing impact of eugenic thought in the postrevolutionary period (3). For Alexandra Stern, biotypology functions in part as a continuity of the eugenic project ("Mestizofilia" 59–60), while Beatriz Urías Horcasitas emphasizes differences between the two, but still notes the racist underpinnings of the work of the biotypologists ("Fisiología" 373–74).

2. Eraso refers here to the Argentinian context, also influenced by the Italian school of biotypology in the same period.

3. As a related example, the study of US immigration policy at Ellis Island during the late nineteenth and early twentieth centuries shows the influence of classification systems such as the Binet-Simon test, which would lead to an increasingly prevalent use of the test's specific and numerically based terminology: "moron," "imbecile," and "idiot," as well as to actual application of the test (Birn 302–306; Dolmage 33; Mitchell and Snyder 852).

4. Boletin No. 1 de la 'Sociedad Eugénica Mexicana para el Mejoramiento de la Raza,' 22 agosto 1932.

5. Ignacio Méndez Ramírez highlights the importance of Fisher's work in the evolution of statistical methods, points to Mexico's slower incorporation of changes in this discipline, and mentions that Emilio Alanís Patiño was the first Mexican to return to his country after completing postgraduate work abroad. He returned from Italy to Mexico in 1933. Joel Vargas refers to the complexity of the transnational role of statistics in this period, in his analysis of a 1937 biometric study of the Otomíes, by José Rulfo. Rulfo makes extensive references to the (limited) statistical studies of US-based authors, yet dismisses his own results as being statistically insignificant (Vargas 10). Rulfo, a Berkeley-trained veterinarian and member of the Mexican Eugenics Society, most likely acquired his knowledge of statistics abroad. In the same year,

Rulfo assisted José Gómez Robleda in a biotypological study of Mexican schoolchildren (Stern, "Mestizofilia" 86). It is thus plausible that Gómez Robleda's own knowledge and applications of statistics were shaped through this collaboration.

6. A statistic, according to Fisher, was an estimate of a parameter (such as the median, or the mean) derived from a collection of measurements, but not equivalent to the actual, underlying parameter (Salzburg 65).

7. Dilan Mahendran describes epidermalization in this context as "the processual intertwining of the 'historico-racial schema' and 'racial epidermal schema.' The 'historico-racial schema' are the sedimented and knotted fabric of self experiences of anti-black racism and its interpellating discourses, sort of the pre-reflective consciousness memory of lived experiences of racist violence. The 'racial epidermal schema' is the immediately manifest intelligibility of blackness or showing up as such" (192n2).

8. Merleau-Ponty writes, for example, "we shall need to reawaken our experience of the world as it appears to us in so far as we are in the world through our body, and in so far as we perceive the world with our body. But by thus remaking contact with the body and the world, we shall also rediscover ourself, since, perceiving as we do with our body, the body is a natural self and, as it were, the subject of perception" (206).

9. Also see chapter 1 for further reference to Siebers's work in this area.

10. For example: "Con los datos obtenidos en 1926–7 en la Casa del Estudiante Indígena se formaron cuadros comparativos con las pruebas de Fay, Ebbinghaus y Descoeudres y otro comparando esos resultados con los obtenidos en las escuelas de México." [With the data obtained from 1926–7 in the Indigenous Student House, comparative charts were made with the Fay, Ebbinghaus, Descouedres tests, and one other, comparing these results with those obtained in Mexican schools.] (Rafael Santamarina, Carta a José Manuel Puig Casauranc (3).

11. As Deborah Dorotinsky describes, this photographic work was commissioned in 1939 by Lucio Mendieta y Nuñez, director of the Instituto de Investigaciones Sociales, and would extend until 1946 (352). The "México Indígena" photographic archive is still held at the Instituto de Investigaciones Sociales at the UNAM. The two photographs I discuss here were most likely also taken by Raúl Estrada Discua. However, the name of the photographer is not specified in the article, and these two images do not appear in the archival collection.

12. See for example González Ponce 21–23, Buffington 49–50, and del Castillo Troncoso 93.

13. The same photograph appears in the book *Pescadores y campesinos Tarascos* (1943) by Gómez Robleda and his coauthors, though with a different subtitle.

14. For example, the widely criticized 2009 promotional advertisement from the organization Autism Speaks, "I am autism," included the statement: "I know no color barrier, no religion, no morality, no currency." Note that this video is no longer available on the Autism Speaks website. See Find Yaser.

15. As Ríos Molina also notes, schizophrenia was clearly a topic of interest to Gómez Robleda, as evidenced in his 1933 short novel *Esquizofrénico*.

16. Anne McGuire notes that Kanner ultimately considered autism to be an innate condition but adds that his speculations on the role of parenting and his images of cold parents would be later taken up by Bruno Bettelheim, who argued that autism was acquired through environmental influence (38–39).

17. In accordance with Urías Horcasitas's analysis, it is this notion of structural causality that defines the role of biotypology in twentieth-century Mexico, based on biological determinism but tied directly to explorations of the issues of poverty and marginalization—and their causes and effects—in relation to Mexican national character (*Historias secretas* 56).

18. Waltz points out that two of the eleven children in Kanner's study were Jewish, while only 2% of the US population is Jewish; for the mainstream public, this discrepancy linked autism to Jewishness. She notes further that the association became especially strong in Russia, where autism was initially viewed as a disease of both Jewishness and capitalism (68).

19. Although Gómez Robleda is the author of the text, research for the larger project of which the article formed a part was conducted by a team.

20. The Hippocratic facies, for example, refers to the appearance of the face with signs of impending death. In 1935, Dr. Mathilde Rodríguez Cabo, who served at the time as head of child psychiatry at La Castañeda hospital, described some of the children in her care in the following terms: "los labios gruesos y entreabiertas contribuyen a hacer más estúpida la facies asimétrica e inexpresiva" (146); [The thick and partially open lips contribute to the stupid appearance of the assymetrical and inexpressive facies.]. In the same article, Dr. Rodríguez Cabo advocates for the euthanasia of some of these children, arguing that they are "incapaces de desarrollar ninguna actividad útil, reducidos únicamente a la vida vegetativa y destinados a ser lastre perpetuo y carga continua para el Estado" (146), [incapable of developing any useful activity, reduced only to a vegetative life and destined to be a perpetual burden to the State].

21. It is likely that Gómez Robleda refers here to the work of Guillaume Duchenne de Boulogne, specifically his 1862 *The Mechanism of Human Facial Expression*. Duchenne's influential work refers repeatedly to the soul as root of facial expressions, an idea he attempted to demonstrate through the photography of faces under electrical stimulation. Darwin's *The Expression of the Emotions in Man and Animal* is also an important reference here. Darwin studied varying expressions and solicited surveys of those who had the opportunity to observe facial expressions in diverse "races" around the world. While interested in the question of cultural and acquired variation, Darwin emphasizes the universal similarities of expression. As Darwin writes: "All the chief expressions exhibited by man are the same throughout the world. This fact is interesting, as it affords a new argument in favour of the several races being descended from a single parent-stock" (361). In contrast to Darwin's emphasis on universal similarities of expression, Gómez Robleda focuses on what he sees as distinct aspects of the Tarasco's facial expressions and bodies.

22. The teaching and research of Ada D'Aloja, Gómez Robleda's teacher and collaborator, was influential in the development of biotypology in twentieth-century Mexico. As Robert Buffington suggests, however, the practice of biotypology did

not represent an innovative approach in anthropology or criminology. Here, he cites from a 1945 study of human skull measurements: "the different schools of Biotypology . . . are not, in the final analysis, anything but continuers and developers of the ideas of Lombroso" (159).

23. In the introduction I also discuss the relevance of Samuels's work and the distinctions it helps to highlight between US and Mexican contexts.

24. Urías Horcasitas focuses on the period between 1930 and 1950, particularly following the establishment of the 1931 Penal Code, replacing the prior 1929 code (*Historias secretas* 159).

25. Also see Elisa Speckman Guerra for a detailed contextualization of Roumagnac's work in relation to crime and childhood in the *porfiriato*. Gómez Robleda's study of the Tarasco, discussed above, does not focus specifically on the issue of criminality, yet during the same period the Instituto de Investigaciones Sociales of the UNAM, in which he carried out his research, was directly involved in the study of criminal sociology, often in relation to indigenous groups (Urías Horcasitas *Historias secretas* 163).

26. *Don Justo* offers short pedagogically oriented chapters and follows the story of the teacher and his students over the course of their studies. The book concludes with the death of the teacher, beloved and revered by many generations of students. It is likely that Gómez Robleda was inspired in the creation of don Justo by the figure of Justo Sierra, Mexican historian, political figure, and pedagogue under Porfirio Díaz. Sierra served as minister of public instruction and fine arts from 1905 to 1911, was the author of a number of history books for primary school students, and was a key promoter of obligatory primary school education at the national level. In 1948, the year of publication of *Don Justo*, and the centenary of Justo Sierra's birth, the statesman's remains were transferred from the Panteón Francés to the Rotunda de Personas Ilustres in Mexico. In Gómez Robleda's concluding pages, don Justo's body, we learn, will be draped in the national flag "para que comprendamos, todos, que el Gobierno de la República lo considera como un hijo predilecto de la Patria" (416) [so that we all understand that the Government of the Republic considers him a favorite son of the fatherland]. It is interesting that Gómez Robleda does not refer directly to Justo Sierra in his text, thus eliding the political transformation of the Mexican revolution that separates the work from its inspiration.

27. In using the name "Guillaume" Gómez Robleda likely refers here to the nineteenth-century French neurologist Guillaume-Benjamin-Amand Duchenne de Boulogne. Addison's disease, caused by adrenal insufficiency, may result in darkening of the skin. This condition is not clinically related to albinism.

28. A key difference between Fanon's reading and the structure suggested in Gómez Robleda's works is the role of scientific authority in the latter, which shapes the readers' impressions of the othered, voiceless subject through diagnosis.

Chapter 5

1. As Yvette Jímenez de Báez notes in her reading of the novel, and in reference to Juan Bruce Novoa's prologue to the 1987 edition, this portion of the text

also juxtaposes the automobile to railway travel, when the car crosses the railroad tracks, and thus creates a complex dynamic between nineteenth- and twentieth-century modes of transport (325–26).

2. Both John Hall and Jaime Martínez Martín suggest that the novel takes the form of a bildungsroman. In this sense, the pedagogical aspect of the work becomes inevitable, and extends from the individual to the collective in the context of the revolution.

3. For example, Horacio Legrás describes the film *¡Vámonos con Pancho Villa!* as "the story of the increasingly relentless construction of a firm nationalist identity" (172).

4. Kuppers bases her reading here on Deleuze and Guattari's *Anti-Oedipus*, in dialogue with Merleau-Ponty's concept of body scheme.

5. For further analysis of the impact of Deleuze and Barthes in Aguilar Mora's work, see Pineda.

6. This is a reference to the same portion of Deleuze's *Logic of Sense* cited by Garoian.

7. Here the reader may recall my discussion in chapter 2 of the contrast and complementarity between linear and cyclical time in Vasconcelos's writing and in the language of the anti-alcohol campaign.

8. Deleuze here gives the example of a commentary on Ginsberg's poetry, in which accidents suffered by the pathologized subject refer to prior historical incidents, such as a pogrom, or the bombing of Guernica or Hanoi.

9. "At least 270 Chileans have been wounded in the eyes as a result of Carabineros shooting directly in the face in anti-government protests, a record in world statistics" (Telesur Nov 19).

10. As Parra notes, in this sense Muñoz's work contrasts sharply with that of Martín Luis Guzmán, in which empathy for Villa and his violent acts is absent (99).

11. In Parra's reading this kind of complication is further achieved through the scene in which Villa murders Tiburcio's wife and daughter, shocking the reader and yet instilling heightened fidelity in Tiburcio. Legrás for his part, reads *Vámonos* the film (though not the novel) as an homage to loyalty and bravery, but not to Villa himself: "*Vámonos* is an attempt to wrestle these qualities from Villa in order to transfer them to the sphere of state representation" (172).

12. In *¡Vámonos con Pancho Villa!* the leader in question is Villa himself, while in *Se llevaron el cañón para Bachimba*, it is Pascual Orozco, largely represented through the fictional general, Marcos Ruiz.

13. Carolyn Fornoff offers a brilliant analysis of the affective roles of nature and landscape in Muñoz's novel. As she notes, "The environment's logic, temporality and scope concurrently subvert and uncannily echo the organization of human life and the revolution itself" (107).

14. As Deleuze writes in *Difference and Repetition*, "A scar is the sign not of a past wound but of 'the present fact of having been wounded.' We can say that it is the contemplation of the wound, that it contracts all the instants that separate us from it into a living present" (98–99).

15. Lennard Davis sees this concern as unfounded (*End of Normal* 100), while for Alison Davis: "Terminally ill and incurably disabled people are those most at risk of having their lives deemed 'not worth living.'"

16. This kind of description is not unique to the Mexican Revolution. As Robert Goler writes, in his analysis of disabled US Civil War veterans, "Embodying loss, the Civil War veteran amputee remained an ambiguous figure, simultaneously epitomizing survival and death, victory and bereavement" (162).

17. This is the case in James's reading of Gwendolyn Brooks's work, where she argues that the poet "creates an 'othered' space where these bodies might give voice to an alternative view of war" (247).

18. Huerta was the general who defeated the rebel army of Pascual Orozco at the battles of Rellano and Bachimba, both of which are represented in Muñoz's later novel *Se llevaron el cañón para Bachimba*.

19. In the cinema version of this scene, one of the most dramatic sequences in the feature-length film, Espinosa is played by Muñoz, author of the novel, and the character has not lost an arm (see Aguilar Mora, *El silencio de la revolución*, 125).

20. The film version of this novel concludes here and avoids reference to events in the second half of the novel, including Villa's murder of Tiburcio's wife and daughter.

21. Aguilar Mora's interpretation celebrates Tiburcio's allegiance, while Parra more cautiously notes the novel's problematic and violent sacrifice of women (Tiburcio's wife and daughter) in the name of male honor.

22. Both Deleuze and Derrida employ this phrase from Shakespeare's Hamlet in their respective discussions of temporality.

Epilogue

1. I elaborate further on this topic in a brief reflection, titled "Andamio higiénico," available at https://diecisiete.org/expediente/andamio-higienico/

Works Cited

Abbondanza, Ermanno. "*Eugenia* (1919) de Eduardo Urzaiz Rodríguez: Apuntes para una lectura entre líneas." Ponencia Central, II Congreso Internacional de Literatura Iberoamericana. Cartografías Literarias: Rutas, trazos y miradas. Universidad Santo Tomás. Facultad de Filosofía y Letras. Bogotá-Colombia, septiembre 22 al 25 de 2010. Web.

Acevés García, Norma. "El modelo social de la discapacidad ¿qué es y cómo va su adopción en México?" *Nexos, (Dis)capacidades. Blog sobre otros cuerpos y mentes,* Sept. 30, 2018. https://discapacidades.nexos.com.mx/?p=672

"Acta Final del Quinto Congreso Panamericano del Niño, Habana, Cuba, 1927." Archivo General de la Nación. Fondo de la Secretaría de Educación Pública, Departamento de Psicopedagogía e Higiene. Caja 35485, ref. 138 exp. 1, p. 47.

Adorno, Theodor. "Functionalism Today." *Rethinking Architecture. A Reader in Cultural Theory.* Edited by Neil Leach. Routledge, 1997, pp. 6–19.

Agostoni, Claudia. "Introducción." *Curar, sanar y educar. Enfermedad y sociedad en México, siglos XIX y XX.* Coordinated by Claudia Agostoni. Universidad Nacional Autónoma de México, 2008, pp. 5–13.

Agostoni, Claudia. *Monuments of Progress: Modernization and Public Health in Mexico City, 1876–1910.* U of Calgary P, 2003.

Aguilar Ferreira, Melesio. "El espíritu de la asistencia pública." Archivo Histórico de la Secretaría de Salud Pública. Fondo: Beneficencia Pública. Sección: Asistencia. Serie, Dirección General, Leg-12, exp-4. Boletín de los Servicios Coordinados de Salubridad y Asistencia Públicas en Michoacán. Año I. num 2, febrero de 1940, Tomo I, pp. 17–18.

Aguilar Mora, Jorge. "Novela sin joroba." *Revista de Crítica Literaria Latinoamericana,* año 33, no. 66, 2007, pp. 225–48.

Aguilar Mora, Jorge. *Una muerte sencilla, justa, eterna: Cultura y guerra durante la revolución mexicana.* Era, 1990.

Aguilar Mora, Jorge. *El silencio de la revolución y otros ensayos.* Era, 2011.

Aguirre Beltrán, Gonzalo. *Antropología médica.* Centro de Investigaciones y Estudios Superiores en Antropología Social, 1986.

Albarrán, Elena Jackson. *Seen and Heard in Mexico: Children and Revolutionary Cultural Nationalism*. U of Nebraska P, 2014.

Alonso Gutiérrez, José Félix, coord. *Guía de la Sección de Asistencia del Fondo Beneficencia Pública en el Distrito Federal*. Centro de Documentación y Archivo. Archivo Histórico. Serie: Guías, num. 6, enero 1988.

Amador, José. *Medicine and Nation Building in the Americas, 1890–1940*. Vanderbilt UP, 2015.

Andrade Briseño, Magdalena et al./Taller 1932. *Utopía—no utopía: La arquitectura, la enseñanza y la planificación del deseo*. Museo Casa Estudio Diego Rivera y Frida Kahlo, 2005.

Antebi, Susan. "Andamio higiénico." *Fragmentos hallados a nuestro paso*. 17 Instituto de Estudios Críticos, April 2020. https://diecisiete.org/expediente/andamio-higienico/

Antebi, Susan. *Carnal Inscriptions: Spanish American Narratives of Corporeal Difference and Disability*. Palgrave Macmillan, 2009.

Antebi, Susan. "El haplotipo cósmico: discapacidad, mestizaje y el Mapa del Genoma Mexicano." *Heridas abiertas: Biopolítica y representación en América Latina*. Edited by Mabel Moraña and Ignacio Sánchez Prado. Iberoamericana Vervuert, 2014, pp. 225–46.

Aréchiga Córdoba, Ernesto. "Educación, propaganda, o 'dictadura sanitaria': Estrategias discursivas de higiene y salubridad públicas en el México posrevolucionario, 1917–1945." *Estudios de historia moderna y contemporánea de México*, vol. 33, 2007, pp. 57–88.

Arrellano Belloc, Alberto. "Juicio crítico sobre los trabajos de médico de zona con algunas sugestiones para su mejoramiento." Archivo General de la Nación. Fondo de la Secretaría de Educación Pública. Departamento de Psicopedagogía e Higiene. Caja 35516, 17-13-1-175, 1935.

Bach, Caleb. "Art and Anger of Juan O'Gorman." *Americas*, vol. 58, no. 6, 2006, pp. 48–55.

Barad, Karen. *Meeting the Universe Halfway: Quantum Physics and the Entanglement of Matter and Meaning*. Duke UP, 2007.

Barthes, Roland. *Mythologies*. Translated by Annette Lavers, Hill and Wang, 1984.

Bartra, Roger. *La jaula de la melancolía: Identidad y metamorfósis del mexicano*. Random House Mondadori, 2011.

"Bases generales para estructurar la nueva organizacion escolar de la Beneficencia Pública en el Distrito Federal." Archivo Histórico de la Secretaría de Salud Pública. Fondo, Beneficencia Pública, Sección, Asistencia, Serie, Departamento de Acción Educativa y Social. Leg. 5, exp. 16, 21 octubre 1936, hojas 3–6.

Benjamin, Walter. "The Work of Art in the Age of Mechanical Reproduction." *Illuminations*. Translated by Harry Zohn. Schocken, 1985, pp. 217–51.

Bergson, Henri. *Creative Evolution*. Translated by Arthur Mitchell. Modern Library, 1944.

Berlant, Lauren. "Slow Death (Sovereignty, Obesity, Lateral Agency)." *Critical Inquiry*, vol. 33, no. 4, 2007, pp. 754–80.

Birn, Anne-Emanuelle. "Six Seconds Per Eyelid: The Medical Inspection of Immigrants at Ellis Island, 1892–1914." *Dynamis*, no. 17, 1997, pp. 281–316.

Blacher, Jan, and Lisa Christensen. "Sowing the Seeds of the Autism Field: Leo Kanner (1943)." *Intellectual and Developmental Disabilities*, vol. 49, no. 3, June 2011, pp. 172–91.

Bojórquez Urzaiz, Carlos E. *Entre mayas y patriotas: José Martí en Yucatán*. Universidad Autónoma de Yucatán, 2008.

Bojórquez Urzaiz, Carlos E., and Fernando Armstrong Fumero. "Estudio preliminar." *La familia, cruz del Apóstol (Ensayo psicoanalítico sobre José Martí)*. Compania Editorial de la Península, 2004, pp. 8–34.

Boletín Semanal. Departamento de Salubridad Pública. 1.17, febrero 8–14, 1931.

Boletín Semanal. Departamento de Salubridad Pública. 1.19, febrero 22–28, 1931.

Bravo Gómez, Pedro. "Asunto: Informa sobre las condiciones higiénicas pedagógicas en que se encuentra el centro 13–11." Archivo General de la Nación. Fondo de la Secretaría de Educación Pública. Departamento de Psicopedagogía e Higiene. Caja 35540, 17-13-5-86, 1933, folio 1–2.

Bravo Gómez, Pedro. "Higiene escolar y educación moderna." Archivo General de la Nación. Fondo de la Secretaría de Educación Pública. Departamento de Psicopedagogía e Higiene. Caja 35529, 23-1-5-58, 1934.

Brogna, Patricia. "Las representaciones de la discapacidad: la vigencia del pasado en las estructuras sociales presents." *Visiones y revisiones de la discapacidad*. Edited by Patricia Brogna. Fondo de Cultura Económica, 2009, pp. 157–87.

Buffington, Robert. *Criminal and Citizen in Modern Mexico*. U of Nebraska P, 2000.

Burian, Edward R. "The Architecture of Juan O'Gorman: Dichotomy and Drift." *Modernity and the Architecture of Mexico*. Edited by Edward R. Burian. U of Texas P, 1997, pp. 127–49.

Burian, Edward R. "Modernity and Nationalism: Juan O'Gorman and Post-Revolutionary Architecture in Mexico, 1920–1960." *Cruelty and Utopia. Cities and Landscapes of Latin America*. Edited by Jean-François Lejeune. Princeton Architectural Press, 2003, pp. 210–23.

Butler, Judith. *Frames of War: When Is Life Grievable?* Verso, 2009.

Cabrera, Miguel. "Informe del médico escolar." Archivo General de la Nación. Fondo de la Secretaría de Educación Pública. Departamento de Psicopedagogía e Higiene. Caja 35498, 17-13-1-127, 1935.

Cabrera, Miguel. "Informe sobre las condiciones higiénicas de la escuela 13–9." Archivo General de la Nación. Fondo de la Secretaría de Educación Pública. Departamento de Psicopedagogía e Higiene. Caja 35540, 17-13-5-94.

Campobello, Nellie. *Cartucho. Relatos de la lucha en el norte de México*. Era, 2009.

Canguilhem, Georges, *The Normal and the Pathological*. Translated by Carolyn R. Fawcett. Zone Books, 1991.

Carranza, Luis. *Architecture as Revolution: Episodes in the History of Modern Mexico*. U of Texas P, 2010.

Carrillo, Ana María. "Inicio de la higiene escolar en México. Congreso higiénico pedagógico de 1882." *Revista Mexicana de Pediatría*, vol. 66, no. 2, 1999, pp. 71–74.

Castillo Troncoso, Alberto. "Médicos y pedagogos frente a la degeneración racial: La niñez en la ciudad de México, 1876–1911." *De normas y transgresiones: Enfermedad y crimen en América Latina (1850–1950)*. Edited by Claudia Agostoni and Elisa Speckman Guerra. UNAM, 2005, pp. 83–107.

Chaoul Pereya, María Eugenia. *Entre la esperanza de cambio y la continuidad de la vida: El espacio de las escuelas primarias nacionales en la ciudad de México, 1891–1919.* Instituto de Investigaciones Dr. José María Luis Mora, 2014.

Chapman, Chris, Allison C. Carey, and Liat Ben-Moshe. "Reconsidering Confinement: Interlocking Locations and Logics of Incarceration." *Disability Incarcerated: Imprisonment and Disability in the United States and Canada.* Edited by Liat Ben-Moshe, Chris Chapman, and Allison C. Carey. Palgrave Macmillan, 2014, pp. 3–24.

Charcot, Jean-Martin. *Charcot in Morocco.* Introduction, notes, and translation by Toby Gelfand. U of Ottawa P, 2012.

Cházaro, Laura. "Reproducción y muerte de la población mexicana: cálculos estadísticos y preceptos higiénicos a fines del siglo diecinueve." *De normas y transgresiones: Enfermedad y crimen en América Latina (1850–1950).* Edited by Claudia Agostoni and Elisa Speckman Guerra. Universidad Nacional Autónoma de México, 2005, pp. 55–81.

Chen, Mel. *Animacies: Biopolitics, Racial Mattering, and Queer Affect.* Duke UP, 2012.

Clare, Eli. *Brilliant Imperfection: Grappling with Cure.* Duke UP, 2017.

Courtis, Christian. "Discapacidad e inclusion social." *Nexos,* 1 octubre, 2004, https://www.nexos.com.mx/?p=11274

Dalton, David S. *Mestizo Modernity: Race, Technology, and the Body in Postrevolutionary Mexico.* U of Florida P, 2018.

Dalton, David S. "Science and the (Meta)physical Body: A Critique of Positivism in the Vasconcelian Utopia." *Revista Canadiense de Estudios Hispánicos,* vol. 40, no. 3, 2016, pp. 535–59.

Darwin, Charles. *The Expression of The Emotions in Man and Animals.* John Murray, 1872.

Davidson, Michael. "Pregnant Men: Modernism, Disability, and Biofuturity." *Sex and Disability.* Edited by Robert McRuer and Anna Mollow. Duke UP, 2012, pp. 123–44.

Davis, Alison. "A Disabled Person's Perspective on Euthanasia." *Disability Studies Quarterly,* vol. 24, no. 3, 2004, n.p.

Davis, Lennard. *Bending Over Backwards: Disability, Dismodernism, and Other Difficult Positions.* New York UP, 2002.

Davis, Lennard. *The End of Normal: Identity in a Bicultural Era.* U of Michigan P, 2013.

Delaporte, François. *Anatomy of the Passions.* Translated by Susan Emanuel. Stanford UP, 2008.

Del Castillo Troncoso, Alberto. "Médicos y pedagogos frente a la degeneración racial: la niñez en la ciudad de México, 1876–1911." *De normas y transgresiones: Enfermedad y crimen en América Latina (1850–1950).* Edited by Claudia Agostoni and Elisa Speckman Guerra. Universidad Nacional Autónoma de México, 2005, pp. 83–107.

Deleuze, Gilles. *Difference and Repetition.* Translated by Paul Patton. Continuum, 2004.

Deleuze, Gilles. *The Logic of Sense.* Translated by Mark Lester. Columbia UP, 1990.

Deleuze, Gilles, and Félix Guattari. *A Thousand Plateaus. Capitalism and Schizophrenia,* Translated by Brian Massumi. U of Minnesota P, 1987.

Derrida, Jacques. *Spectres of Marx. The State of the Debt, the Work of Mourning, and the New International.* Translated by Peggy Kamuf. Routledge, 2006.

Didi-Huberman, Georges. *Invention of Hysteria. Charcot and the Photographic Iconography of the* Salpêtrière. Translated by Alisa Hartz. MIT P, 2003.

Dolmage, Jay. *Disabled Upon Arrival: Eugenics, Immigration, and the Construction of Race and Disability.* Ohio State UP, 2018.

Dorotinsky, Deborah. "Para medir el cuerpo de la nación: Antropología física y visualidad racialista en el marco de la recepción de la biotipología en México." *De normas y transgresiones: Enfermedad y crimen en América Latina (1850–1950).* Edited by Claudia Agostoni and Elisa Speckman Guerra. Universidad Nacional Autónoma de México, 2005, pp. 331–65.

Draper, Susana. "Las prisiones del archivo: pasado y presente de Lecumberri en Cementerio de papel." *MLN,* vol. 128, 2013, pp. 352–72.

Duchenne de Boulogne, Guillaume Benjamin Amand. *The Mechanism of Human Facial Expression.* Edited and translated by R. Andrew Cuthbertson. Cambridge UP, 1990.

Dziubinskyj, Aaron. "Eduardo Urzaiz's 'Eugenia': Eugenics, Gender, and Dystopian Society in Twenty-Third-Century Mexico." *Science Fiction Studies.* Nov. 2007, pp. 463–72.

Eggener, Keith L. "Contrasting Images of Identity in the Post-War Mexican Architecture of Luis Barragan and Juan O'Gorman." *Journal of Latin American Cultural Studies,* vol. 9, no. 1, 2000, pp. 27–45.

Eggener, Keith L. "Settings for History and Oblivion in Modern Mexico, 1942–1958." *Cruelty and Utopia. Cities and Landscapes of Latin America.* Edited by Jean-François Lejeune. Princeton Architectural Press, 2003, pp. 224–39.

Eggener, Keith L. "Juan O'Gorman versus the International Style: An Unpublished Submission to the JSAH." *Journal of the Society of Architectural Historians,* vol. 68, no. 3, 2009, pp. 301–7.

Eistenstein, Sergei, director. *¡Qué viva México!* Mosfilm, 1979.

Eraso, Yolanda. "Biotypology, Endocrinology, and Sterilization: The Practice of Eugenics in the Treatment of Argentinian Women during the 1930s." *Bulletin of the History of Medicine,* vol. 81, no. 4, winter 2007, pp. 793–822.

Erevelles, Nirmala. *Disability and Difference in Global Contexts: Enabling a Transformative Body Politic.* Palgrave Macmillan, 2011.

Erevelles, Nirmala. "Thinking with Disability Studies." *Disability Studies Quarterly,* vol. 34, no. 2, 2014.

Esposito, Roberto. *Bios. Biopolitics and Philosophy*. Translated by Timothy Campbell. Minnesota UP, 2008.

Esquivel, Aureliano. "1932–1936, Programas de enseñanza y proyectos." Archivo Histórico de la Secretaría de Salud Pública. Fondo, Beneficencia Pública, Sección, Asistencia, Serie, Departamento de Acción Educativa y Social. Leg-4, Exp-9. 20 septiembre 1932, hojas 1–18.

Fanon, Frantz. *Black Skin, White Masks*. Translated by Charles Lam Markmann. Grove, 1967.

Fernández Manero, Victor. "Carta sobre la escuela primaria #17–9, 'Jaime Nunó.'" Archivo General de la Nación. Fondo de la Secretaría de Educación Pública. Departamento de Psicopedagogía e Higiene. Caja 35540, 17-13-5-134. 22 de marzo 1930.

Ferrante, Carolina. "Usos, posibilidades y dificultades del modelo social de la discapacidad" *Revista Inclusiones*, vol. 1, no. 3, 2014, pp. 31–55.

Fisher, Ronald Aylmer Sir. *Statistical Methods for Research Workers*. Oliver and Boyd, 1928.

Fornoff, Carolyn. "The Nature of Revolution." *Mexican Literature in Theory*. Edited by Ignacio Sánchez Prado. Bloomsbury, 2018, pp. 93–110.

Foucault, Michel. *Abnormal. Lectures at the Collège de France, 1974–1975*. Translated by Graham Burchell. Picador, 2003.

Foucault, Michel. *The Birth of Biopolitics. Lectures at the Collège de France, 1978–1979*. Translated by Graham Burchell. Picador, 2010.

Foucault, Michel. *Society Must Be Defended. Lectures at the Collège de France, 1975–76*. Translated by David Macey. Picador, 2003.

Fraser, Valerie. *Building the New World. Studies in the Modern Architecture of Latin America 1930–1960*. Verso, 2000.

Frenk, Julio M. "México en el umbral de la era genómica: impacto en la salud pública." FUNSALUD, 2001.

Freud, Sigmund. "Fragment of Analysis of a Case of Hysteria." Standard Edition of the Complete Psychological Works of Sigmund Freud. Vol. VII. Hogarth Press, 1905, pp. 3–63.

Gallo, Rubén. *Mexican Modernity: The Avant-Garde and the Technological Revolution*. MIT P, 2005.

Galton, Francis. *Inquiries into Human Faculty and its Development*. Macmillan, 1883.

García de Mendoza. "Teoría de las probabilidades y la estadística de la medicina." *Boletín de la Sociedad Eugénica Mexicana*, no. 25, April 30, 1933.

Gamio, Manuel. *Forjando patria*. Porrúa, 2006.

García González, Armando. "El desarrollo de la eugenesia en Cuba." *Asclepio*, LI–2, 1999, pp 85–100.

Garland-Thomson, Rosemarie. *Staring. How We Look*. Oxford UP, 2009.

Garoian, Frank R. *The Prosthetic Pedagogy of Art: Embodied Research and Practice*. SUNY P, 2013.

Gelfand, Toby. "Introduction." *Charcot in Morocco*. Introduction, notes, and translation by Toby Gelfand. U of Ottawa P, 2012.

Gilly, Adolfo. *La revolución interrumpida*. Era, 2004.

Gilman, Sander. *The Jew's Body*. Routledge, 1991.

Goetz, Christopher G. "Visual Art in the Neurologic Career of Jean-Martin Charcot." *Archives of Neurology*, vol. 48, April 1991, pp. 421–25.

Goler, Robert I. "Loss and Persistence of Memory: 'The Case of George Dedlow' and Disabled Civil War Veterans." *Literature and Medicine*, vol. 23, no. 1, 2004, pp. 160–83.

Gómez Robleda, José. *Características biológicas de los escolares proletarios*. Instituto Nacional de Psicopedagogía, 1937.

Gómez Robleda, José. "La cara de los Tarascos." *Revista Mexicana de Sociología*, vol. 3, no. 2, 1941, pp. 83–91.

Gómez Robleda, José. *Don Justo*. Secretaría de Educación Pública, 1948.

Gómez Robleda, José. *Esquizofrénico*. Imprenta Mundial, 1933.

Gómez Robleda, José. *El güero*. Imprenta Mundial, 1933.

Gómez Robleda, José. *Un ladrón*. Imprenta Mundial, 1933.

Gómez Robleda, José. *Noúmeno*. Imp. A. Mjares y Hno, 1942.

Gómez Robleda, José, and Ada d'Aloja. *La familia y la casa*. Instituto de Investigaciones Sociales, Universidad Nacional, 1959.

Gómez Robleda, José, and Luis Argoytia. *Deportistas*. Departamento de Psicopedagogía y Médico Escolar, 1940.

Gónzalez Ponce, Citlalli. "Tres instantáneas de la relación entre fotografía científica y antropología en México." *Encartes antropológicos*, vol. 1, no. 2, 2018, pp. 13–35.

González Stephan, Beatriz. "The Teaching Machine for the Wild Citizen." *The Latin American Subaltern Studies Reader*. Edited by Ileana Rodríguez, Duke UP, 2001, pp. 313–40.

Goodley, Dan. "Dis/entangling Critical Disability Studies." *Disability and Society*, vol. 28, no. 5, 2013, pp. 631–44.

Gudiño Cejudo, María Rosa. "Educación higiénica y consejos de salud para campesinos en *El Sembrador* y *El Maestro Rural*, 1929–1934." *Curar, sanar y educar. Enfermedad y sociedad en México, siglos XIX y XX*. Coordinated by Claudia Agostoni. Universidad Nacional Autónoma de México, 2008, pp. 71–98.

Guzmán, Martín Luis. *La sombra del caudillo*. Porrúa, 1985.

Hacking, Ian. *The Taming of Chance*. Cambridge UP, 2014.

Hall, John. "Epic and Irony in a Novel of the Mexican Revolution: Rafael Felipe Muñoz's *Se llevaron el cañón para Bachimba*." *Romance Notes*, vol. 9, issue 1, 1991, pp. 83–96.

Hatfield, Elia. *La representación del ejército mexicano en la literatura y el cine*. Juglaría, 2010.

Haywood Ferreira, Rachel. *The Emergence of Latin American Science Fiction*. Wesleyan UP, 2011.

"Higiene escolar en México." Archivo General de la Nación. Fondo de la Secretaría de Educación Pública. Departamento de Psicopedagogía e Higiene. Caja 35476, 17-14-6-203, 1937.

"Informe de labores de 1 sept 1934 a 31 agosto 1935." Archivo General de la Nación.

Fondo de la Secretaría de Educación Pública. Departamento de Psicopedagogía e Higiene. Caja 35498, 17-13-1-45.

"Informe de la última sesión de la Sociedad Eugénica Mexicana." *Boletín de la Sociedad Eugénica Mexicana*, no. 25, 30 de abril, 1933, p. 5.

"Distribucion de los mendigos, 1 de julio de 1931." Archivo Histórico de la Secretaría de Salud Pública. Fondo: Beneficencia Pública. Sección: Asistencia. Serie: Departamento de Acción Educativa y Social. Leg, 1, Exp, 10, hoja 2.

Instituto Nacional de Psicopedagogía. Secretaría de Educación Pública, Departamento de Psicopedagogía y médico escolar, 1936.

James, Jennifer C. *A Freedom Bought with Blood: African American War Literature from the Civil War to World War II.* U of North Carolina P, 2007.

Janzen, Rebecca. *The National Body in Mexican Literature: Collective Challenges to Biopolitical Control.* Palgrave Macmillan, 2015.

Jiménez, Carlos. "El papel del médico, la enfermera y de los maestros para la realización de los fines de la higiene escolar." Archivo General de la Nación. Fondo de la Secretaría de Educación Pública. Departamento de Psicopedagogía e Higiene, Caja 35514, ref. 139, exp. 28, leg 4, 1925.

Jímenez de Báez, Yvette. "Escritura y proyección en *La sombra del caudillo* de Martín Luis Guzmán." *Actas de XI Congreso de Asociación Internacional de Hispanistas.* Coordinated by Juan Villegas. Vol. 5, 1994, pp. 323–30.

Jullian Montañez, Christian Giorgio. "Palos de ciego. La Escuela Nacional de Ciegos y Sordomudos: Historia del fracaso de un proyecto anacrónico (1928–1937). 2013. Universidad Nacional Autónoma de México, PhD dissertation.

Kafer, Alison. *Feminist, Queer, Crip.* Indiana UP, 2013.

Kanner, Leo. "Autistic Disturbances of Affective Contact." *Nervous Child*, vol. 2, no. 2, 1943, pp. 217–30.

Kim, Eunjung. *Curative Violence: Rehabilitating Disability, Gender, and Sexuality in Modern Korea.* Duke UP, 2016.

Kuppers, Petra. *The Scar of Visibility: Medical Performances and Contemporary Art.* U of Minnesota P, 2007.

Lavín, Emiliano. "Carta al C. Administrador de la Escuela de Ciegos y Sordo-Mudos, 20 de marzo de 1932." Archivo Histórico de la Secretaría de Salud Pública. Fondo de Beneficencia Pública. Sección: Asistencia, Serie: Departamento de Acción Educativa y Social. Leg, 4, exp. 3, hoja 5.

Louça, Francisco. "Emancipation through Interaction: How Eugenics and Statistics Converged and Diverged." *Journal of the History of Biology*, vol. 42, no. 4, 2009, pp. 649–84.

Legrás, Horacio. *Culture and Revolution. Violence, Memory, and the Making of Modern Mexico.* U of Texas P, 2017.

Longmore, Paul K. *Telethons: Spectacle, Disability, and the Business of Charity.* Oxford UP, 2016.

Lombardo, Paul, "Eugenic Sterilization Laws." Eugenicsarchive.org. Web. 20 June 2016.

Lomnitz, Claudio. *Deep Mexico, Silent Mexico: An Anthropology of Nationalism.* Minnesota UP, 2001.

López Beltrán, Carlos. "Escenarios de la patologización racial: La anomalía amerindia en una nación enferma." *Metatheoria*, vol. 8, no. 2, 2018, pp. 181–93.

López Beltrán, Carlos and Vivette García Deister. "Scientific Approaches to the Mexican Mestizo." Translated by Catherine Jagoe. *Historia Ciência, Saúde— Manguinhos*, vol. 20, no. 2, 2013, pp. 391–410.

López Carrillo, Ximena. "Retraso mental." *Los pacientes del manicomio La Castañeda y sus diagnósticos. Una historia de la clínica psiquiátrica en México, 1910–1968.* Coordinated by Andrés Ríos Molina. Universidad Nacional Autónoma de México, 2017, pp. 123–64.

López-Durán, Fabiola. *Eugenics in the Garden: Transatlantic Architecture and the Crafting of Modernity.* U of Texas P, 2018.

Lozano Garza, Alberto. "Algunas palabras en favor de los niños anormales." *Memoria del Primer Congreso Mexicano del Niño.* El Universal, 1921, pp. 267–69.

Lozano Garza, Alberto. "Ideas generales sobre la higiene escolar." Archivo General de la Nación. Fondo de la Secretaría de Educación Pública. Departamento de Psicopedagogía e Higiene. Caja 35483, ref. 135, exp. 6, 1925.

Lund, Joshua. *The Mestizo State: Reading Race in Modern Mexico.* U of Minnesota P, 2012.

Mahendron, Dilan. "The Facticity of Blackness: A Non-conceptual Approach to the Study of Race and Racism in Fanon's and Merleau-Ponty's Phenomenology." *Human Architecture: Journal of the Sociology of Self Knowledge*, vol. 5, issue 3, 2007, pp. 191–203.

Maldonado Ramírez, Jhonatthan. "Capacidad organotópica." *Heterotopías del cuerpo y el espacio.* Coordinated by Verónica Rodríguez Cabrera, Chloé Constant, María Guadalupe Guacuz Elías, and Jaqueline García Bautista. La Cifra Editorial, 2017, pp. 37–62.

Martínez Martín, Jaime. "Alegato politico y discurso literario en ¡*Vámonos con Pancho Villa!* y *Se llevaron el cañón para Bachimba* de Rafael F. Muñoz." *Anales de Literatura Hispanoamericana*, vol. 41, 2012, pp. 191–211.

McDonald, Brent. "A Bullet to the Eye Is the Price of Protesting in Chile." *New York Times*. Nov. 19, 2019.

McGuire, Anne. *War on Autism: On the Cultural Logic of Normative Violence.* U of Michigan P, 2016.

McLaren, Angus. *Our Own Master Race: Eugenics in Canada, 1885–1945.* U of Toronto P, 2014.

McRuer, Robert. *Crip Theory: Cultural Signs of Queerness and Disability.* New York UP, 2006.

McRuer, Robert. *Crip Times: Disability, Globalization, and Resistance.* New York UP, 2018.

Memorias del Primer Congreso Higiénico Pedagógico reunido en la Ciudad de México en el año de 1882. Imprenta del gobierno, en palacio, 1883.

Mendez Ramírez, Ignacio. "Una mirada a la estadística en México." *El Universal.* April 12, 2013.

Merleau-Ponty, Maurice. *Phenomenology of Perception.* Translated by Colin Smith. Routledge and Kegan Paul, 1966.

Mesa Editorial Merca2.o. "Eli Lilly México se lleva el oro en los premios Aspid 2008." Sept. 11, 2008. https://www.merca20.com/eli-lilly-mexico-se-lleva-el-oro-en-los-premios-aspid-2008/

Michalko, Rod. *The Difference that Disability Makes*. Temple UP, 2002.

Millán, Ignacio. "Clave de enfermedades observadas con mayor frecuencia entre escolares." Archivo General de la Nación. Fondo de la Secretaría de Educación Pública. Departamento de Psicopedagogía e Higiene. Caja 35519, 1934.

Miller, Marilyn Grace. *The Rise and Fall of the Cosmic Race: The Cult of Mestizaje in Latin America*. U of Texas P, 2004.

Mitchell, David, and Sharon Snyder. *The Biopolitics of Disability: Neoliberalism, Ablenationalism, and Peripheral Embodiment*. U of Michigan P, 2018.

Mitchell, David, and Sharon Snyder. "The Eugenic Atlantic: Race, Disability and the Making of an International Eugenic Science, 1860–1945." *Disability & Society*, vol.18, no. 7, 2003, pp. 843–64.

Mitchell, David, and Sharon Snyder. "Introduction: Ablenationalism and the Geo-Politics of Disability." *Journal of Literary and Cultural Disability Studies*, vol. 4, no. 2, 2010, pp. 113–26.

Mitchell, David, and Sharon Snyder. *Narrative Prosthesis: Disability and the Dependencies of Discourse*. U of Michigan P, 2001.

Mitchell, David, and Sharon Snyder. "Posthumanist T4 Memory." *The Matter of Disability: Materiality, Biopolitics, Crip Affect*. Edited by David T. Mitchell, Susan Antebi, and Sharon L. Snyder. U of Michigan P, 2019, pp. 249–72.

Mitchell, David T., Susan Antebi, and Sharon L. Snyder. "Introduction." *The Matter of Disability: Materiality, Biopolitics, Crip Affect*. U of Michigan P, 2019, pp. 1–36.

Morán, Francisco. *José Martí, La justicia infinita: Notas sobre ética y otredad en la escritura martiana (1875–1894)*. Verbum, 2014.

Moreno Figuera, Mónica, and Emiko Saldívar Tanaka. "We Are Not Racists, We Are Mexicans: Privilege, Nationalism, and Post-Race Ideology in Mexico." *Critical Sociology*, vol. 42, nos. 4–5, 2016, pp. 515–33.

Morlock, Forbes. "The Very Picture of a Primal Scene: *Une leçon clinique à la Salpêtrière*." *Visual Resources. An International Journal on Images and Their Uses*, vol. 23, nos. 1–2, 2007, pp. 129–46.

Morones, Elvira. "Clasificación escolar." Archivo Histórico de la Secretaría de Salud Pública. Fondo: Beneficencia Pública, Sección: Asistencia, Serie: Dirección General, Lg-6, Exp-3, 11 de septiembre 1933.

Muñoz, Rafael F. *Se llevaron el cañón para Bachimba*. Planeta DeAgostoni, 2004.

Muñoz, Rafael F. *¡Vámonos con Pancho Villa!* Factoría Ediciones, 2010.

Navarrete, Federico. *México racista: Una denuncia*. Grijalbo, 2016.

Obregón, Diana. "The Anti-Leprosy Campaign in Colombia: The Rhetoric of Hygiene and Science, 1920–1940." *História, Ciêncas, Saúde—Manguinhos*, vol. 10, supplement 1, 2003, pp. 179–207.

Ocaranza, Fernando. "Límites de la eugenesia." *Boletín de la Sociedad Eugénica Mexicana*, no. 34, tomo 2, 4 diciembre, 1933.

O'Gorman, Juan. "Arquitectura funcional." *La palabra de Juan O'Gorman*. Edited by

Ida Rodríguez Prampolini, Olga Sáenz, and Elizabeth Fuentes Rojas. Universidad Nacional Autónoma de México, 1983, pp. 122–24.

O'Gorman, Juan. "Conferencia en la sociedad de arquitectos mexicanos." *La palabra de Juan O'Gorman*. Edited by Ida Rodríguez Prampolini, Olga Sáenz, and Elizabeth Fuentes Rojas. Universidad Nacional Autónoma de México, 1983, pp. 101–17.

Oliver, Michael. "The Social Model in Action: If I Had a Hammer." *Implementing the Social Model of Disability: Theory and Research*. Edited by Colin Barnes and Geof Mercer. The Disability Press, 2004, pp. 18–31.

Oliver, Michael, and Colin Barnes. "Disability Studies, Disabled People and the Struggle for Inclusion." *British Journal of Sociology of Education*, vol. 31, no. 5, 2010, pp. 547–60.

Olsen, Patrice Elizabeth. *Artifacts of Revolution: Architecture, Society, and Politics in Mexico City, 1920–1940*. Rowman and Littlefield, 2008.

O'Rourke, Kathryn E. "Guardians of Their Own Health: Tuberculosis, Rationalism, and Reform in Modern Mexico." *Journal of the Society of Architectural Historians*, vol. 71, no. 1, 2012, pp. 60–77.

Ortiz, Fernando. *Los negros brujos*. Ediciones Universal, 1973.

Owens, Janine. "Exploring the Critiques of the Social Model of Disability: The Transformative Possibility of Arendt's Notion of Power." *Sociology of Health and Illness*, vol. 7, no. 3, 2015, pp. 385–403.

Palou, Pedro Ángel. *El fracaso del mestizo*. Ariel, 2014.

Pani, Alberto. *La higiene en México*. J. Ballescá, 1916.

Pani, Alberto. *Hygiene in Mexico: A Study of Sanitary and Educational Problems*. Translated by Ernest L. de Gogorza. G. P. Putnam's Sons, 1917. Reprinted by General Books, 2010.

Parra, Max. *Writing Pancho Villa's Revolution: Rebels in the Literary Imagination of Mexico*. U of Texas P, 2005.

Patiño Guadarrama, Ariadna. "Juegos infantíles: el símbolo lúdico en los murales de Julio Castellanos en Coyoacán." *Encauzar la mirada: Arquitectura, pedagogía e imágenes en México, 1920–1950*. Coordinated by Renato González Mello and Deborah Dorotinsky Alperstein. UNAM, Instituto de Investigaciones Estéticas, 2010, pp. 145–68.

Paz, Octavio. *El laberinto de la soledad y otras obras*. Penguin Books, 1997.

Paz, Octavio. *The Labyrinth of Solitude and Other Writings*. Translated by Lysander Kemp, Yara Milos, and Rachel Phillips Belash. Grove Press, 1985.

Pérez-Gómez, Alberto. "Mexico, Modernity, and Architecture. An Interview with Alberto Pérez-Gómez." *Modernity and the Architecture of Mexico*. Edited by Edward R. Burian. U of Texas P, 1997, pp. 13–60.

Peza, Juan de Dios. *La beneficencia en México*. Imprenta de Francisco Díaz de León, 1881.

Pierce, Gretchen. "Small Alcohol Producers and Popular Resistance to Mexico's Anti-Alcohol Campaigns, 1910–1940." *Alcohol in Latin America: A Social and Cultural History*. Edited by Gretchen Pierce and Áurea Toxqui. U of Arizona P, 2014, pp. 161–84.

Pineda, Adela. "El pensamiento francés y la obra crítica de Jorge Aguilar Mora." *Revista de Crítica Literaria Latinoamericana*, vol. 39, issue 78, 2013, pp. 43–55.

Preston, V. K. "Baroque Relations: Ballet of the Americas." *Oxford Handbook of Dance and Reenactment*. Edited by Mark Franko. Oxford UP, Dec. 2017, pp. 1–30.

Puar, Jasbir K. *The Right to Maim: Debility, Capacity, Disability*. Duke UP, 2017.

Quintana Navarrete, Jorge. "La utopía a prueba: formas heterogéneas de vida en *Eugenia* de Eduardo Urzaiz." *Revista Canadiense de Estudios Hispánicos*. Forthcoming.

Ramírez H, Juliana. "Mito y nación: La ex nominación de la burguesía." Spanish 386 final paper, University of Toronto, Dec. 6, 2012.

Ramos, Julio. *Divergent Modernities: Culture and Politics in Nineteenth-Century Latin America*. Translated by John D. Blanco. Duke UP, 2001.

Ramos, Samuel. "Perfil del hombre y de la cultura en México." *Obras Completas de Samuel Ramos*. Universidad Nacional Autónoma de México, Dirección General de Publicaciones, 1975, pp. 87–184.

Razack, Sherene. "Timely Deaths: Medicalizing the Deaths of Aboriginal People in Police Custody." *Law, Culture and the Humanities*, vol. 9, no. 2, 2013, pp. 352–74.

Ríos Molina, Andrés. *Cómo prevenir la locura. Psiquiatría e higiene mental en México, 1934–1950*. Siglo veintiuno, 2016.

Ríos Molina, Andrés. "Esquizofrenia y psicosis maniaco-depresiva." *Los pacientes del manicomio La Castañeda y sus diagnósticos. Una historia de la clínica psiquiátrica en México, 1910–1968*. Coordinated by Andrés Ríos Molina. Universidad Nacional Autónoma de México, 2017, pp. 71–122.

Rivera, Diego, and Emilo Portés Gil. "Propaganda Anti-Alcoholica." *El Sembrador*, no. 4, 5 de junio de 1929, pp. 8–9.

Rodríguez Cabo, Mathilde. "La eutanasia de los anormales." *Criminalia*. Año II, núm. 11, 1935, pp. 145–50.

Rodríguez Prampolini, Ida. "El creador, el pensador, el hombre." *Juan O'Gorman 100 años. Temples, dibujos y estudios preparatorios*. Edited by Cándida Fernández de Calderón and Carlos Monroy Valentino. Conaculta, 2005, pp. 197–228.

Rojas, Jesús, A. "Registro escolar del alumno." Archivo General de la Nación. Fondo de la Secretaría de Educación Pública. Departamento de Psicopedagogía e Higiene. Caja 35479, ref. 134, exp. 21, 1923.

Ruiz Escalona, Alfonso. "Un símbolo en la higiene de la raza." *Eugenesia*, Tomo 3, no. 37, enero de 1942, pp. 11–15.

Saade Granados, Marta. "¿Quiénes deben procrear? Los medicos eugenistas bajo el signo social (México 1931–1940)." *Cuicuilco*, vol. 11, no. 31, 2004, pp. 1–36.

Sáenz, Moisés. *México íntegro*. Fondo de Cultura Económica, 1982.

Salsburg, David. *The Lady Tasting Tea: How Statistics Revolutionized Science in the Twentieth Century*. Holt, 2002.

Samuels, Ellen. *Fantasies of Identification: Disability, Gender, Race*. NYU Press, 2014.

Sánchez, Carlos Alberto. *Contingency and Commitment: Mexican Existentialism and the Place of Philosophy*. SUNY P, 2016.

Sánchez Prado, Ignacio M. "El mestizaje en el corazón de la utopía: La raza cósmica entre Aztlán y América Latina." *Revista Canadiense de Estudios Hispánicos*, vol. 33, no. 2, 2009, pp. 381–404.

Sánchez Prado, Ignacio M. *Naciones intelectuales: Las fundaciones de la modernidad literaria mexicana, 1917–1959*. Purdue UP, 2009.

Santamarina, Rafael. "Bases para la higiene mental escolar." *Memoria del Primer Congreso Mexicano de Pediatría*. Dir. Alfonso G. Alarcón. Editorial Nipios, 1938, pp. 223–28.

Santamarina, Rafael. "Carta a José Manuel Puig Casauranc, Secretario de Educación Pública." 31 August, 1927. Archivo General de la Nación. Fondo de la Secretaría de Educación Pública. Departamento de Psicopedagogía e Higiene. Caja 42787, 4-8-9-223.

Santamarina, Rafael. "La clasificación del Dr. Santamarina." Archivo General de la Nación. Fondo de la Secretaría de Educación Pública. Departamento de Psicopedagogía e Higiene. Caja 35514, Ref. 139, exp. 16, Folio 20, 1927.

Santamarina, Rafael. "Conocimiento actual del niño mexicano desde el punto de vista médico-pedagógico." *Memoria del Primer Congreso Mexicano del Niño*. El Universal, 1921, pp. 264–66.

Santamarina, Rafael. "La cuestión de los anormales." Archivo General de la Nación, Fondo de la Secretaría de Educación Pública, Departamento de Psicopedagogía e Higiene, caja 35514, ref. 139. Exp. 16.

Santamarina, Rafael. "Ensayo de clasificación médico-pedagógica de los niños en edad escolar." *Memoria del Primer Congreso Mexicano del Niño*. El Universal, 1921, pp. 274–78.

Santamarina, Rafael. "3 de febrero, 1928." Archivo General de la Nación. Fondo de la Secretaría de Educación Pública. Departamento de Psicopedagogía e Higiene. Caja 35513, ref 142, exp. 85, 1928.

Scarry, Elaine. *The Body in Pain: The Making and Unmaking of the World*. Oxford UP, 1987.

Schalk, Sami, "Reevaluating the Supercrip." *Journal of Literary and Cultural Disability Studies*, vol. 10, no. 1, 2016, pp. 71–86.

Sedgwick, Eve Kosofsky. *Tendencies*. Routledge, 1994.

Siebers, Tobin. *Disability Aesthetics*. U of Michigan P, 2013.

Siegel, Irwin M. "Charcot and Duchenne: Of Mentors, Pupils and Colleagues." *Perspectives in Biology and Medicine*, vol. 43, no. 4, Summer 2000, pp. 541–47.

Sola, Jesús. "El desarrollo del niño mexicano" (thesis). Archivo General de la Nación. Fondo de la Secretaría de Educación Pública. Departamento de Psicopedagogía e Higiene. Caja 35514, ref. 139, exp. 28, leg. 6, 1926.

Solís Quiroga, Roberto. "Carta de 17 oct 1936." Archivo General de la Nación. Fondo de la Secretaría de Educación Pública. Departamento de Psicopedagogía e Higiene. Caja 35489. fondo III/201.5 (063)/-1.

"Sombras." CMV Publicidad. Eli Lilly México. Web. 27 junio 2013.

Soto Martínez, M. Adriana. "La discapacidad y sus significados: Notas sobre la (in) justicia." *Política y Cultura*, 2011, no. 35, pp. 209–39.

Speckman Guerra, Elisa. "Infancia es destino. Menores delincuentes en la ciudad de México (1884–1910)." *De normas y transgresiones: Enfermedad y crimen en América Latina (1850–1950).* Edited by Claudia Agostoni and Elisa Speckman Guerra. Universidad Nacional Autónoma de México, 2005, pp. 225–53.

Stepan, Nancy Leys. *The Hour of Eugenics. Race, Gender and Nation in Latin America.* Cornell UP, 1991.

Stern, Alexandra. *Eugenic Nation: Faults and Frontiers of Better Breeding in Modern America.* U of California P, 2005.

Stern, Alexandra. "'The Hour of Eugenics' in Veracruz, Mexico: Radical Politics, Public Health, and Latin America's Only Sterilization Law." *Hispanic American Historical Review,* vol. 91, no. 3, 1991, pp. 431–33.

Stern, Alexandra. "Mestizofilia, biotipología y eugenesia en el México posrevolucionario: Hacia una historia de la ciencia y del Estado, 1920–1960." *Relaciones. Estudios de Historia y Sociedad,* vol. 21, no. 81, 2000, pp. 58–91.

Stern, Alexandra. "Responsible Mothers and Normal Children: Eugenics, Nationalism, and Welfare in Post-revolutionary Mexico, 1920–1940." *Journal of Historical Sociology,* vol. 12, no. 4, 1991, pp. 369–97.

Stern, Alexandra. "Unravelling the History of Eugenics in Mexico." *Archives: Institute for the Study of Academic Racism.* August 1, 1998, https://ferris-pages.org/ISAR/archives2/sources/mexico.htm

Suárez y López Guazo, Laura. *Eugenesia y racismo en México.* Universidad Nacional Autónoma de México, 2005.

Suárez y López Guazo, Laura. "Evolucionismo y eugenesia en México." *Boletín Mexicano de Historia y Filosofía de la Medicina,* vol. 12, no. 1, 2009, pp. 19–23.

Taylor, William B. *Drinking, Homicide and Rebellion in Colonial Mexican Villages.* Stanford UP, 1979.

teleSur. "Chile's Police Suspend Use of Pellets after 270 Eye Injuries." *teleSur English,* Nov. 19, 2019.

Titchkosky, Tanya. *The Question of Access: Disability, Space, Meaning.* U of Toronto P, 2011.

Torres Puga, Gabriel. "'Documentar, preservar . . . ¿y la difusión?' (una crítica a la iniciativa de la Ley General de Archivos)." *Nexos, Blog de Redacción,* 5 dec. 2016. https://redaccion.nexos.com.mx/?p=7930

Tucker, Irene. *The Moment of Racial Sight.* U of Chicago P, 2012.

Turda, Marius. *Modernism and Eugenics.* Palgrave Macmillan, 2010.

Turda, Marius, and Aaron Gillette. *Latin Eugenics in Comparative Perspective.* Bloomsbury, 2014.

Urías Horcasitas, Beatriz. "Fisiología y moral en los estudios sobre las razas mexicanas: continuidades y rupturas (siglos xix y xx)." *Revista de Indias,* vol. 65, no. 234, 2005, pp. 355–74.

Urías Horcasitas, Beatriz. *Historias secretas del racismo en México, (1920–1945).* Tusquets, 2007.

Urzaiz, Eduardo. *Antología.* Ediciones del Gobierno del Estado de Yucatán, 2006.

Urzaiz, Eduardo. "El desequilibrio mental." Tésis profesional presentada ante la Facultad de Medicina y Cirugía de Yucatán. Imprenta de la lotería del Estado de Yucatán, 1902.

Urzaiz, Eduardo. *Eugenia. Esbozo novelesco de costumbres futuras.* Ediciones de la Universidad de Yucatán, 1947 [1919].

Urzaiz, Eduardo. *Eugenia. A Fictional Sketch of Future Customs. A Critical Edition.* Edited and translated by Sarah H. Buck Kachaluba and Aaron Dziubinskyj. U of Wisconsin P, 2016.

Urzaiz, Eduardo. *La familia, cruz del Apóstol. (Ensayo psicoanalítico sobre José Martí).* Compilación, estudio preliminar y notas por Carlos E. Bojórquez Urzaiz y Fernando Armstrong Fumero. Compañía Editorial de la Península, 2004.

Urzaiz, Eduardo. "Los hormones sexuales. Conferencia sustentada por el Dr. Eduardo Urzaiz la noche del 21 de 1921, por invitación del Círculo de Estudiantes de Medicina de Yucatán." Universidad Autónoma de Yucatán, 2002.

Urzaiz, Eduardo. *Nociones de antropología.* Mérida: Talleres gráficos y editorial Zamná, 1948.

Urzaiz, Eduardo. *Reconstrucción de hechos. Anécdotas Yucatecas Ilustradas.* Editorial de la Universidad Autónoma de Yucatán, 1992.

Vargas Domínguez, Joel. "Conexiones internacionales en fisiología, eugenesia y nutrición: la investigación sobre el metabolismo otomí en el México posrevolucionario." *Ludus Vitalis,* vol. 23, no. 43, 2015, pp. 83–104.

Vargas Parra, Daniel. "Fisiología lúdica de la higiene." *Encauzar la mirada: Arquitectura, pedagogía e imágenes en México, 1920–1950.* Coordinated by Renato González Mello and Deborah Dorotinsky Alperstein, UNAM, Instituto de Investigaciones Estéticas, 2010, pp. 33–73.

Vasconcelos, José. *The Cosmic Race: A Bilingual Edition.* Translated by Didier T. Jaén. Johns Hopkins UP, 1997.

Vasconcelos, José. "Estética." *Obras completas.* Vol. 5, Libreros Mexicanos Unidos, 1957, pp. 1111–734.

Vasconcelos, José. "Ética." *Obras completas.* Vol. 5. Libreros Mexicanos Unidos, 1957, pp. 665–1109.

Vasconcelos, José. "Prometeo vencedor." *Obras Completas.* Vol. 1. Libreros Mexicanos Unidos, 1957, pp. 239–86.

Vaughan, Mary Kay. *Cultural Politics in Revolution: Teachers, Peasants, and Schools in Mexico, 1930–1940.* U of Arizona P, 1997.

Velasco, Sherry M. *Male Delivery: Reproduction, Effeminacy, and Pregnant Men in Early Modern Spain.* Vanderbilt UP, 2006.

Vergara, Anastasio. "Relato general de la semana de estudios eugenésicos organizada por el Ateneo de Ciencias y Artes de México y por la Sociedad Eugénica Mexicana." *Boletín de la Sociedad Eugénica Mexicana,* no. 1, 22 agosto, 1932.

Victoria Maldonado, Jorge A. "El modelo social de la discapacidad: Una cuestión de derechos humanos." *Revista de Derecho UNED,* no. 12, 2013, pp. 817–33.

Weiss, Gail. *Body Images: Embodiment as Intercorporeality.* Routledge, 1999.

Williams, Gareth. *The Mexican Exception: Sovereignty, Police, and Democracy.* Palgrave Macmillan, 2011.

Waltz, Mitzi. *Autism: A Social and Medical History.* Palgrave Macmillan, 2013.

Wolff, Sula. "The History of Autism." *European Child & Adolescent Psychiatry*, vol. 13, no. 4, 2004, pp. 201–8.

Yaser, Find. "I am Autism Commercial by Autism Speaks." *YouTube*, 20 April 2016. https://www.youtube.com/watch?v=9UgLnWJFGHQ

Zavala, Adriana. "Mexico City in Juan O'Gorman's Imagination." *Hispanic Research Journal*, vol. 8, no. 5, 2007, pp. 491–506.

Index

Note: entries followed by *f* indicate a figure